THE GREEN GUIDE TO PROFITABLE MANAGEMENT

◆

THE GREEN GUIDE TO PROFITABLE MANAGEMENT

◆

Kit Sadgrove

Gower

© Kit Sadgrove 1992

All rights reserved. No part of this publication may be reproduced, stored in a retrieval system, or transmitted in any form or by any means, electronic, mechanical, photocopying, recording, or otherwise without the permission of the publisher.

Published by
Gower Publishing
Gower House
Croft Road
Aldershot
Hants GU11 3HR
England

Gower
Old Post Road
Brookfield
Vermont 05036
USA

CIP catalogue records for this book are available from the British Library

Made with Recycled Fibre

Printed on recycled paper. Content: 100% minimum recycled waste. Mixed de-inked and unprinted waste. Oxygen (non chlorine) bleached. Hot melt adhesive may be recycled. Boards 100% recycled material.

ISBN 0 566 07288 2 – HBK
0 566 07542 3 – PBK

Typeset in 11pt Garamond by Photoprint, Torquay, Devon and printed in Great Britain at the University Press, Cambridge

TO MY GREEN-EYED ALEXANDRA

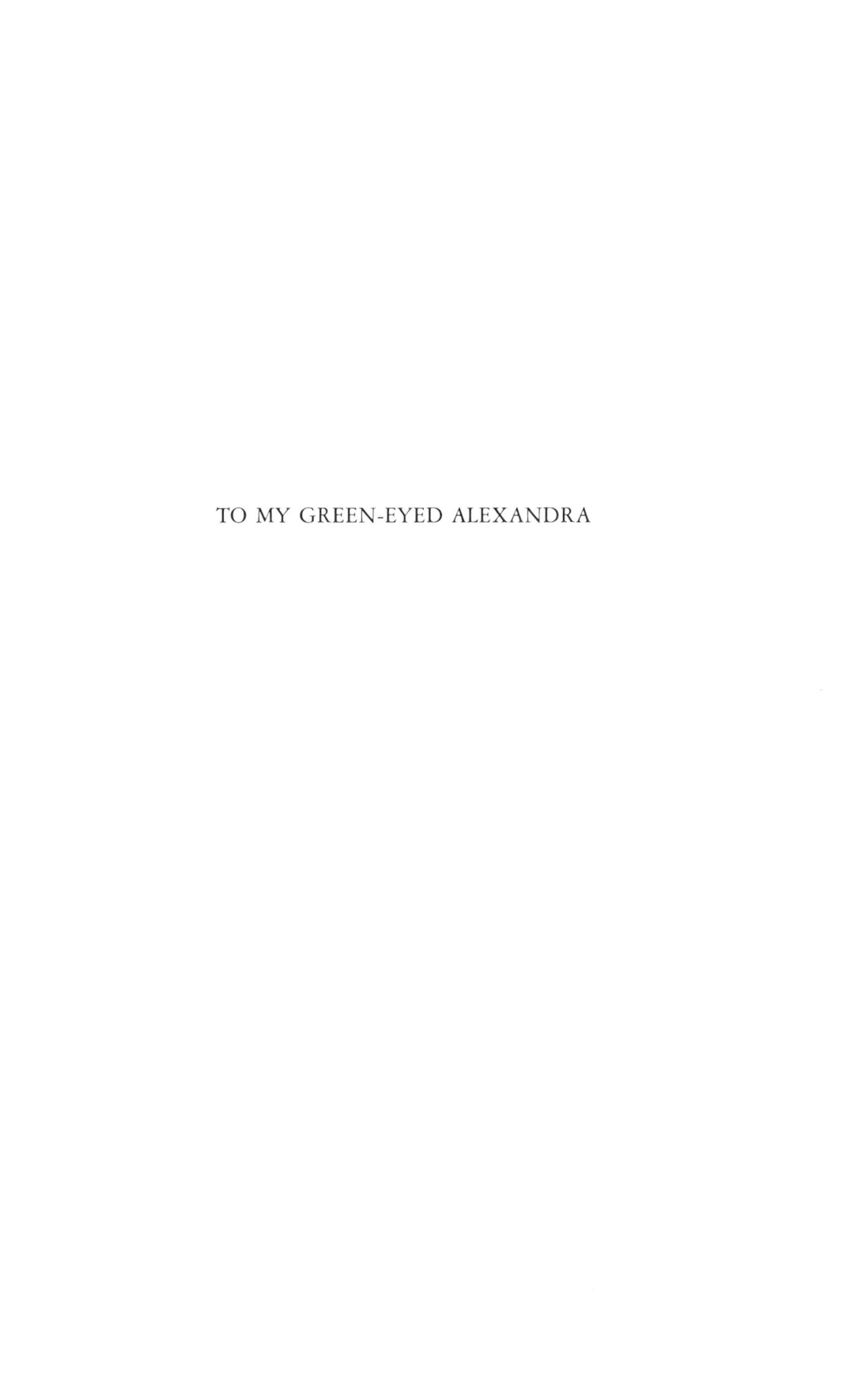

CONTENTS

♦

List of checklists	xi
List of illustrations	xiii
Foreword	xv
Preface	xvii
Acknowledgements	xix

1. **Going Green** — 1
   Attitudes among business people — The new legislation — Who is to blame? — Industry's reaction — When to start

2. **The Environmental Audit** — 18
   Which audit? — Planning the audit — Measuring the environmental record — Data analysis — Drawing up an environmental policy — Establishing targets

3. **Land and Buildings** — 34
   When refurbishment is better than new build — Maintenance materials — Site appearance and building exteriors — Litter — Land use — Land holdings — Contaminated land — Helping larger and rarer forms of wildlife — Assessing environmental impact — Hazards found in specific locations — Green new buildings — Green office assessment

4. **The Office** — 52
   The sick office — VDUs — Other occupational health and safety matters — Office drinks — Buying recycled stationery — Recycling your used paper — Other consumables and recycling — Fixtures, fittings and equipment — Energy use — The washroom — Teleworking

5. **Buying** — 69
   A buying policy — Criteria for purchasing — Better information — Assessing competing arguments — Packaging — Timber — Paper

6. **Production**   81
   Attitudes to pollution — The new legislation — Air pollution — Landfill — Incineration — Water pollution — Noise — Hazardous substances — How to minimize the risk — Other aspects of safety

7. **Engineering**   98
   Reducing waste and pollution — Recycling the waste — Energy use — Insulation and draughts — Lighting — Space and water heating — Machinery and equipment — Combined heat and power — Renewable energy — Reducing water use

8. **Transport**   119
   Purchase factors — Green car factors — General issues — Better car use — The bicycle option — Maintenance — Lorries and distribution — Disposal of waste — Inland waters — Sea transport

9. **Research and Development**   136
   Information gathering — A green R&D programme — Growth markets — Product improvement — Substituting new components — Unpopular products — Testing times — Making claims that can be proved

10. **Marketing**   146
    Defining the audiences and their attitudes — Marketing analysis — Developing a green brand — After-sales support — Packaging — Labelling — Communication and ethical marketing — Using the environment in promotion — Sales literature and direct mail — Setting standards for business associates

11. **Public Relations**   163
    Defining the environmental impact — Taking action — Community involvement — Better PR communications — Handling critics

12. **Personnel**   175
    Commitment from the top — In-house versus external auditors — The Environmental Affairs Manager — Getting staff commitment — Revising responsibilities — Reducing waste in staff communications — Environmental training — Health and Safety Manager

13. **The Cafeteria**   190
    A green food strategy — Food sources — The cafeteria — Educating the diner — Entertaining at work — Behind the scenes

14. Medical 197
    The healthy diet strategy — The healthy lifestyle strategy — The prevention strategy — The healthy management strategy — The healthy treatment strategy

15. Finance 203
    Costing the future — A new form of accounting — Expenditure strategy — How much to invest — Information systems — Annual Report — Acquisitions — Insurance — Ethical investment — Payroll giving

16. Putting It All Together: The Environmental Management System 215
    Internal information — External information — The Audit — Assessment and report — A policy — Objectives and targets — The action plan — Points common to all parts of an EMS

Appendix I   UK Environmental Law   227
Appendix II   Prescribed Processes and Substances   232
Appendix III Hazardous Substances   236
Appendix IV   Glossary   241
Appendix V   Useful Addresses   244

Index   247

Related resources from Gower   253

LIST OF CHECKLISTS

◆

Introductory checklist	17
Corporate strategy	33
Building maintenance	37
Site appearance	39
Litter	40
Landscaping	43
Environmental impact	46
New projects	47
New buildings	51
Air quality	54
VDU	55
Office health and safety	56
Drinks	58
Paper	62
Office consumables	64
Office equipment and energy	65
Washroom	67
Telecommuting	68
Purchasing system	75
Packaging	76
Air pollution	87
Solid waste disposal	89
Water pollution	91
Noise	93
Hazards	95
Scrap and waste	102
Recycling	107
Energy strategy	111
Insulation	112
Lighting	112
Heating	113
Equipment	114
Renewable energy	118

Water use	118
Car choice	123
Transport	127
Bicycle and pedestrian	128
Distribution strategy	131
Waste disposal – distribution	131
Shipping	134
R&D strategy	137
Product development	145
Marketing research	149
Marketing analysis	150
Marketing strategy	152
Pack	154
Green claims	157
Green information	161
PR strategy	165
Local residents	165
Community involvement	167
Communications	172
Complaints	174
Personnel strategy	178
Environmental manager	181
Human resources	187
Safety	189
Cafeteria	193
Behind the counter	196
Medical	201
Environmental costing	209
Information systems and acquisitions	211
Insurance	212
Investment	214
Environmental management system	226

LIST OF ILLUSTRATIONS

♦

1.1	World interest in green issues	2
1.2	Attitudes towards green business issues	5
1.3	Environmental pressures	7
1.4	Business in the environment	8
1.5	Global issues	9
2.1	A strategic response	19
2.2	The environmental audit	21
2.3	Environmental impacts	24
2.4	SWOT analysis	28
2.5	NAP analysis	29
3.1	Buildings and maintenance	35
4.1	Key environmental issues in the office	53
5.1	A green buying policy	70
6.1	Environmental process chart	81
6.2	Emissions	85
7.1	Waste reduction options	99
7.2	Breaking down energy use	109
8.1	The green car agenda	120
8.2	Car tactics	124
8.3	Green transport and logistics audit	132
10.1	The green marketing agenda	147
10.2	The audiences	148
12.1	Attitudes towards the environment	176
12.2	Environmental responsibilities and communications	179
12.3	An environmental training course	186
15.1	Strategic options	204
15.2	The impact of selected environmental protection measures on short- and long-term profits	207
15.3	Environmental cost analysis	208
15.4	Factors in the investment analysis	209
16.1	The conservation concept	216

16.2	Comparison between quality and environmental systems	217
16.3	An environmental management system	218
16.4	Departmental involvement	225

FOREWORD
by David Bellamy

◆

JUNGLE, WE USED TO CALL IT

Jungle, we used to call it. It was a treacherous place where Tarzan lived. Now we call it rainforest. We know it holds medicinal plants, threatened native peoples and precious forests.

How our knowledge has grown in the last 20 years! New words like global warming, deforestation and the ozone layer are in common use. We may not always know *precisely* what these new words mean (even the scientists disagree among themselves). But the general thrust is clear.

Unless we change our behaviour, we'll end up living on a bare planet, surrounded by piles of rubbish. The rivers will smell, the air will be poisoned, and the beaches will be full of dead fish.

An unlikely prospect? If you think so, it shows how much we've changed. Everyone today is more concerned about their environment. I still see people dropping rubbish in the street. But in ten years time that will be a rare sight. Most of us know that the plastic wrappers we discard will clog the drains or last for centuries in a landfill site.

At one time we thought water simply came from a tap, and electricity from a switch. Now we know that electricity comes from smoking power stations, and our sewage is fouling the rivers.

We in the West have come a long way. Not so the poorer countries, alas. Too many of them are burdened with debt to Western banks. For every £1 they receive in aid, they're repaying £3 in interest charges.

In the Philippines, they're chopping down their irreplaceable forests to pay off grandiose loans that a former dictator took out 15 years ago.

As a manager, you can help. You can use your organization's purchasing power, its investments, its humanity and its influence to improve the conditions in the South and to reduce pollution.

This book isn't just for people who buy from the Third World, or those who work in traditional smokestack industries. It's for anyone who works in an organization that employs people or has an office.

Take the government, for example. At national and local level, its staff buy huge quantities of goods and services. The way that money is spent has a big bearing on the environment. Consider two very different examples: home insulation and traffic calming. Both are very simple ideas, and both make an excellent contribution to environmental protection. But the extent of these schemes varies enormously from one area to another.

The legislators have been busy. There's more environmental legislation than even the most committed conservationist would once have dreamed of. A recycling idea that Germans or Danes adopt today ends up as EC legislation five years later.

But getting back to industry, if companies are taking the blame for pollution, they should also get credit for the way they've improved. Lots of companies are pressing ahead with new investment to reduce their discharges and emissions.

It's easy for conservationists to forget that industry is the workhorse of the modern world. If we want books, clothes, homes and buses, we must make them. But their manufacture should involve the least environmental impact. We should walk on tip-toe around the earth, not clamber all over it in hobnail boots.

For people who run industry, the opportunities are tremendously exciting. That's really what this book is about. It shows how you can improve the world by improving your business. It means using fewer resources, buying sensibly, and avoiding waste. To me, that sounds like good housekeeping.

Perhaps you, the reader, are responsible for the £3 million spent annually on paper by one British bank?

Perhaps you're in charge of a fleet of lorries that run between Washington and New York every week?

Perhaps you oversee the design department of an engineering company, where blueprints for new machines are on the drawing board?

Perhaps you manage the buildings and lands of a local authority?

The opportunities for going green are as exciting as in the pioneering days of industry when Isambard Kingdom Brunel was discovering how to drive tunnels through hills.

And the impact of your work could be as far reaching as his was.

You aren't alone. In every company I visit, the Chairman tells me of the initiatives he is undertaking. He says, 'They're being spearheaded by Jones. He's a closet greenie.'

All over the country, these closet greenies are creating change.

Now it's your turn.

David Bellamy

PREFACE

♦

Industry has always had to adapt. It has always faced change in consumer demand, technology and legislation. The environment is simply the latest change. Flexible, pragmatic and far-sighted companies will respond positively. Those that meet the challenge are the ones that will prosper.

Many environmental solutions can only be created by the government. They include fiscal incentives, better public transport, and greater investment in renewable energy sources.

But there is much that businesses can do: and the purpose of this book is to show that going green is good business sense.

We cannot ignore the environment. We cannot pretend that environmentalists are all cranks (though the green movement has its share of them). Nor can we dismiss environmentalism as a passing fad. Concern for the environment is here to stay.

There are costs involved in becoming a greener organization, just as there are costs involved in raising quality. But the green company will be cleaner, more confident, and better placed to face the future.

There are even greater costs involved in *not* being green. They include waste disposal bills, excessive energy costs, reduced consumer demand, possibly even catastrophic disasters.

In *The Green Guide to Profitable Management*, environmental impact is defined as any activity that affects the air, water, land or living things. This is a broad definition, which means that the book touches on health and safety, diet, quality, and some other surprising areas.

Many green concerns have a range of effects. A hazardous chemical can harm staff, local residents, animals and the water supply. So *The Green Guide to Profitable Management* covers green food, green landscaping and employee health, as well as more obvious concerns such as air pollution and waste paper.

The chapters of this book are organized on a departmental basis, reflecting corporate structure. This will help companies introduce change more effectively. Some issues cross functional barriers, and these have been allocated to the department most greatly affected.

Some departments, such as production, are heavily involved with the environment, while others have a smaller role to play. But the company that wants to go green will need environmental awareness throughout the business and in each department.

Much of this book reflects 'best practice' in industry, and many of the examples show the reader how far other companies have gone. Part of the book relates to manufacturing industry, but most of it applies equally to service organizations, whether building societies, hospitals or local authorities.

Situations vary widely, so it is impossible to cover all eventualities. No responsibility can be taken for any loss or damage arising as a result of reading this book. If in doubt consult a specialist, such as an environmental consultant or a solicitor. The word 'he' is used throughout for the sake of convenience; it should be taken to mean male or female.

ACKNOWLEDGEMENTS

♦

Thanks are due to many people at P-E International including Vernon Snellock and Barry Luke, and especially to Ralph Hepworth for his continuing guidance and support. Thanks also to Dr. Stuart Gregory and everyone else at David Bellamy Associates for their help. Responsibility for defects is mine alone.

My thanks are due to numerous publishers including ENDS, *Works Management*, the *Guardian*, the *Independent*, and *Marketing Week*. I am also indebted to the many companies who supplied information, and to trade associations such as the Chemical Industries Association. Thanks also to the Departments of Energy and Environment, and the Board of Trade.

Thanks are particularly due to my family, who put up with my absence during the writing of this book: thank you Alexandra, Charlotte, Katherine, John-John, Rosalind and Christabel. Thanks also to my parents, Rhona and Victor, for their encouragement and help.

I would also like to thank you, the reader, for buying this book. If you have thoughts on green business issues, or you're carrying out green innovations at work, I would be delighted to share your views. You can contact me at the address below.

Kit Sadgrove
Springwater Cottage
Mill Lane
Mere
Wiltshire

1
GOING GREEN

♦

Concern about the environment is not new. In Britain the 1956 Clean Air Act, now largely forgotten, was an environmental milestone. It swept away the smoking chimneys and the pea-soup fogs that we associate with Victorian England but which were actually common up to that year. 4 000 people died in the London fogs of 1952.

In the early 1970s, environmental consciousness was surprisingly strong. In June 1972 1 200 delegates from 110 countries attended a UN conference on what was quaintly called 'The Human Environment'. Prime Minister Harold Wilson, not remembered as an ecologist, set up a Royal Commission on Environmental Pollution. It reported alarming statistics about pollution in estuaries, the skies, rivers and fields.

But concern for the environment slumped during the early 1980s as the 'me' ethos took over. One disaster after another filled people's television screens. TV documentaries showed growing deserts, acid rain and the extinction of species. There was famine in Ethiopia, a chemical explosion in India. But though Friends of the Earth complained, the population was unmoved.

Then in 1985 the world's media announced two particularly alarming pieces of news. Human pollution had punctured a hole in the atmosphere, and the same human pollution was actually causing the weather to change for the worse. Suddenly, the earth seemed rather fragile, and its protection became important.

Opinion formers were alarmed, and by 1988 the message got through to everyone else. The environment burst into public awareness in the autumn of 1988. The following year the captain of the *Exxon Valdez* sailed into the history books by pouring 2 million gallons of oil on to the unspoilt Alaskan shoreline. The green issue had arrived.

The changing level of interest can be seen in Figure 1.1, which shows the number of column centimetres devoted to environmental issues over the last 25 years. It is taken from the index of Keesings Contemporary Archives, which records month by month the topics being discussed around the world. In the 1960s, the subject was simply not on the world's agenda. As the illustration shows, 1986 was a watershed year.

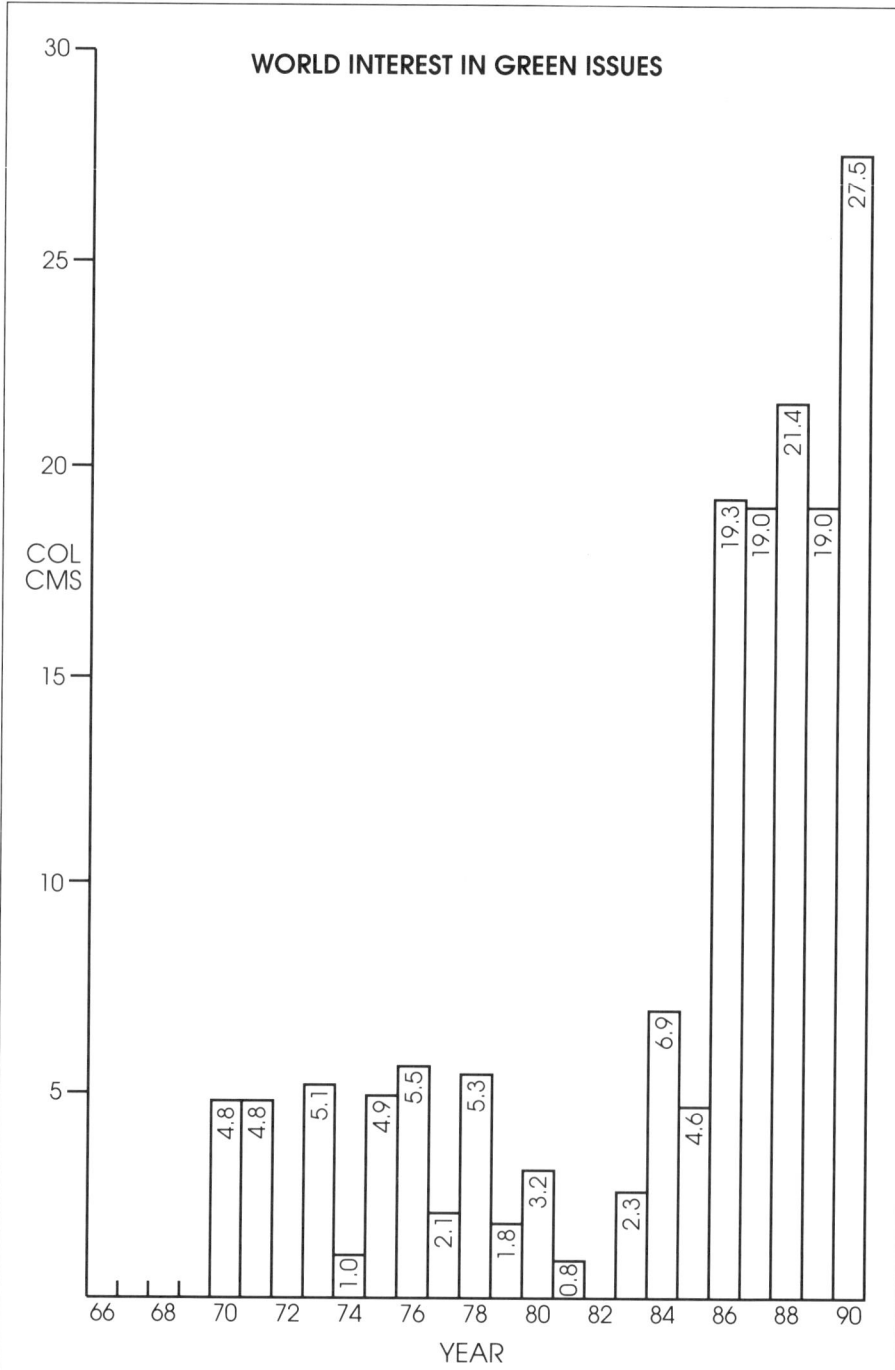

Figure 1.1: World interest in green issues. The level of interest in green issues is reflected in the index of Keesings Contemporary Archives.

DISASTER AND CHANGE

Ever since the Old Testament plagues afflicted Egypt, there have been prophets and disasters. Here are some of the more recent ones.

1977 The UN calls for a convention to protect the ozone layer. The call is ignored for another 12 years.

1982 After pressure from conservationists, the International Whaling Commission votes for a ban on whaling.

1984 Famine in Africa, magnified by military conflict, deforestation, overgrazing and desertification.

1984 2 800 people are killed by a gas leak at a Union Carbide pesticide plant in Bhopal, India.

1985 In Villach, Austria, 100 scientists, assembled by the UN and the World Meteorological Organisation, warn that the world's climate might be warming.

1985 British Antarctic Survey finds a hole in the protective ozone layer. This leads to international agreement four years later to ban CFCs.

1986 An explosion destroys the Chernobyl nuclear reactor in the USSR, casting doubts on the wisdom of nuclear energy.

1986 The river Rhine is heavily polluted by a chemical spillage. This causes a re-think on environmental protection and hazards throughout Europe.

1988 Scandals about illegal transportation of toxic waste. Attention focuses on the *Karin B*. The search is on for a better strategy for waste.

1988 Climatic disaster around the world and growing scientific evidence lead more people to accept the idea of climate change.

1989 2 million gallons of oil hit the Alaskan coast from the *Exxon Valdez*. 2 000 sea birds and 300 sea otters die despite a ruinously expensive mop-up operation by the company.

1990 The 1 000 scientists of the Intergovernmental Panel on Climate Change forecast sea level rises and significant climate change due to greenhouse gases.

1991 The world's first act of environmental terrorism: Saddam Hussein sets fire to Kuwait's oil wells.

Now, according to Mintel, 39 per cent of adults in the UK buy green products as far as possible, and a further 20 per cent buy them whenever they see them. Research by MORI shows that 35 per cent of the population rate the environment as the most important issue facing the country, making it the biggest issue on the political agenda.

According to another survey conducted by Gallup for *Green Magazine*:

○ 9.5 million out of Britain's 20.8 million households say they are 'very concerned' or 'extremely concerned' about green issues.

- Nearly all the rest are 'concerned', with a mere 8 per cent expressing indifference.
- 2.3 million people are committed greens, belonging to organizations and buying books about the subject.
- Men and women are equal in expressing concern.
- Green concerns are not merely a youthful trend. Buying habits are more affected in the 16–34 age group but organization membership is strongest in the 35–54 age group. People of all ages were equally concerned about the issue.

Concern about the environment is no longer confined to long-haired students who wear sandals. It has reached every part of society.

Membership of environmental groups has grown enormously. Greenpeace has reported a 50 per cent rise in European membership since 1988. And corporate subscriptions to the World Wide Fund for Nature (formerly World Wildlife Fund) have risen from £300 000 in 1984 to £1.8 million in 1991.

A survey by Avon County Council in 1990 showed that 93 per cent of local residents wanted environmental issues to have a high priority; and 100 per cent said that pollution control was important. Of the 1 717 responses, there were virtually no adverse comments such as 'waste of money'.

ATTITUDES AMONG BUSINESS PEOPLE

Environmental concern is not restricted to the consumer. In research by 3M among business people in Spain, Sweden, West Germany and the Netherlands, one in five of all respondents said that 'concern for the environment' was the most important attribute they would look for in a prospective supplier. This was ahead of 'value for money', 'useful products', and 'help with customer problems'.

Far-sighted business leaders are equally concerned. E.S. Woolard, Chairman of Du Pont, believes that avoiding environmental incidents 'is the greatest imperative facing business today'.

KEEN ON THE ENVIRONMENT, BUT MEASURES ARE UNPLANNED

Companies are keen to protect the environment. According to a survey conducted by the author for David Bellamy Associates, 65 per cent would consider certifying their business to the new British Standards Institution (BSI) environmental standard.

The survey investigated attitudes among 176 organizations with turnovers of between £2 million and £2 billion. The overwhelming majority of businesses (94 per cent) thought that environmental pressure would increase, and they had

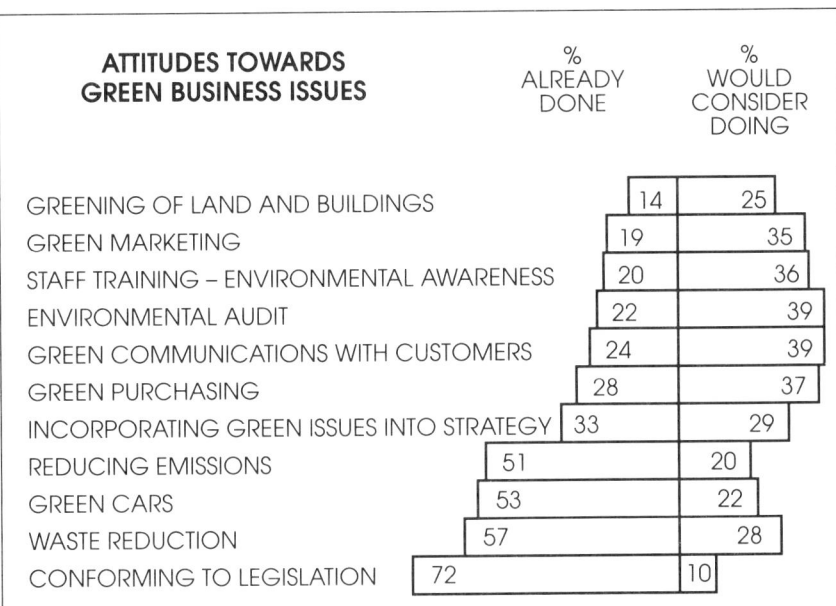

Figure 1.2: Attitudes towards green business issues. The chart shows the areas that companies have targeted, or will do so in the future.

introduced a range of measures, especially pollution control, waste reduction, and greener cars. Recycling systems were becoming widely adopted.

Responses to selected business issues are shown in Figure 1.2. Areas in which companies had taken least action were green buildings marketing and communications, staff training, and an environmental audit. Over one-third of respondents said they would consider taking action on these points.

Even companies which had not implemented green improvements were interested to learn about them. In many cases, twice as many companies would consider undertaking green measures as have already done so.

A majority of respondents thought the environment was 'very important' to them personally (63 per cent), but only 'quite important' to their businesses (51 per cent). This means that executives consider the environment more important in their personal lives than in their work.

These figures also suggest that business people are selling products whose environmental performance is lower than consumers would wish.

There was a lack of sound data. Nearly three-quarters of respondents (72 per cent) claimed they were conforming to legislation. But hardly any had taken formal steps to assess their legal position.

Likewise, 22 per cent of companies had carried out an environmental audit. But

> deeper investigation revealed that most of the audits were not independent, co-ordinated or comprehensive. Very often the departmental manager had audited his own department.
>
> The proportion of companies which had commissioned an independent audit was more like 3 per cent. The lack of objectivity that affected the majority of audits meant that companies were not able to use the results as a marketing device.
>
> Companies also thought that using unleaded petrol meant that they were 'green'. Few had a comprehensively green car or transport policy.
>
> Companies' activities were mostly restricted to spontaneous initiatives by individuals. There was generally a lack of management systems (no planning, co-ordination, controls or an action plan). However, 53 per cent of businesses said they would consider introducing an environmental management system into their business.
>
> The individual charged with environmental responsibility tended to operate in isolation from the rest of the company and had little understanding of the environmental implications and activities of other departments.
>
> The respondents covered a variety of job functions, including facilities, personnel, engineering, production, quality assurance, marketing and operations.

THE NEW LEGISLATION

Consumer-orientated businesses have found the environment an added selling benefit, and have adapted their products. But for many other companies, the environment has been irrelevant and conservationists merely an irritation. The real issue has been cost. For many companies, environmental protection costs money and adds nothing to the bottom line. When pollution was free, business could afford to ignore the problem – but things have changed.

The arrival of harsh new laws, some of which are outlined in Appendix I, has changed the way business thinks. Pollution has become expensive, and its enforcement rigorous. Beset by demands from environmentalists, consumers and legislators (Figure 1.3), business people are having to find new solutions. In the UK three new pieces of legislation have been particularly significant:

- 1988 The COSHH (Control of Substances Hazardous to Health) regulations have made many businesses reconsider the safety of their plants.
- 1989 The Water Act brought the National Rivers Authority into existence. Though many people thought it would be a paper tiger, it turned into a determined watch-dog. Businesses have found that water pollution is much more stringently controlled.
- 1990 The Environmental Protection Act has exposed businesses to the public gaze through public registers of consents. It has imposed controls on larger polluters, and given local authorities new powers to

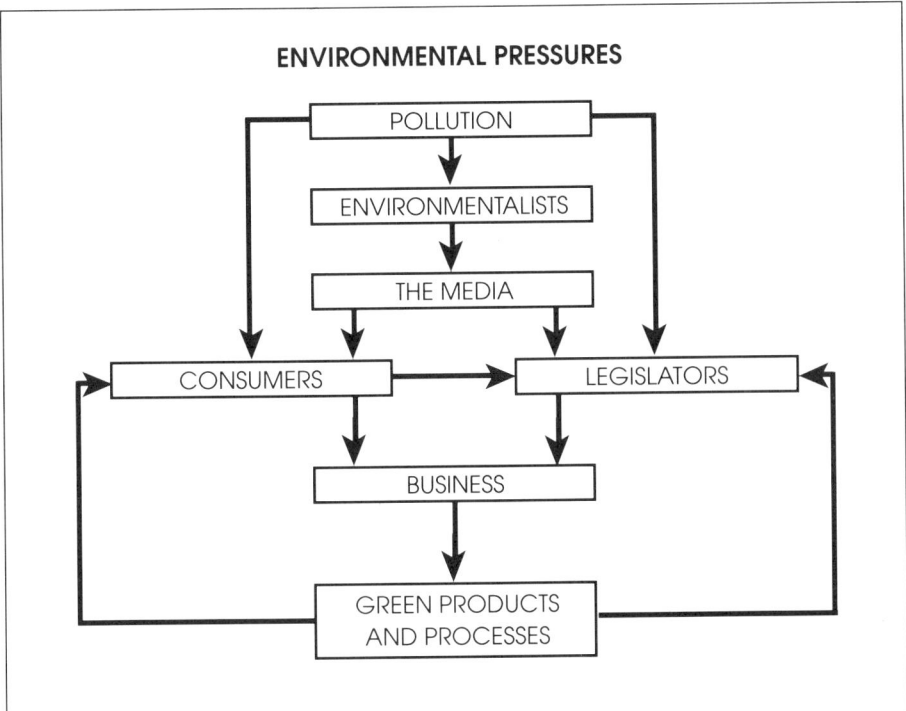

Figure 1.3: Environmental pressures. Environmentalists only achieve their objectives if they gain the support of consumers and legislators. Green products and processes will reduce the pressure on businesses.

regulate smaller polluters. It has also added regulations on waste and noise. All have considerable implications for business.

In the past, businesses concentrated on customers, staff and shareholders. More thoughtful companies also took into account their suppliers and business associates. Now, as Figure 1.4 shows, businesses are having to include the environment in their strategic thinking. But will green issues fade away, like all the other fads?

ARE GREEN ISSUES A PASSING FAD?

The importance of the environment varies in the mind of the public, depending on what else is happening in the world. Interest slumped during the Gulf War, with only 5 per cent rating it the most important issue. The UK Green Party's vote has also fallen, partly because of the growing emphasis placed on ecology by the other parties.

So is the environment likely to disappear as an important issue? Will it fade, just as the mystical movements of the 1960s did? The answer is no, for two

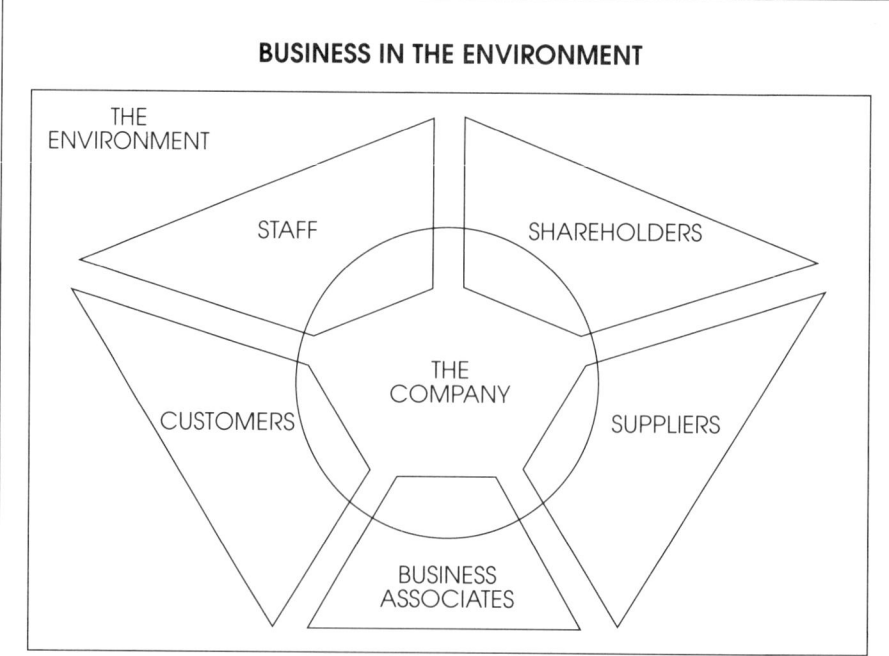

Figure 1.4: Business in the environment. Business now has to take into account the environment as well as its traditional concerns.

main reasons. Firstly, environmentalism is not based on issues of personal development, but on real problems that will not go away.

Global warming, depletion of the ozone layer, growing deserts, destruction of the rain forests, loss of species – the evidence is reported all the time. And these problems will grow worse unless serious action is taken.

Secondly, legislation is being passed in Westminster and Brussels, in Washington and Addis Ababa, that will change forever the way we do business. Even Russia has introduced a law that fines polluting factories. So even if consumer fervour lapsed tomorrow, business would still have to comply with the new legislation.

Still more legislation is in the pipeline. Whether this is passed depends partly on the speed at which industry pre-empts it with voluntary schemes.

THE NATURE OF THE PROBLEM

The keys issues are shown in Figure 1.5. A few facts indicate the scale of the problem:

- Global temperature could rise by 3°C before the end of the next century with a consequent sea level rise of 65cm. Some inhabited islands could disappear altogether, and the shape of Britain would

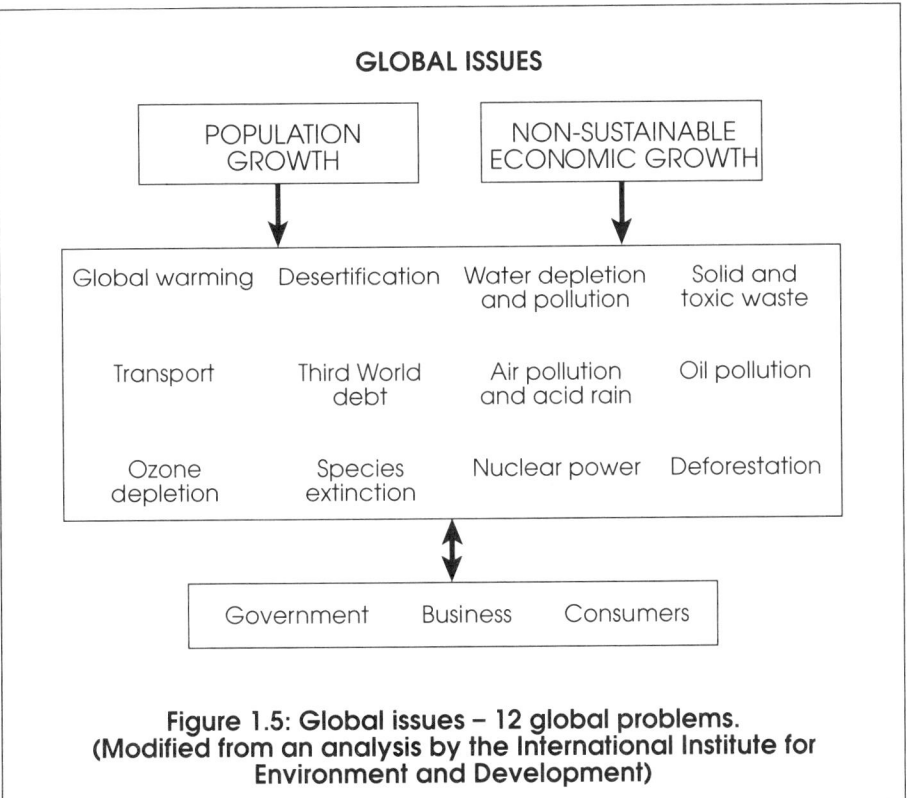

**Figure 1.5: Global issues – 12 global problems.
(Modified from an analysis by the International Institute for Environment and Development)**

alter. People in low lying areas could lose their homes and businesses to the sea.
- Over 2 million seabirds and 100 000 sea mammals die every year, trapped or injured by discarded rubbish.
- Only 400 mountain gorillas remain in the wild.
- Only 48 kakapos, New Zealand's giant flightless parrots, are left to continue the species.
- World industrial output is seven times what it was in 1950; and we use energy at a rate equivalent to 10 000 million tonnes of coal a year.
- The tropical forests, the world's store of rare species, are being reduced at the rate of 17 million hectares a year. Ninety-three per cent of Madagascar's forests has been destroyed or degraded.
- Since 1977, 1.7 billion tonnes of overworked American farm land have disappeared each year, due to soil erosion.
- Scandinavian lakes are dead and their forests are dying because of acid rain.
- Seven million tonnes of pollutants enter Romania's rivers annually. 200 000 hectares of farm land are totally unproductive due to pollution, with another 900 000 seriously polluted.

- In Britain, there is a growing shortage of landfill sites, and their use is becoming increasingly criticized. Other methods of disposal, such as dumping at sea, are increasingly restricted.

THE PROBLEMS BUSINESS FACES

The regulatory bodies are determined to stop pollution of every type. Shell was fined £1 million for the oil slick on the Mersey which killed 200 birds and contaminated another 2 000.

In the USA the fines are even heavier: ICI was fined $2.3 million for pollution caused at its Louisiana plant, while Monsanto was fined $1 million for a leak of hydrochloric acid at its Massachusetts plant. Europe is also getting tough: Sandoz had to pay SF40 million in compensation when in 1986 it polluted the Rhine with pesticides.

Punitive action is not restricted to the large oil and chemical companies. Up and down the country smaller breaches are coming to court, and the unfavourable publicity is often worse than the fines.

WHO IS TO BLAME?

Everyone who drives a car, washes their hands or opens a carton of milk is to blame. All consumption involves the expenditure of energy, and the reduction of some natural resource. Even the innocents are guilty. The grandmother sitting in front of her gas fire is using a non-renewable resource. The child on her bicycle has caused greenhouse gas emissions through the making of the steel.

We cannot turn our back on progress, nor live like medieval hermits. But we can reduce waste, re-process spent material, and use renewable resources. And in so doing we will build a better world for ourselves and our children.

According to the CBI, manufacturing industry creates 30 per cent of CO_2 emissions in the UK. Much of this could be reduced by energy efficiency and conservation, producing cash savings for business at the same time.

WHY INDUSTRY NEEDS TO BECOME GREEN

Many benefits flow from a good environmental record. They include:
- **Higher sales**. Increasingly aware of green issues, consumers are consciously choosing green products. The same applies to business-to-business markets. Industrial users do not want products that produce by-products, waste and pollution.
- **Better distribution**. Retailers are putting pressure on manufacturers to provide green products. Those that conform will win better distribution and achieve higher sales.
- **New product opportunities**. New products can be created by

identifying a green market opportunity, which in turn comes from a greater environmental awareness. Some firms have developed saleable products from their waste, or from environmental technologies they have developed. Demand for recycled plastic products in the US is growing at 44 per cent a year, according to the Freedonia Group.

- **A Unique Selling Point**. Competitors who develop a greener product or service will gain a competitive advantage. Recycled lavatory paper simply did not exist a few years ago. Now it takes a substantial share of the market.
- **Easier staff recruitment**. As population trends make staff more difficult to find, the green company will find it easier to attract good people. People will not want to work for a company that pollutes.
- **Reduced staff turnover**. Many members of staff have a personal interest in environmental protection. Allowing them to reduce pollution helps their careers and gives them personal satisfaction as well as helping the company. By contrast, one cigarette company faces regular staff resignations.
- **A reduced threat of law suits**. Companies that pollute face legal action from consumers or regulatory authorities (such as the National Rivers Authority). An environmental audit will identify or anticipate problems, and allow the company to take preventative action.
- **A legal defence**. Written procedures and records of inspection could be a defence in any future legal action.
- **Cheaper and more accessible insurance**. Lack of proper controls may prevent companies from obtaining insurance cover against environmental accidents.
- **Easier access to finance**. In the USA following the 'Fleet Factors' case, bankers may be held liable for clean-up costs in pollution incidents caused by their clients. In the UK and elsewhere, bankers are evaluating the environmental impact of proposals.
- **Reduced abatement control costs**. A company that has less waste or fewer emissions will not have to conduct clean-up operations.
- **Reduced risk of disaster**. Environmental catastrophes occur regularly, bringing serious problems to the companies who let them happen. Disasters are less likely to happen to companies which have introduced environmental controls or have opted for less contentious markets. It is vital to identify areas of weakness and rectify them.
- **Improved technical excellence**. In improving standards, the company will become stronger and better able to meet change.
- **Improved relationships with the local community**. Safer systems and reduced noise and pollution will reduce the friction between companies and their communities. Reduction of this distraction will allow management to concentrate on managing the business.
- **Reduced energy costs**. Significant savings can be made from reduced energy use.
- **Reduced waste disposal costs**. Disposal costs are estimated to have

jumped 300 per cent in the USA during the last decade. The UK's Environmental Protection Act could have the same effect. There is a growing trend to prevent trans-frontier shipments of toxic waste, the *Karin B* being an example of this. Missouri has banned the landfilling of waste oil and large consumer appliances.

- **Other savings.** 3M reckons to have saved $462 million worldwide since it started its environmental programme in 1975. This figure is conservative, being based on first year savings only. In the UK, the company has saved £10 million as a result of 80 projects.
- **Improved corporate image.** An improvement in a business's image has all kinds of beneficial effects, not least a better stock market value.
- **Greater international competitiveness.** Unless British firms become proactive about the environment, they will fall behind continental companies, particularly those from Germany, the Netherlands and Scandinavia. Many firms in those countries are further advanced in environmental issues, giving them a competitive advantage. There is also a danger that EC laws may prevent British companies from selling current products without substantial alterations.

Having spent millions on environmental safeguards, industrialists in Germany are fighting to toughen up EC legislation to prevent 'dirty companies' from competing with them on unfair terms. It is not all one-sided. Dutch and German firms also pollute the sea. But the times are changing, and polluters will soon either have to pay or be stopped from operating.

HOW AWARENESS AND ATTITUDES HAVE CHANGED

The index of a leading conservation book published in 1982 does not list the words 'global warming', 'greenhouse effect' or 'ozone layer'. It believes zoos 'have an important part to play in educating the public'. It also claims 'long periods of drought are rare in Britain, and that of 1975–6 was exceptional'. Maritime disposal of wastes 'has little effect' on the sea.

It was not alone in these attitudes. In 1981 the House of Lords Select Committee on Hazardous Waste Disposal (The Gregson Committee) said, 'No major changes on dumping hazardous wastes at sea are needed.' It also said, 'Landfill is an acceptable disposal method for a wide range of waste.' At that time, 78 per cent of chemical waste was buried in waste tips.

Since then, we have discovered a hole in the ozone layer and the problems of a warmer climate. Today, we are more aware of the dangers of methane explosions from the 1 300 old dumps that exist across Britain, and the environmental damage caused by dropping toxic waste in the sea. Now legislators are severely restricting what may be dumped at sea and in landfill sites.

Conservation has changed greatly in a single decade, and the next decade will be no different. It will bring renewed legislation, more controls, and greater inspection of corporate activities.

THE DANGERS OF INACTION

Doing nothing is a dangerous choice. Though little will happen in the short term, events will surely catch up with companies that take no action. The problems will include:

- **Increasing cost of compliance**. It costs more to 'back fit' technology to stop waste or pollution than it does to integrate it into new plant. Failure to act now could mean that one day the company will find itself unable to achieve the required standards. This could result in unacceptably heavy pollution-control costs or even closure.
  EC Directives oblige the UK to reduce sulphur emissions by 60 per cent by 2003 and nitrogen oxides by 30 per cent by 1998. To comply, the UK government will make life difficult for polluting companies. According to a CBI survey, less than 50 per cent of British firms think that EC law will have any influence. In the words of one observer, 'They are in for a rude awakening.'
- **Cost of non-compliance**. Companies face unlimited fines in the Crown Court, and their directors face a maximum two-year prison sentence. Fines for pollution under the Water Act have increased from £2 000 to £20 000.
- **Boycott or demonstrations from the national or international community**. The last thing a company needs is a concerted consumer attack, such as Nestlé faces over its sale of baby milks to Third World countries. Some of these attacks will be based on emotion rather than logic, and pressure groups will ignore scientific arguments.
- **The vocal locals**. Residents and pressure groups will increasingly make their voice heard. Such pressure can lead to a range of difficulties, from a complete shutdown to the company's failure to win planning permission for expansion when it needs it.
- **Reduced access to landfill sites**. Land disposal of waste will become increasingly restricted and costly. By 1995 more than half of all US cities will no longer use landfill sites. Companies that have not reduced their output of waste will be at a competitive disadvantage.
- **Early write-off of capital**. Failure to take the environment into account could lead management to buy the wrong type of plant, which could soon become redundant.

INDUSTRY'S REACTION

Many companies are taking positive steps to protect the environment. The entire chemical industry is making huge investments in environmental protection. But in other industries some companies are reluctant to get involved in environmental issues. The main reasons they quote are as follows, together with some green responses:

'Our machinery is a fixed asset – we can't simply get rid of it'

An environmental plan does not necessarily entail changing machinery. It might involve muffling it or adding guards. It might entail putting different raw materials through it. Or it might be about getting higher yields to reduce waste.

'We can't afford to invest – our profits are too low'

The Forum of Private Business, which represents 18 000 small firms in the UK, believes that the government is unrealistic in asking companies to become environmentally friendly, because its member companies do not have the money to spend. As we have seen, however, the environmental plan may start with no-cost or low-cost actions (insulation and draught-proofing, for example). Many companies find that an environmental programme brings significant savings in energy or waste-disposal costs. Green products will gain a bigger market share and will command higher prices.

'We all support the ideal of a green world, but it isn't our main priority'

If the regulatory bodies decide to become involved in your business, the company may have to take action that will be considerably more expensive than a phased action plan. The green company is an efficient one, which is why the environment should be a priority.

'We're not a big polluter'

Until someone takes an objective look at a company's operation, it cannot determine how clean it is. Most companies can become 'greener' without much difficulty. And going green will have beneficial spin-offs on staff morale and your corporate image. Universal Office Supplies, for example, Britain's largest office supplies company, has carved out a special position for itself as a green organization following the publication of its Green Office Guide.

'We're in the middle of a redundancy/quality/buyout/JIT programme – we don't want to be distracted'

The environment is a critical issue that cannot be ignored or postponed. Neither will it disappear from the agenda. The first stage in addressing it, the audit, can be helped through by outside consultants, thereby minimizing company executives' time.

'I don't want to lose control, and especially not to some green extremists'

When a company is facing a green audit for the first time, managers may be suspicious that they will lose power, and that they will have to implement expensive and irrelevant solutions. In fact, the audit will merely indicate possible problem areas, and it is usually up to the line manager to decide what to do about it. The auditors have to convince the Chief Executive that they are business-minded people, or they will not be appointed.

'I don't want my weaknesses exposed'
When they start thinking about a green programme, all companies are nervous about exposing their weaknesses, especially to an outside audit team. The auditors should advise the manager that the audit is participative and forward-looking, and that it will not apportion blame. This is in the auditors' interest: they need the manager's help and they like to see solutions implemented. It is all too easy for a manager to sabotage an audit by discrediting it.

'Many customers buy on price. That gives polluting companies (the cowboys) and dirty countries (like Eastern Europe) an advantage'
Within a decade, dirty companies will be legislated out of business. Environmental criteria are already appearing in the purchasing policies of large companies and local authorities. And most companies expect their suppliers to pass a quality threshold. Concern for the environment is one aspect of quality.

HOW INDUSTRY CAN HELP

Industry can help to improve the environment in numerous ways:

- **As a property and land owner.** It can protect and enhance the built and rural environment, and conserve energy.
- **As an investor.** It can invest its money in environmentally sound organizations.
- **By reducing pollution.** Companies can reduce their output of waste to land, air and water by using cleaner techniques, cleaner raw materials, better management controls, and recycling.
- **As an opinion former.** Companies can provide information about environmental issues, and educate the public about local and global issues.
- **As a consumer.** Industry can encourage its suppliers to provide environmentally sound products.
- **As an employer.** Companies can harness employees' enthusiasm for environmental protection to reduce pollution and waste.
- **As an innovative organization.** Companies can share their advances, and communicate 'best practice' to the rest of the world.
- **As a repository of expertise.** Every company has experts in environmental issues, ranging from chemists to architects. This expertise may be made available to the community.
- **Through transport decisions.** The company car and the lorry fleet contribute to pollution and congestion. With sensitive handling, the company can reduce the environmental impact of its operations.
- **With environmentally friendly products.** Companies can introduce products that biodegrade, that do not harm nature, and that last longer.

○ **In conforming to the highest standards.** Companies should meet or exceed the highest standards set for protecting the environment.

LOCAL AUTHORITIES

'Local authority' is a misnomer for organizations which purchase £3 billion worth of goods and services a year, and which employ thousands of people. Newcastle City Council alone is responsible for £15 million worth of goods.

Local authorities are in the forefront of environmental thinking, and many have commissioned audits. With local authorities buying everything from food to street furniture, their policies can have a significant impact on the environment.

Though authorities are restrained through the tendering process in certain ways (for example 'country of origin' cannot be a discriminator), products can be specified on the ground of their nature or means of production.

Local authorities are also able to discriminate against products not produced to BS 5750, the British quality standard. Moreover, the COSHH (Control of Substances Hazardous to Health) regulations require authorities to purchase the least toxic chemicals and to audit those in use.

Moreover, national government has said that local authorities need not fear criticism for spending money on goods that are less damaging to the environment, even if they cost more.

Much of this book is wholly relevant to local authorities. The only exceptions are certain manufacturing processes. But as regulatory authorities and purchasing bodies, public sector managers will find it useful to understand manufacturing problems and their solutions.

Local authorities have a wider ambit than commercial businesses. Their concerns include transport conditions, public health, housing, education and leisure facilities. An environmental strategy can be equally applied to each of these areas. It is a matter of assessing the current situation, determining what needs to be done, setting objectives, and defining a plan to achieve them.

WHEN TO START

Some companies have a long and honourable tradition of environmental protection: 3M has been running its anti-pollution programme since 1975. Others only wake up to the problem when it knocks on their door in the form of a Health and Safety Executive inspector.

One thing is certain. The sooner a company sets up a green policy and implements it with an action plan, the sooner it lessens the risk of a serious incident. And when environmentalists and regulators start asking questions, the company will have facts and figures to show the steps it is taking.

Environmental protection takes time to get started. It can take five years for a company to get its house in order. So the sooner a company starts, the sooner its operations will become 'clean'.

There are two ways to act. One is to adopt minor and uncontroversial activities — a bit of paper recycling in the office, and a quick tidying of site litter. The other way is to adopt a thorough and co-ordinated approach, starting with an environmental audit.

People will see through a half-hearted effort, if only because they can observe other companies doing better. And as people become environmentally literate, they will know what questions to ask. Just as the consumer is receiving increasing amounts of information on product labels, so in time she will get more information about companies' impact on the environment.

As Ciba Geigy has said, 'A sceptical public will not allow its doubts to be allayed by declarations of intent, public relations exercises or glossy brochures.'

INTRODUCTORY CHECKLIST

- Assess what environmental legalization is relevant to your business, and whether you are complying with it.
- Evaluate the benefits that going green could bring, including financial savings and higher sales.
- Evaluate the problems that corporate pollution could bring.
- Determine what objections to going green managers and staff might raise, and consider how they might be overcome.

2
THE ENVIRONMENTAL AUDIT

♦

Having decided to take environmental action, the first step is usually an environmental audit. 'Audit' is only a new buzz-word for an old-fashioned business activity, namely a systematic analysis of one aspect of the business, in this case its impact on the environment.

The audit is a method of collecting information, a fact-finding activity; without facts, you are just another person with an opinion. The audit also helps to ensure that the environment is tackled in an organized and professional way, rather than in a superficial or piecemeal manner.

BENEFITS OF AN ENVIRONMENTAL AUDIT

○ Provides a factual basis for decision making

○ Increases employee awareness of green issues

○ Identifies cost savings

○ Increases the company's credibility among outsiders

○ Allows management to identify and reward good environmental performance

○ Provides data when seeking insurance cover or additional finance

○ Provides an early warning of impending disaster

Technically, the first analysis of a company's environmental impact is called a review, rather than an audit. You cannot audit a company where no system

A STRATEGIC RESPONSE

STAGE	PROCESS	METHOD	CHARACTERISTICS
1	Data gathering	Environmental audit	Comprehensive Systematic Regular
2	Policy making	Environmental policy	Formally defined Available to all Quantified goals
3	Execution	Environmental plan	Involves everyone Integrated into the business Monitored/reviewed

Figure 2.1: A strategic response. The three stages of a planned environmental strategy.

exists, whether financially or environmentally. The review may recommend setting up new systems and procedures, whose effectiveness can be checked in future audits. That said, most companies use the word 'audit' alone, partly because it has become a fashionable management term.

Companies should not assume that an audit will solve their problems. The audit does not provide answers: it merely collects information and identifies problems. The solutions come later. As Figure 2.1 shows, the audit forms part of a wider environmental strategy, which includes an environmental policy and a plan.

DEFINITION

Environmental audit: a systematic and comprehensive analysis of the company's impact on the environment.

In carrying out the audit, the company will discover the extent of the problem (if one exists). It can then define an environmental policy or objectives, and produce a plan that will help the company achieve that policy.

Environmental audits started in the USA as a means of assessing compliance with environmental regulations. The US Environmental Protection Agency found that management weaknesses rather than technical failure were primarily responsible for environmental damage. With many offending firms it introduced a compulsory independent audit as part of the settlement.

WHICH AUDIT?

Most companies think of the environmental audit as one type of analysis. But as the audit has become more common, it has spawned various options. Just as a motorist can buy a saloon car, an estate, a 4×4 or a sports car, so the green audit is available in a range of types. The main ones are listed below. Each concentrates on a different business need, or varies in its thoroughness.

- **Scoping audit**: An introductory audit. It will analyse the strategic issues, but it will not include measurements.
- **Site audit**: Looks at a specific factory or office.
- **Corporate audit**: Examines the activities of the entire business. Like a site audit, only more extensive.
- **Compliance audit**: Evaluates whether a plant is conforming to legislation or company standards.
- **Take-over audit**: Checks the potential environmental costs of an acquisition. The reverse of this is a divestiture audit, which will consider which activities to halt or sell in order to reduce the company's involvement with ecologically suspect activities.
- **Activity audit**: Checks a specific activity that may cover more than one site. Waste disposal is one such example.
- **Issue audit**: Checks how the company is handling one particular issue of public concern, such as CFCs or greenhouse gas emissions.
- **Supplier audit**: Checks the environmental standard of suppliers. It may also be called an associate audit when carried out on other business contacts such as contractors.
- **Environmental Impact Assessment**: An EIA checks the impact of a new plant or product on the environment. The words 'Environmental Impact Assessment' relate specifically to a new development.

Each audit overlaps the others. For example, a standard site audit may include a check on whether the site is complying with legislation.

Many companies need a straightforward corporate or site audit. Some are looking to protect themselves from protesters (an issue audit). Others want to check that an acquisition does not cost them more than they bargained for (a take-over audit).

Carrying out the investigation can take many days; its follow-up (in terms of analysis, report writing, planning and training) can last much longer. In fact, the audit is just the first step towards a long-term objective of environmental efficiency.

As Figure 2.2 shows, the company's first environmental audit (or review) will be different from subsequent audits, and will take longer. The auditors will need to obtain new types of information, set up new documentation and procedures, and start an education process.

Subsequent audits will review the company's compliance with previously set goals, and will check for deviations from agreed procedures. They will also

THE ENVIRONMENTAL AUDIT

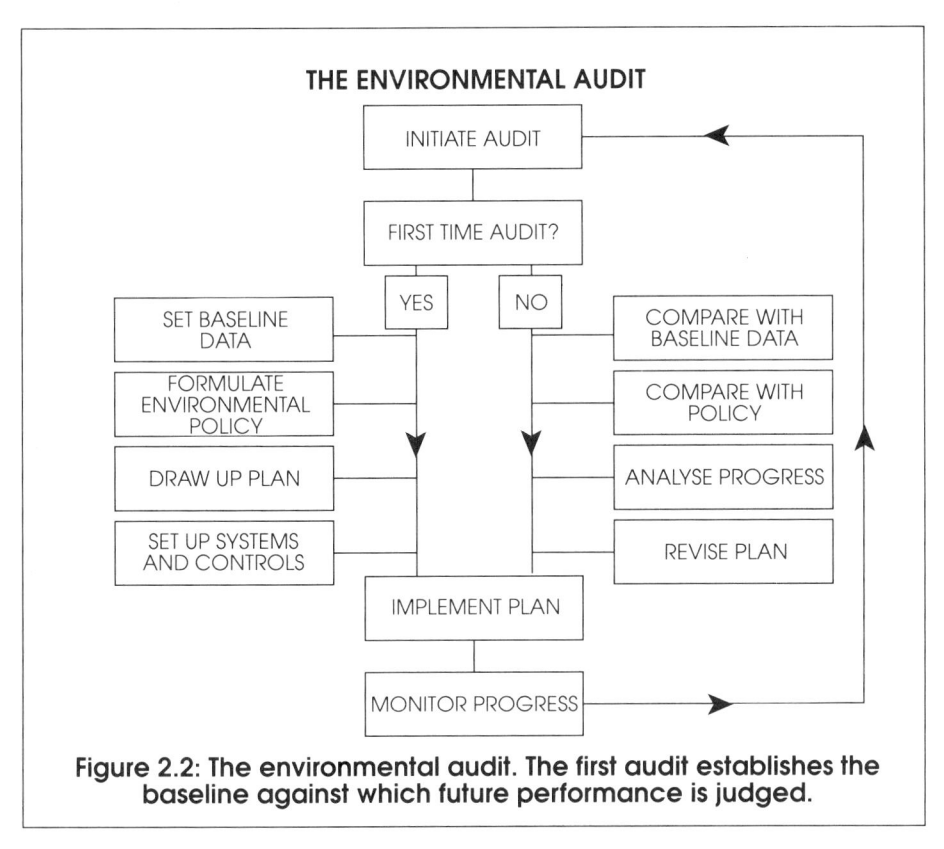

```
                    INITIATE AUDIT  ←─────────────┐
                          ↓                       │
                    FIRST TIME AUDIT?             │
                      ↙       ↘                   │
                   YES         NO                 │
   SET BASELINE ──┤             ├── COMPARE WITH  │
       DATA                         BASELINE DATA │
   FORMULATE    ──┤             ├── COMPARE WITH  │
   ENVIRONMENTAL                    POLICY        │
   POLICY                                         │
   DRAW UP PLAN ──┤             ├── ANALYSE PROGRESS
   SET UP SYSTEMS─┤             ├── REVISE PLAN
   AND CONTROLS                                   │
                    IMPLEMENT PLAN                │
                          ↓                       │
                    MONITOR PROGRESS ─────────────┘
```

Figure 2.2: The environmental audit. The first audit establishes the baseline against which future performance is judged.

assess whether external changes have taken place, such as new legislation or technical innovations.

PLANNING THE AUDIT

A pilot survey can be useful in checking that the auditors time will be properly used, and that company staff are prepared for the audit. A pilot survey will also help to assess which data should be checked.

The audit should be formally planned, and a written plan should include the topics shown in the box below.

TOPICS FOR AN AUDIT PLANNING DOCUMENT

- Objectives of the audit
- Scope (area and processes to be covered, topics to be excluded)

- ○ Key issues
- ○ Names of audit team members, with allocated tasks (see p. 177)
- ○ Announcement to staff about the audit, its purpose and schedule
- ○ Itinerary
- ○ Method of collecting internal and external data
- ○ List of people to be interviewed, together with job titles
- ○ Timing
- ○ Method of presenting findings
- ○ Follow-up action (for example, defining an environmental policy)

The audit should be simple and quick. Evidence from ICI and IBM suggests that bureaucratic or excessive auditing becomes unworkable, and such companies are changing to flexible, faster audits.

METHODS OF GATHERING INFORMATION

There are several ways of gathering information for the audit. The auditors can inspect the different departments by walking around the site, and they can question staff. They can also analyse whatever data are collected by the business (such as discharge statistics), and they can consult their databases and outside experts on technological developments and legal requirements.

Inspections

During the inspections, which comprise a site tour, the auditors will look for signs of emissions, hazardous materials, unsafe practices or waste. Visits will be made to all departments, and a description made of all processes and materials.

Interviews

The auditors will talk to staff at all levels of the company, and in all areas of the firm. The auditors also need to check the site's history. Staff must be briefed to give the interviewers their time, and they should provide access to information. The value of the audit will be severely weakened if information is not forthcoming or the auditors are faced with hostility.

Checklists are generally used to ensure that all topics are covered. Suitable checklists are provided throughout the book for this purpose. There is a list of checklists on pages xi–xii.

Internal Records

The auditor will analyse the company's performance as measured by environmental data collected on the site. Typically, these will be emissions and discharges. In the initial audit, not all the data will be available. Some will not yet be collected. (See 'Measuring the environmental record' below.) One of the main benefits of an initial audit is that it identifies which data should be collected, and how collection should be undertaken.

The first audit will set baseline data – a snapshot showing the current levels of emissions, time lost from injuries and so on. Audits in the following years will compare latest results against the baseline data, and assess the success of the company's environmental plan.

External Records

The auditor will check his database for relevant legislation, and for problems encountered by other companies in the same industry.

Setting up an external data-gathering system is another benefit of the first audit. The EC has introduced an array of directives and laws, which are only now coming into force. Many companies are still unaware of their impact. It is vital to monitor relevant legislation, both new and proposed. Smaller companies will only need to do this annually.

TOPICS FOR AN ENVIRONMENTAL AUDIT

A site audit is usually a wide-ranging study. It will examine the impact of all the company's activities on all aspects of the environment (Figure 2.3). Here are the topics to be included, along with some of the main issues.

- **Business associates**: Do contractors, agents or retailers perform their work in a way that is environmentally acceptable?
- **Cafeteria**: Is company food healthy and wholesome?
- **Complaints**: How are complaints handled?
- **Corporate strategy**: Policy, targets, standards and plans that relate to the environment.
- **Emissions and discharges**: Their volume and composition. Consents. What steps are being taken to reduce emissions and discharges?
- **Energy**: Can energy use be reduced?
- **Finance**: Has any provision been made for liabilities or losses that could stem from environmental legislation or from an ecological disaster? What are the costs and revenues of implementing change? Is money invested in an environmentally sound way?
- **Hazards**: Dangers to staff, in terms of work practices or materials used. COSHH regulations. Accident plans.
- **Human Resources**: Who is responsible for environmental issues? Does a job description exist? What environmental training is carried out? Who has line responsibility for ensuring that environmental standards are met? Do all individuals have specific responsibilities? Occupational health.
- **Internal communication**: How are the company's practices and policies communicated to staff?

ENVIRONMENTAL IMPACTS

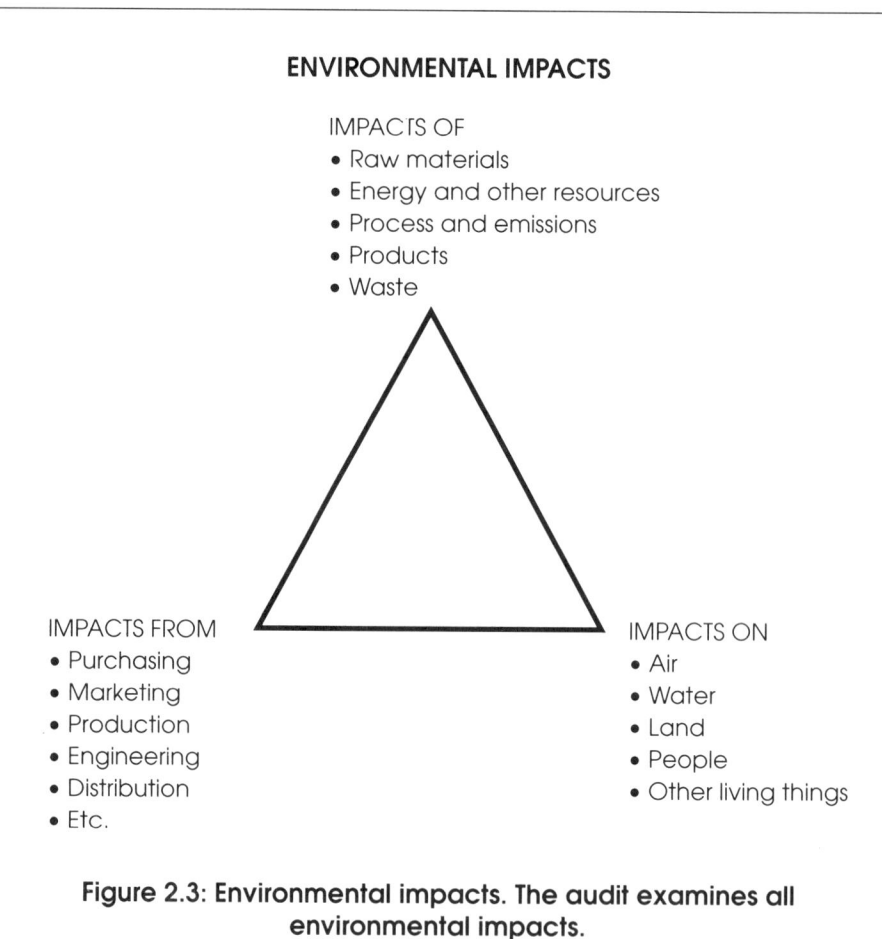

IMPACTS OF
- Raw materials
- Energy and other resources
- Process and emissions
- Products
- Waste

IMPACTS FROM
- Purchasing
- Marketing
- Production
- Engineering
- Distribution
- Etc.

IMPACTS ON
- Air
- Water
- Land
- People
- Other living things

Figure 2.3: Environmental impacts. The audit examines all environmental impacts.

- **Land and buildings**: Design of energy-efficient buildings. Litter. Maintenance. Impact of new developments. Protection of wildlife.
- **Legal**: What legislation (current and proposed) impinges on the company's activities? Does the business conform to legislation and consents? Is compliance monitored?
- **Management information**: What information is gathered? Is it adequate? How are environmental standards monitored and reported?
- **Marketing strategies and plans**: Have they taken into account customers' attitudes to the environment? Green products, and the withdrawal of damaging products. Better packaging. What research is carried out? Marketing communication. Competitor activity.
- **Medical**: What responsibility does the company accept for employee health? How is this borne out?
- **Office**: Checks on 'sick building syndrome' and repetitive strain injury

(RSI). Recycled materials, and recycling them after use. Energy efficiency.
- **Past activities**: The investigation will also consider previous dumping or landfill activities, so that action can be taken and future problems avoided. Is the company liable for past products or practices?
- **Public relations**: Listening to and communicating with the public at large, and local inhabitants in particular.
- **Processes**: What technology is used? What chemicals are used in non-productive processes (such as solvents used in cleaning machinery)? Can more ecologically sound manufacturing activities be introduced? Checks on safety, reliability and control equipment. What balance exists in terms of raw materials, processes, products and losses?
- **Products**: Safety, quality and impact on the environment. The entire life of the product must be evaluated 'from the cradle to the grave'. Are particular products likely to suffer from new legislation or green attitudes?
- **Purchasing**. What environmental information exists about products bought? Can better products be bought? What is the environmental record of suppliers?
- **Raw materials**. Are they dangerous or toxic? Use of sustainable vs. non-renewable resources. Where are they sourced? How are they stored, handled and disposed of?
- **R&D**: Design of eco-friendly products. Laboratory safety. What further technical analysis needs to be done?
- **Transport**: The company's use of cars and lorries.
- **Waste**: Production and disposal of waste. Can it be reduced?

Since 1980, Hoffman-La Roche has carried out 200 environmental audits throughout the company. The audits are conducted by a team from the safety and environmental protection department in Basle. It checks compliance with company directives, examines particular problems and suggests remedial measures. Typically it takes four auditors about three days to conduct an audit. The report is sent to Basle together with a series of recommendations and a timespan within which improvements should be made.

MEASURING THE ENVIRONMENTAL RECORD

Gathering data is a key task. The data will tell the company the extent to which environmental problems exist, and where the problems are greatest.

It is also vital to have a baseline against which environmental progress can be measured.

There are many ways to check environmental performance, and the choice will depend on the type of plant. The checklist below shows some of the measurements that can be taken.

When the first environmental audit is undertaken much of the data will have to be captured for the first time. This will entail setting up recording systems.

ENVIRONMENTAL INDICES

Health and safety, staff

Annual lost time injuries (actual number; number per million hours worked)

Number of staff receiving environmental training, total hours of training

Noise

Peak and mean noise levels, within the working areas and at the site boundary

Air emissions

Annual emissions of specific pollutants (compared with consent levels)

Number of deviations from consent or target emission values

Number of complaints about air quality, smoking chimneys or odours

Water discharges

Maximum pH value of water (compared with consent)

Quantity of different substances in water (compared with consent); for example, concentrations of lead or aluminium

Number of spills recorded

Waste

Scrap as percentage of total production

Percentage of waste recycled

Quantity of waste sent for dumping as a ratio of total volume

Energy

Units of energy consumed (per standard unit of output)

Wildlife

Number of species of plants, animals, birds or insects present

Number of trees by type and maturity

Number of trees planted each year

Area of grass (m^2)

Other

Add your own measures here:

_____

_____

_____

_____

Once these indicators have been established, the company can set targets for their improvement (see 'Establishing targets' below).

DATA ANALYSIS

By this stage you will have assembled all relevant information about your business and the environment. The next stage is a SWOT analysis, assessing the company's strengths and weaknesses, along with the opportunities and threats posed by external forces. This will include the PEST factors – political, economic, social and technological. Figure 2.4 shows an outline SWOT analysis. It is a useful way of analysing the company's present position, and evaluating what is happening outside the firm.

Another way of analysing the situation is through a NAP analysis (Now – Aim – Plan). A NAP analysis for another company is illustrated in Figure 2.5. This analysis is useful in helping management develop a plan of action. At its simplest, the NAP analysis uses three large sheets of paper. They are headed respectively Now, Aim and Plan.

The first sheet describes the current problems. It outlines the status of the company – the stage it has reached.

The second sheet describes management's goals. It tells where the company would like to be in five years' time. Management will want to have removed the problems described in the first chart.

The third sheet shows how management will progress from the first chart to the second. It is the plan of action.

SWOT ANALYSIS

	POSITIVE	NEGATIVE
PRESENT/INTERNAL	**STRENGTHS** Main products do not damage the environment Environmental committee set up BS5750 gained recently	**WEAKNESSES** Lack of green packaging/promotion Substantial emissions Some ageing plant No checks on raw material sourcing No environmental policy
FUTURE/EXTERNAL	**OPPORTUNITIES** Investment programme – new plant Availability of cleaner processes Green audit planned Customers' interest in green issues	**THREATS** Green activities by competitors New legislation Threat of consumer hostility

Figure 2.4: SWOT analysis. This analysis shows that the company is aware of many green issues. A SWOT analysis can be done for each division, product or department.

Another way of making sense of the data is to gather it into logical structures:

○ Review of relevant management plans, controls, systems and procedures
○ Use of natural resources (raw materials, water, air, land, fuel and energy)
○ Analysis of the manufacturing processes, from raw material to finished product
○ Socio-cultural review (the company's beliefs, values, style, skills and structure)
○ Performance analysis (emissions, energy costs, legal compliance, competitor comparisons).

REPORTING THE FINDINGS

By this stage the audit team should have identified the key findings. They can have a preliminary discussion with management to check that they have not missed any important issues. Then they can make a formal presentation, supported by a written report. Copies of the report should go to all appropriate

NAP ANALYSIS

NOW	AIM	PLAN
Dependent on declining products	New range of environmentally sound products	Set up new product development programme
Air pollution satisfactory	Maintain	Monitor
Water pollution increasingly criticized	No water pollution	Devise pollution reduction plan
Rising energy costs	Reduce to <250kWh/m²/yr	Appoint Energy Manager
Local residents hostile to our operations	Harmony between residents and company	Carry out research: set up public affairs committee
Substantial scrap levels	Reduce landfill waste to 2% of output	Investigate quality programme, recycling programme
Fragmented responsibility	Secure management control	Implement environmental management system

Figure 2.5: NAP analysis. A NAP analysis concentrates on what needs to be done. This makes it an extremely effective management tool.

staff, whose input should be requested for the next stage of the action: defining the environmental policy.

DRAWING UP AN ENVIRONMENTAL POLICY

Defining an environmental policy (see above, Figure 2.1) helps the company determine its attitude towards the environment. The policy is a set of principles that tell the world how green the company plans to be. It helps employees know what is expected of them, and ensures that everyone in the company has the same objectives. It prevents the company from operating 'by the seat of the pants', and guides the company in all its activities.

As Figure 15.1 shows (p. 204), a company may decide simply to comply with legislation, or it might seek to become a leader in its field. The policy will have to balance environmental considerations against commercial objectives.

One guiding principle is that of 'sustainable development'. This avoids the twin excesses of the throw-away, high growth economy on the one hand, and the zero-growth medieval economy on the other.

Sustainable development means that the company should operate in a way that meets the needs of today without affecting the abilities of future generations to meet their needs. It should husband any scarce or non-renewable resources, avoid polluting the planet and creating deserts or slums, and not expect future generations to clear up its messes.

The environmental policy or charter should be given to all employees, to opinion formers, and to all other relevant people.

SPECIMEN ENVIRONMENTAL POLICY

Our attitude: We recognize our responsibility to the environment, and all living things, wherever we operate. We bear a special responsibility to our customers, staff and local residents. We aim to ensure a safe, healthy and sustainable environment, on which we have the least possible impact.

Goals: We will set goals for safety and environmental performance. These goals will be quantified by targets which will be annually raised.

Audits: We will regularly audit our compliance with legislation and this policy, measure progress, and strive to improve.

Standards: We will select and conform to the most stringent international environmental standards. Wherever possible we will surpass those standards. We will aim continually to raise our standards. We will work for fair and sound legislation.

Conservation: We will aim to conserve natural resources by minimizing the use of non-renewable materials, by recycling materials, by minimizing energy use, and by using recycled products and packaging.

Products: We aim to produce products/services that are useful or beneficial. Wherever possible, our products will be recyclable. We will not produce or sell products that harm people or the world.

Production: Our production methods will strive to achieve waste-free production, and to avoid polluting the land, air or water. We will avoid hazardous processes or materials where alternatives are available. We will reduce waste and losses by being efficient, and we will take all reasonable steps to prevent pollution at its source.

R&D: Our research and development programme will seek to improve current products and to introduce new ones that are better still. We will undertake 'cradle to grave' responsibility for our products. We will stay abreast of new technologies, and uncover new business opportunities that are compatible with the environment.

Workplace: Our factories and offices will be safe, healthy and attractive places in which to work. We will avoid hazardous practices. We will assess the environmental impact of all major proposed changes and reduce their environmental effects.

Transport: We will adopt an environmentally sound transport policy.

Communication: We will communicate openly about our operations to all relevant bodies, and provide appropriate statistical information even when not required by law. We will provide information to consumers and the trade about the contents of our products and the nature of our activities. We will not make misleading or exaggerated environmental claims, and we will oppose and expose such information.

The community: We will be a responsible neighbour, acting promptly to correct incidents or conditions that endanger health, safety or the environment. We will report them to the authorities promptly, and inform everyone who may be affected.

Society: We recognize a duty to share solutions with the rest of society. To that end we will communicate openly and participate in efforts to improve the environment.

Staff: We will ensure that all our employees are aware of their environmental responsibilities. We will provide proper training and involve them in decision making on environmental issues. At each of our sites there will be an individual with responsibility for environmental protection.

Suppliers: We expect high environmental standards from suppliers and contractors who work for us, and we will monitor their performance.

A comprehensive set of principles. Some companies may prefer a set of shorter one-line goals. The policy should also refer to issues that are important to its industry. For example, a printing works will want to mention using recycled paper wherever possible, while an electricity company might highlight its intention to educate customers in energy conservation.

HOW GREEN DO WE HAVE TO BE?

Some products are clearly not environmentally sound. The nuclear power industry, for example, threatens our children's future. Although its safety record is better than that of the coal industry, nuclear power has the capacity to devastate the land for generations to come. It also requires our descendants to guard our nuclear waste. This contravenes the concept of sustainable development, because it restricts the choices of future generations.

Weapons manufacture is another difficult issue. It may be reasonable to sell guns to the Navy to protect our shores against invaders. But it is not acceptable to sell those same guns to an unstable military regime which will use them against its own starving people. Military spending also diverts money from areas like healthcare and education.

A third category of products is widely used by the public, but their use causes feelings of guilt. Such products include pesticides and cars. Demand will continue, but market share will switch to companies whose brands are less harmful to the environment.

Other products can be environmentally positive or negative, depending on the way they are managed. If organized purely for profit, the forestry industry grows regimented rows of conifers that damage ecologically important areas and provide poor wildlife habitats. If conservation becomes an added objective, the same forests can become a haven for wildlife, can fit attractively into the landscape, and will provide a social amenity. Either way, forests serve to reduce the import of timber products, which is Britain's fourth highest import bill, costing nearly £7 billion a year. The timber industry also employs 40 000 people; and these economic arguments cannot be ignored.

Companies should look at their product and market portfolio; they should develop a corporate strategy, and take steps to implement that strategy. This may require product or factory improvement. It may require divestment or acquisition. It may lead to investment in one part of the market, and withdrawal from another.

Most companies are in less contentious markets than those mentioned above, but they still have the capacity to go green. The builders' merchant can check where its supplies come from. The yoghurt company can provide an organic range. The finance company can provide an investment policy based on green principles. No company is perfect, but all can help to make the world a better place. To seek environmental gains that are commercially achievable is surely a realistic aim for any business.

ESTABLISHING TARGETS

Having decided on a policy, the company will need to agree a set of targets. These will provide a measure by which the company can judge its progress. The targets can be categorized by department, division or type of pollution. They can have short-, medium- and long-term aims, but each should be quantified and have an achievement date. Most will relate to the environmental indices discussed above in 'Measuring the Environmental Record'. The targets of 3M include:

- elimination of 85 per cent of the company's US air emissions by mid-1992, with further reductions after that
- reduction of annual hydrocarbon emissions by more than 55 000 tonnes
- setting the annual trigger level for action at 100 tonnes of hydrocarbons for existing plants and 40 tonnes at new plants. This means new plants are expected to operate much more efficiently than existing plants.
- moving closer to the ideal of zero pollution.

Many goals will involve reaching a certain standard by a certain date. This means identifying the standards relevant to your operation. You may also have to set standards in cases where none exist. Over time these could become the industry standard.

AN INTERNATIONAL PERSPECTIVE

Different standards apply in different countries, with a knock-on effect for companies who operate internationally. Many Third World countries have much less legislation than the west. Thailand, for example, has become a centre for the export of wild animals. Before the US embargo of 1988, Panama's merchant fleet was the largest in the world, with over 12 500 ships flying the Panamanian flag, avoiding payment of corporate income tax and free from interference by maritime unions.

A company cannot maintain high standards in the west and low ones in the Third World without being accused of double standards. While it is reasonable to provide rates of pay that are appropriate to each country, it is not acceptable to operate unsafe practices.

Setting higher standards can cause problems of competitiveness, but this problem has been faced and overcome by companies in Germany, the US and Scandinavia. Moreover, many industry leaders believe they should set high standards for others to follow. Such companies see themselves as agents of change, and believe they are better placed to face the future.

CORPORATE STRATEGY CHECKLIST

- Conduct an initial environmental review.
- Commit the business to regular environmental auditing.
- Include all matters which could damage people, other living things or the planet.
- Collect and analyse information about emissions and discharges.
- Check what legislation is relevant to the business, and evaluate its compliance.
- Decide which corporate positioning to adopt.
- Draw up an environmental policy and strategy to guide the company's future actions.
- Create an environmental action plan to rectify problems and to monitor future progress.
- Set quantifiable goals.
- Review progress regularly, and take corrective action.

Once the environmental policy has been agreed, the company can develop an action plan, which is discussed in Chapter 16. Before that we will look at each function in turn, examining how the audit should be applied, and considering what steps each department can take.

3
LAND AND BUILDINGS

◆

The way we use land and buildings has an important impact on the environment. Construction, maintenance and landscaping can help or harm the world, but they are rarely neutral activities.

As Figure 3.1 shows, we can separate new development from the treatment of existing buildings. In this chapter, we start by looking at the maintenance of older buildings. Then we consider land use and appearance, before turning to new development.

WHEN REFURBISHMENT IS BETTER THAN NEW BUILD

Renovating an existing building often uses fewer resources than demolishing and rebuilding. Buildings built before 1945 are often solidly built and on a human scale, as well as having a greater lived-in charm than modern buildings.

Although they were never designed to cope with today's modern services, older buildings can be adapted to provide a more interesting workspace. Renovating is never as simple as building from scratch, but sympathetic and intelligent use of old buildings can provide major advantages in terms of cost and lifestyle.

Some British companies today are buying Georgian mansions and converting them into offices. This gives employees a peaceful and rather grand place of work, with plenty of green space, a clean environment and lots of parking space. However, these buildings are often poorly served by public transport, and this causes an increase in car use.

When refurbishing an existing building, especially a period one, consider using second-hand building materials. They blend more easily into the building, they recycle raw materials, and their worn look is often aesthetically pleasing. Contact an architectural salvage company for doors, gates, windows, railings and other objects.

Do not throw out old architectural items: offer them to an architectural salvage company. This will avoid wasting valuable materials, and you will receive money for them. Even if you do not like the 1950s partitions, 1940s

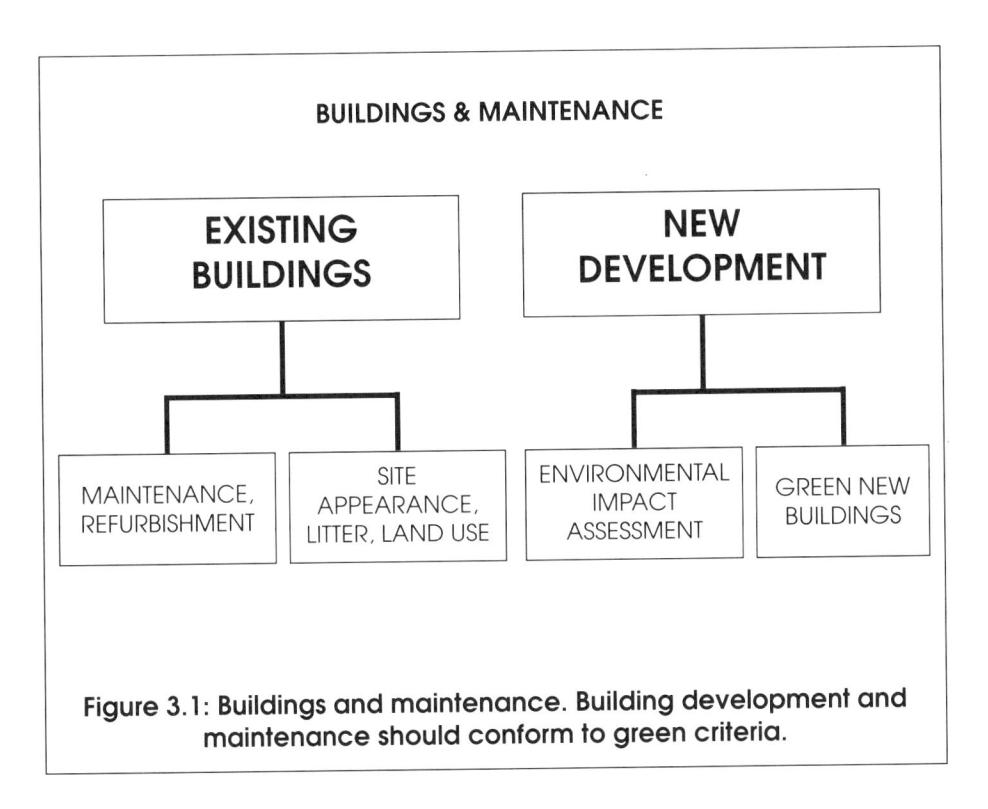

```
                    BUILDINGS & MAINTENANCE

        ┌──────────────────┐              ┌──────────────────┐
        │     EXISTING     │              │       NEW        │
        │    BUILDINGS     │              │   DEVELOPMENT    │
        └──────────────────┘              └──────────────────┘
           │          │                      │            │
   ┌───────────┐  ┌──────────┐        ┌─────────────┐  ┌──────────┐
   │MAINTENANCE│  │   SITE   │        │ENVIRONMENTAL│  │GREEN NEW │
   │REFURBISH- │  │APPEARANCE│        │   IMPACT    │  │BUILDINGS │
   │  MENT     │  │LITTER,   │        │ ASSESSMENT  │  │          │
   │           │  │LAND USE  │        │             │  │          │
   └───────────┘  └──────────┘        └─────────────┘  └──────────┘
```

Figure 3.1: Buildings and maintenance. Building development and maintenance should conform to green criteria.

desks, 1930s fireplaces and 1920s doors, someone else will. Twenty years ago, London skips were full of Victorian baths; now they are expensive and sought after.

Be especially careful about ripping out original multi-paned windows, and replacing them with flat sheets of glass. Though this can be done effectively, the building can easily lose its style. Some twentieth-century buildings, especially those of the 1930s, are still too modern for us to evaluate their architectural merit.

If the windows are reasonably solid, it is safer to leave them for another decade, and let the next generation of directors decide on their aesthetic value. One thing is for sure: once they have been taken out, these features can never be replaced. Unnecessary modernization will also cost more than simple maintenance.

MAINTENANCE MATERIALS

In the battle against rain, damp and wood-boring insects, we have equipped ourselves with a deadly arsenal of substances that are sometimes out of proportion to the problem. This can be most clearly seen in the garb of pest control contractors who come equipped for a moon walk rather than killing beetles.

Wood preservatives and woodworm killers often contain toxins which are barely degradable, for which we lack long-term experience, and for which nature lacks an equivalent. PCP, which is used to prevent fungi, can cause cirrhosis of the liver, while lindane is a poisonous insecticide. Over 100 000 buildings in the UK are treated annually with lethal chemicals.

Fungi cannot exist in timber whose moisture level is below 20 per cent. If fungi exists, it is important to discover the cause, rather than treat the effect. In other words, by keeping wood dry you will eradicate fungal attack. Timber can be protected against moisture by ensuring that the building is sound. It can also be protected against moisture by applying varnish, lacquer or beeswax.

Insects can live in relatively dry wood, though excess dryness and heat will kill them. Ensure you are not simply fighting boreholes of a former infestation. Signs of active infestation are fresh wood dust.

For insect treatment, timber can be treated with preparations containing borax, acetic acid or soda. According to Auro, which makes a range of organic paints and wood treatments, hot air is better than chemical application, because it does not damage the environment and guarantees total elimination. The company also makes an insect repellent which is free from all chemical fungicides and insecticides. Its repellent effect is due to the essential oil extracted from the cembra pine.

Alternatively consider synthetic pyrethroid insecticides, such as permethrin and cypermethrin, which are less toxic to mammals. But whatever can harm insects can also harm humans and other life forms. This should dissuade you from unnecessary use of toxic chemicals.

Take special care in treating roof spaces, for fear of damaging a bat habitat. Since 1981, it has been an offence to kill, injure or disturb any bat or damage their roosts. A single bat can eat thousands of midges and mosquitoes every summer night.

Many paints, varnishes and glues use organic solvents. These can cause breathing difficulty, eye irritation and other complaints. Some paints also contain titanium dioxide, a white pigment whose production causes a range of undesirable by-products (including heavy metals and chlorinated hydrocarbons). These are often discharged into rivers, harming wildlife.

In Denmark, 90 per cent of paint used in building is water-based. ICI Paints is phasing out its use of organic solvents, and plans to have switched to water-based paints by the end of the decade.

Wallpaper paste often incorporates a fungicide: alternatives that are free from fungicide can be found.

Chipboard and insulation foam in cavity walls can contain formaldehyde. This slowly releases a gas that can cause defects of the nervous system and severe memory loss in adults. Canada has now outlawed insulation foams that contain formaldehyde.

Paint thinners and strippers contain hydrocarbon solvents. They quickly evaporate and cause ground-level ozone, which is a pollutant.

Aerosols now rarely contain CFCs. However, they are all highly packaged and their propulsion gases are dangerous.

People are talking nowadays about 'gentle chemistry'. Organic paints, for example, are made from natural raw materials such as pine resin, linseed oil, chalk, rubber, indigo and essential oils. Their waste products are compost and oxygen. Plant pigments will eventually fade, but people will increasingly come to see vivid colours as artificial.

Avoid non-porous artificial materials wherever possible. Natural products like wood, wool and cotton have been used for thousands of years. They are also pollution-free and renewable (though wood is raising questions as a result of unsympathetic afforestation). Porous materials allow moisture and air to diffuse and thereby let the building breathe.

Doors should be made from wood, not woodchips that contain formaldehyde. Smooth floorcovering can be made from linoleum, which is made from linseed oil, rather than thermoplastic vinyl tiles. Carpets should be made from wool, rather than polypropylene which comes from oil.

Shelving should be made from timber rather than plastic-coated chipboard; chair covers should be made of wool, not artificial fibres.

Natural materials are often more expensive than their man-made substitutes, but they may last longer. They also biodegrade harmlessly.

BUILDING MAINTENANCE CHECKLIST

◆ Aim to renovate old buildings rather than building new ones.

◆ Use second-hand building materials in renovation.

◆ Avoid unnecessary modernizing if it entails ripping out solid architectural features.

◆ Check what substances are being used in building maintenance.

◆ Find out the contents of these substances.

◆ Avoid the use of substances that are unnecessarily toxic.

◆ Check whether the building is used by bats or birds, and protect their habitat.

◆ Use natural materials such as wood and wool rather than artificial substitutes.

SITE APPEARANCE AND BUILDING EXTERIORS

Take a fresh look around your site. Does it contain broken old pallets or rusting equipment? Is waste paper blowing across the site? Are windows becoming rotten for lack of a coat of paint?

Introduce a plan to tidy up the plant. Decide what will happen in future to old pallets. Introduce a better maintenance programme for buildings.

Unused buildings should not be left to moulder: they quickly become a blot on the landscape. Buildings should be kept in use wherever possible. If the company has no immediate need for them, alternative uses can be found. Many old industrial buildings could make short-term small business units. When the decision has been been made to sell a building, it should be sold as quickly as possible.

Decaying relics of industry are not a positive or reassuring sight, and bring down the area. Although it can take time for developers to agree plans and obtain planning approval, it need not take a decade – a fate that befalls some buildings.

Pull down old tin sheds which are not serving any purpose, and grass the area. Plant trees and shrubs. Encourage staff to take pride in the area.

It is important to ensure that machinery, plant and buildings are properly maintained. This will prevent unnecessary pollution or safety hazards.

> Built 60 years ago, Ford's 700 acre site at Dagenham originally included its own forge, blast furnace, and even its own power station. Over time, large parts of the site became redundant and were becoming an eyesore. Over the last 15 years, Ford has turned large tracts into a wildlife park and amenity area.
>
> Originally, the company grassed the area, but found that it took longer to get a mower to some parts of the site than to cut the grass. Ford has now made parts of the area self-supporting. Contractors even pay Ford to dump top soil over existing foundations. The company has stocked the lakes with fish, erected 300 bird boxes, and built a lakeside bank to encourage kingfishers to nest. It has also planted 1 500 shrubs and 2 000 trees. As a result of this activity, the area looks better, its amenity value has increased, and 57 species of birds have been sighted.

POLLUTION CASE HISTORY

One dairy company was reported as follows on the front page of the local newspaper:

Faulty pipes caused pollution

Caustic detergent seeped from faulty pipework at St Ivel's factory and polluted West Brook, magistrates heard on Tuesday.

A water authority expert found the stream was black and foaming, and a ditch nearby was cloudy with a milky smell.

Further investigations revealed that the caustic detergent had entered the stream via a surface water drain.

> St Ivel was fined £800 by Shepton Mallet court and ordered to pay £706 costs to the National River Authority after admitting polluting the brook.
>
> Nick Foster, defending, said 'The company was totally unaware of any pollution until it was alerted by a visit from the water authority.'
>
> Since the incident, the company has spent more than £10 000 on repairs and work to prevent a similar accident, the court heard.
>
> There are several factors to note in this case history. The pollution was accidental and not even noticed; the company's products were not of the polluting type; remedial works probably cost more than planned maintenance; the extent of the pollution was considerable; and the bad publicity was probably worse than the fine. It just goes to show that you do not have to be an oil company to create pollution.

SITE APPEARANCE CHECKLIST

- Put derelict buildings back into service, sell them or demolish them.
- Ensure that buildings are being properly maintained.
- Assess whether environmental enhancement could reduce maintenance.

LITTER

Litter forms an important part of the UK's Environmental Protection Act. Certain types of business, such as fast food restaurants, can be obliged to keep their frontages clear of litter. Educational institutions must also keep their ground litter-free.

For the first time, an individual can take a local authority to court by applying to the magistrates' court for a Litter Abatement Order. If prosecuted, the authority will face fines of up to £1 000 plus £50 a day for each day the offence persists.

Likewise, the local authority can serve an order on a business. On conviction, the court can impose a fine of up to £1 000 plus 5 per cent of the fine for every day the area is left uncleared.

The local authority can serve shopkeepers and businesses with a Street Litter Control Notice. This will say how many litter bins must be outside the premises, how many times a day they must be emptied, and what other cleaning tasks must be performed.

LITTER FACTS

- Almost one-third of all litter dropped is smoking related: cigarette ends, used matches and wrapping material.
- Men are ten times more likely than women to appear in court for dropping paper.
- Paper and cardboard account for 22 per cent of litter, and 9 per cent consists of sweet wrappers.
- Cigarettes take 1–5 years to degrade, plastic bags 10–20 years, nylon tights 30–40 years, tin cans 50 years, ring pulls 80–100 years, and glass bottles take 1 million years to degrade.

LITTER CHECKLIST

- How much litter is left outside your premises?
- Does it come from employees, customers or the general public?
- What does the litter consist of?
- Draw up a plan for reducing litter.

LAND USE

Offices and factories usually have immaculate lawns. But the close-cropped grass, routinely sprayed with pesticides and fertilizer, is environmentally barren. A manicured flower-bed sometimes sits in the centre of the grass but, dosed with insecticide, it offers little benefit to the environment.

Biodiversity (having a range of species) is an important environmental concept. It means that a green area is ecologically more valuable if it is home to a range of plants and animals.

Gardeners once regarded brambles and nettles as an abomination. Now people are realizing that these plants are ecologically important, and that a weed is only a plant in the 'wrong' place. Here are a few simple guidelines for creating a more interesting and varied landscape:

- Provide a mix of vegetation: grass, flower-beds, shrubs, and trees; and add a pond. Each has an important and interactive function.
- Let the grass grow long to provide shelter for wildlife. Owls need rough grassland to hunt. Do not worry about the clover that grows among the grasses: the more variety the better. Try a range of traditional grasses, and only cut grass after wild flowers have had a chance to set seed.

LAND AND BUILDINGS 41

- Do not use toxic sprays. The chemicals will kill not only the unwanted insects but also harmless creatures, and will get into the food chain. Dig out weeds by hand – someone among the staff may take on this job for a nominal payment, or you may want to foster participation and set up a rota. Alternatively, set environmental guidelines for the contractor. The EC has a blacklist and the UK a red list of pesticides that should be avoided.
- Think before laying poison. It can kill owls and other creatures. In 1989 alone, out of Britain's 50 breeding pairs of endangered red kites, a dozen died from poisoned baits. There are high fines for illegal use of poisons.
- Plant shrubs which attract wildlife and provide low cover. Grow buddleia and sedum for butterflies; and rowan, crab apple and honey-suckle for birds. Use plants that are already found in the area.
- Plant hedges rather than fences or walls. A total of 65 species of birds nest in hedges, along with 600 species of plant, hundreds of insects, and many mammals, reptiles and amphibians. Hawthorn and blackthorn are good for wildlife.
- Plant native broadleaved trees like oak, birch, willow, apple and elm, rather than pine trees. Native deciduous trees provide a home for many more species of wildlife than do imports. Evergreens have tough leaves and inedible seeds which are no use to wildlife. But do not plant trees which will grow too large and have to be chopped down in a decade. Trees with holes are important for a wide range of creatures. Do not chop one down just because it looks old and gnarled.
- Leave some dead or decaying timber lying on the ground. It provides food and shelter for many creatures.
- Plant wild flowers with strong colours to attract bees and butterflies.
- Build a pond. This will attract water-boatmen, frogs and dragon-flies. Ensure that frogs can get in and out of the pond easily.
- Erect a bird table, and keep it filled with scraps to attract the birds.
- Allow clumps of nettles to survive: they support 15 species of moth, and are the food plant of butterflies and ladybirds. Humans do not go near nettle beds, so that makes them a good habitat. But do not let the nettles take over.
- Keep some brambles: they are the food plant of 40 species of butterfly and moth. They provide ground cover for birds, and their berries are an important food for thrushes and blackbirds.
- Plant a vegetable or herb garden and plant fruit trees. Use the crop in your canteen. It will boost interest in your canteen if customers know that the food comes from their own garden.
- Grow creepers over your building. It will give wildlife a place to rest, feed and nest. It may also make your building look less stark.
- Window boxes make your building look welcoming, especially in an urban setting. They also attract birds, butterflies and bees. Maintenance, however, can be time-consuming.

○ Avoid using peat: its use is causing the destruction of important wetland habitats. These took 10 000 years to form and at current extraction rates, we have less than ten years to save them. In 1850 14 000 hectares of raised bogs existed. Today 96 per cent have gone, mostly since 1945 to afforestation and agricultural improvement as well as peat cutting. Substitutes are available.

Do not let the garden distract you from running the company. Make the garden low-maintenance by selecting plants which look after themselves. Finally, erect a sign saying:

> Wildlife Area
>
> This green space provides a natural habitat for wildlife. No chemicals are used in its upkeep.

This sign will assure visitors that there is a purpose in your slightly overgrown and untrimmed garden.

> At the Rover pressing plant at Swindon, the company has laid out a picnic area for employees. It has also planted trees and built earth mounds to shield neighbouring houses from the industrial noise and sights.

LAND HOLDINGS

The company may own land all over the country or even across the world. In such circumstances, it should audit its land holdings to check for important habitats and to assess how the land can be used to benefit nature.

> At Hydro Polymers Ltd, the site is not fully industrialized and contains grassy and wooded areas, including a large fish pond and a golf course. The company has recorded 18 species of tree, 39 species of nesting bird and 36 other bird species, together with 10 species of butterfly. And 15 species of animal are resident from time to time.

If the business is located near an important wildlife habitat such as wetland, a river, estuary or coast, a survey should establish what wildlife or fish is present. This survey should be repeated annually to establish changes that are taking place.

Even ordinary sites can be home to unusual or rare species, and this may only be discovered with a nature survey. Discussions with conservationists will determine the measures that could be taken to help important wildlife species thrive or become re-established.

Some lichens and ferns are very pollution sensitive, and their abundance or absence can be good pollution indicators. Do not rush to scrape lichens and mosses off stonework: treat them as proof of your clean environment.

> In the greenhouses of Durham University, red spider mites and other pests are now tackled by other predatory bugs instead of with pesticides. The

university has reduced its use of other chemicals, and its estate and woodland is managed to conserve trees and protect wildlife.

CONTAMINATED LAND

Some land may be contaminated by chemicals dumped in a less environmentally sensitive age. The green company will clean up old contamination as soon as possible. The depth and extent of contamination will need to be professionally checked, and the materials either neutralized or removed to a landfill site.

As legislation becomes more stringent, it is better to get rid of polluted materials now rather than wait: in later years the cost will be higher and the task more difficult.

HELPING LARGER AND RARER FORMS OF WILDLIFE

Over the last 150 years, the barn owl population in Britain has decreased by 90 per cent. Several bat species are in danger of extinction. The otter has disappeared from many parts of England and Wales. Three species of dragonflies have become extinct since 1953. And one species of butterfly (the large blue) became extinct in 1979.

Business can help to redress the balance by reducing pollution, by letting land revert to nature, and by providing artificial habitats. The conservation societies can give advice on how to encourage wildlife back to the land.

> RNAS Culdrose is the biggest and busiest helicopter base in Europe. It tries to discourage birds from the runways, for they can collide with aircraft or get pulled into the engine turbines, with possibly lethal effects for birds and pilots alike.
>
> The airfield has a PA system that plays pre-recorded bird distress calls. Bird-scaring cartridges are also fired.
>
> The birds, however, get used to the equipment and soon return to the airfield. So now the site has resident falconers whose birds are trained to swoop towards the runway. The falcons are an invaluable passive deterrent, for bird movements have reduced from 24 500 in 1984 to 2 000 in 1991.

LANDSCAPING CHECKLIST

◆ Create a wildlife area.

◆ Provide a range of habitats, including trees, hedges, wild grass and pond.

◆ Avoid the use of synthetic pesticides.

◆ Audit land holdings.

- Carry out a wildlife survey annually to record changes in wildlife.
- Restore contaminated land to its former condition.

ASSESSING ENVIRONMENTAL IMPACT

Before a site or property is bought or a new factory commissioned, an Environmental Impact Assessment (EIA) should be carried out. This will:

- Assess whether there are any reasons not to buy the site (such as contamination).
- Analyse whether there will be problems in developing the site (such as the presence of rare species which would be destroyed during the development).
- Assess the impact of the project on the environment, wildlife and the local population.
- Check how existing wildlife can be incorporated into the development.
- Determine how environmental gains (improvements to the balance of nature) can be made.
- Provide data for use in any future dispute over environmental degradation of the land.
- Assist in planning site layout so as to optimize site use and minimize environmental problems.
- Analyse whether the planned operation will conform to legislation.
- Provide information and plans for a Planning Application.

The assessment will produce findings and solutions, and these will be contained in an Environmental Impact Statement (EIS). This Statement will help to modify the construction, thereby minimizing problems after construction of the building. The EIS should cover the following subjects:

DESCRIPTION OF THE PROJECT

1. Purpose of the project. Access and transport. Numbers of people to be employed and where they will come from.
2. Land use: during construction, when operational, and after use has ceased.
3. Production processes, including types of raw materials, emissions, including to air, water and land. Levels of noise, light, heat and vibrations.
4. Alternative sites considered. Reasons for final choice.

DESCRIPTION OF THE SITE

1. Existing human population – proximity and numbers.
2. Flora and fauna, especially protected and rare species.

LAND AND BUILDINGS 45

3. Soil, geology, water and air – quality and type.
4. Architectural, historic and archaeological heritage.
5. Landscape and topography.
6. Recreational use.
7. Legislation (for example, national nature reserve, tree preservation orders or local area plan).

ASSESSMENT OF EFFECTS

1. Effects on humans (from visual impact, emissions or development).
2. Effects on flora, fauna and geology (from damage to or loss of habitats).
3. Effects on land (from earth moving or waste disposal).
4. Effects on water (from drainage, altering of water courses, or pollution).
5. Effects on air and climate (from pollution or odours).
6. Indirect effects, through transport, new sewers or housing.

MITIGATING MEASURES

1. Site planning.
2. Technical measures (such as recycling or pollution control).
3. Aesthetic or ecological measures (through design, landscaping, recording of archaeological sites, or protection of habitats).

RISKS OF ACCIDENTS

1. Preventative measures adopted. Emergency plans. Compliance with legislation.

ORGANIZATIONS CONSULTED

1. The needs of environmental organizations and the local community; how their concerns can be accommodated.

NON-TECHNICAL SUMMARY

1. Description of all the above in layman's language.

Wherever possible, the development should achieve 'environmental gain': overall the environment should have more gains than losses from the development. Actions could include the improvement of a habitat, an increase in the number of broadleaved trees, or the removal and re-siting of an environmentally important meadow which is threatened by the development. It might involve the demolition of unsightly buildings, the provision of public amenities, or the creation of a wildlife reserve.

The green company will not normally build on a Site of Special Scientific Interest, nor cause the destruction of an important habitat. Yet in 1989 in Coventry, 30 acres of Herald Way Marsh SSSI was bulldozed to make way for warehouse and industrial units. And in the 2 years to 1990, 3 000 acres of SSSI were taken for building work.

On the other hand, some companies are taking steps to restore the appearance and usefulness of their sites:

> British Coal is restoring the land previously used for open-cast mining – by inserting earthworms into the used sites. The company makes £234 million profit from opencast mining. But for years after they have ceased operating, the used mines are environmentally dead - due mainly to the absence of earthworms. This strengthens the case of protesters at planning enquiries, where half of British Coal's planning proposals are lost.
>
> By aerating the soil, improving drainage and providing food for wildlife, the earthworms are bringing the sites back to life. A single acre can harbour two million worms, weighing half a ton, and the worms attract wildlife such as badgers which live off them. British Coal is now including earthworms in its new contracts, except where the land is being returned to arable: intensive farming kills worms.

ENVIRONMENTAL IMPACT CHECKLIST

In this next checklist, we consider other ways of reducing the environmental impact of a new development:

- The development should allow archaeological digging to be carried out before construction work begins. It should also provide finance for the archaeologists.
- The building should be built on land previously built upon. This will help conserve the green areas.
- The development should incorporate any redundant buildings of good quality.
- Buildings of historic or architectural interest should be retained.
- The buildings should not have garish or obtrusive signs. The natural desire for promotion must be tempered by empathy for the surroundings. In an ugly or soulless area, the new building should seek to improve the quality of the neighbourhood.
- The development should be sited in an area well served by trains and public transport, to minimize the need for private cars.
- The building should be designed or sited so as to retain existing landscaping. It should also keep natural features such as ponds or mature trees.
- Trees should be planted as screens to shut out noise or unattractive yards.
- Shrubs and other vegetation will help to bring wildlife to the area. The development should incorporate bat boxes and owl nesting sites.

- New industrial sites should contain their own waste treatment facilities where practical.
- Out-of-town shopping and leisure facilities should be limited on the ground of non-accessibility, loss of open space and traffic generation.
- New sites should incorporate green open spaces, and/or outdoor leisure facilities.

Most of these considerations do not directly profit the company. But below are three considerations which should be taken into account before a company commits itself to a new development. They could have a direct bearing on its profitability.

HAZARDS FOUND IN SPECIFIC LOCATIONS

There are a range of environmental problems which could dissuade a company from buying the site or remaining there. These are either man-made or artificial hazards which can affect employees' health.

ELECTRICITY PYLONS

The heavy charge of electricity carried on high tension power lines can cause headaches, depression and cancer. If your business is located under or near a pylon you should check employees' health.

Check also for the proximity of electricity generators, and for microwave transmitters including radar, telecommunications, cellular phones and satellite TV. Electromagnetic fields affect radio and TV reception; some people believe they can also affect humans by causing stress and sickness, leading to absenteeism and reduced productivity.

METHANE

Methane gas is produced by decomposing rubbish. It is commonly found at rubbish tips. If your business is close to a rubbish tip, check methane emissions.

RADON

Radon is an invisible gas that seeps from the ground and is a carcinogen. It is particularly prevalent in the South West of England. You can check radon levels by leaving a detector in place for a period of time. The Department of the Environment (DOE) and the National Radiological Protection Board (NRPB) provide information and suggest methods to reduce the effect of radon. Solutions include floor insulation and ducting the gas away using fans.

NEW PROJECTS CHECKLIST

- Conduct an environmental impact assessment on new projects.

- Follow this with an impact statement or plan.
- Ensure that the development maintains or increases local wildlife.
- Ensure that the development does not add unnecessarily to traffic.
- Consider distribution and communications when locating new operations (for example, siting a factory next to a railway line).

GREEN NEW BUILDINGS

New offices should be designed to protect the environment. That means they should consume minimum energy and use ecologically desirable materials. We examine these issues next in more depth.

CONSTRUCTION STRATEGY

The building should fit neatly into its location. It should continue the existing roofscape, and be built from locally available materials. Like a good neighbour, the new building should respect the traditions of the area, rather than despising the locals and behaving like an upstart.

This does not mean it has slavishly to follow the style of dead architects, or adopt a classical facade. It merely imposes a greater challenge on the architects of today. They should understand local construction traditions and create buildings that evolve out of them. 'Design and build' buildings should likewise extend local traditions. A 'shed' is unlikely to improve the area.

The height of the building, its scale, personality and the number of its windows are also important. Environmental care is not simply about wildlife and pollution: it is also about providing ourselves with buildings that are visually attractive, designed on a human scale, and are of the highest quality.

ENERGY USE

Low energy use is essential for a modern building, and insulation should be an important part of the construction strategy. You should know the U values (a measure of insulation) of windows and materials used in the external walls and roof. You should also know what percentage of energy use and cost will come from heating, hot water, lighting, office equipment and other uses. This energy use should come within the limits of the CIBSE Energy Code provided by the Chartered Institute of Building Services Engineers.

The siting and construction of the building should take advantage of passive solar energy. It should be limited in depth to maximize daylighting and allow natural ventilation. Passive solar energy could save Britain £230 million by the year 2035, and four times that figure in the later decades of the next century. Areas of solar gain can be used to warm the building, with shades used to minimize glare and overheating. Daylight is popular with inhabitants, and reduces energy demand.

South-facing walls should have large glazed areas, with overhangs to prevent unwanted solar gain. North-facing walls should have less glazing. Low emissivity glass can be used to reduce heat loss by reflecting heat back into the room.

Perimeter daylighting uses glass in the outside walls. The light is then distributed evenly through baffles or lightshelves. Core daylighting uses roof apertures, atria and courtyards to bring light into the interior of a building.

Heaters should be fitted with thermostats. The heating system should be computer controlled, and it should be powered by an energy-efficient system. Hot water should not be dependent on central boilers, unless they will be required to run throughout the year: you could consider fitting point-of-use electric water heaters.

> The Findhorn Foundation has built green homes in a remote Scottish glen. The walls 'breathe' to eliminate condensation, and are lined with recycled newspaper cellulose for insulation. The roofs are capped with turf to blend with the countryside and to maintain balanced temperatures.

Maximum use should be made of daylight. Artificial lighting should be of the low energy sort: there are many new lighting systems now available.

Cables and equipment should be heavily shielded. This will prevent electromagnetic leakage, which could be harmful to humans.

VENTILATION

The lowest-energy offices are naturally ventilated, while those with high energy costs are fully air-conditioned. So before the building is built, decide whether air-conditioning is really necessary. Though a growing sophistication in the market might encourage it, there are many strategies for reducing a building's heat without the need for electrical assistance. Such strategies can include:

- Grouping heat-emitting machinery such as photocopiers in one well-ventilated room.
- Use low-energy lighting to reduce heat gains.
- Use shades and blinds and window size to reduce solar heat.
- Use openable windows.

Air-conditioning plant should not use CFC refrigerants. There should be a maintenance programme to prevent Legionnaires' Disease. And local areas should have timed switches capable of overriding the air-conditioning.

MATERIALS AND FINISHES

Use timber from sustainably managed sources, and avoid materials that release formaldehyde (for example, chipboards). No asbestos should be used, and extinguishers should be halon free.

Surface treatments should avoid the use of toxic pesticides or dangerous wood preservatives, and insulation materials should not have been blown with CFCs.

> At Bethnal Green in London, 34 new homes have been built to new environmental specifications. They include extra loft insulation, double glazing, cavity wall and internal floor insulation, energy-efficient gas central heating, water saving features, and long life low consumption light bulbs.
>
> All materials have been carefully selected, with no CFCs used in the insulation, and all timber coming from sustainable sources. Yet the environmental extras have cost only about 4 per cent of the total. Tower Hamlets Environment Trust, which oversaw the project, believes that people are happy to pay the extra.
>
> The houses are designed for low-cost ownership, and all have been reserved by local people. Residents buy a 70 per cent share, leaving the Trust with a charge over the remainder but with no rent payable on that share.
>
> Although this is a domestic project, the principles of conservation and cost apply equally to commercial buildings.

HUMAN FACTORS

Recent thinking in office planning suggests that workers should have a village philosophy. Workers should have a private room to work in, a shared space for photocopying and filing, and a street for communal activities. According to the Royal Institute for British Architects (RIBA), the open-plan office stops people from having their own defensible space, so people desperately try to create their own space with pictures and flowers.

In large developments, provision should be made for sports facilities, roof garden and restaurant.

WILDLIFE

Roof tiles that incorporate nesting sites for birds are now available from such companies as Redland and Marley. New commercial buildings can also be designed to allow bats to roost, and can include a nest box for barn owls.

SPECIMEN NEW BUILDING GREEN POLICY

GREEN POLICY: The design and construction of the building shall aim to minimize negative contributions to both the local and world environment, as well as the general health and well-being of the building's occupants.

The following materials shall not be used:

○ timbers of tropical rainforest origin.
○ wood preservatives containing lindane or tributylin oxide.

- ○ asbestos or asbestos-containing products.
- ○ urea formaldehyde foam or materials which may release formaldehyde in quantities which may be hazardous.
- ○ materials generally composed of mineral fibres which have a diameter of 3 microns or less and a length of 200 microns or less.
- ○ high alumina cement.
- ○ calcium chloride admixtures for use in reinforced concrete.

CFCs: The design and construction of the building shall aim to avoid the use of insulation materials which contain CFCs in their manufacture.

This policy is taken from the Quality Standards specification for a new building for the Department of Health. It forms part of a wider quality specification which includes durability, building regulations and fire precautions.

GREEN OFFICE ASSESSMENT

The UK Building Research Establishment (BRE) has introduced an assessment scheme for environmentally-sound new offices. Called BREAM, it checks global, neighbourhood and indoor issues. The checklist covers such items as thermal values, openable windows and avoidance of lead-based paint.

The scheme provides building owners with a 35-point certificate. This can be put on display, and used in the marketing of the building. Unlike other certification schemes, it is not a 'win or lose' situation. Each building gets a certificate showing how many points it achieved.

Even one credit on the certificate indicates that the building will be environmentally superior to normal practice. However, BRE expects applicants will seek to obtain a significant number of credits.

NEW BUILDINGS CHECKLIST

◆ Ensure that any new building suits the local area and is built on a human scale.

◆ Ensure that the building is energy efficient.

◆ Avoid unnecessary air-conditioning.

◆ Use environmentally friendly materials and finishes.

◆ Incorporate wildlife habitats.

4
THE OFFICE

◆

The biggest environmental impact of the office is on the people who work there, and in advanced industrial societies nearly half the adult population has a white collar job. Thus the importance of the office cannot be over-estimated. The green office is vitally important in areas such as banking, finance and insurance; public administration; hotels and catering; the utilities, and education. It is also important to office workers in all other fields.

Figure 4.1 shows the key issues that concern the green office, some of which are interrelated. We start by looking at a topic that has emerged with the advent of air-conditioned buildings: sick building syndrome.

THE SICK OFFICE

The sick building is a twentieth-century concept. Modern air-conditioned buildings with their sealed windows and man-made fibres and foams create a variety of problems. Blocked noses, rashes, headaches and itchy eyes are common. They result mainly from a combination of closed ventilation systems and seeping vapours.

Some office managers dislike the term 'Sick Building Syndrome' (SBS). They prefer to talk about 'a ventilation problem'. This is helpful in that it removes some of the unnecessary mystique and puts the problem in its context. On the other hand, it wrongly implies that the problem can be solved by focusing on the effects rather than their cause.

According to the US Environmental Protection Agency (EPA), one in three offices in the US is considered sick and in need of testing. The most common causes of SBS are:

○ **Formaldehyde** leaks from foam insulation in cavity walls, from plywood boards, and carpets or upholstery made from synthetic fibres. Formic acid can enter the blood stream, causing joint cramps and other symptoms. Apart from tearing up the floorboards, there is not much you can do about this.

ENVIRONMENTAL ISSUES IN THE OFFICE

Sick building syndrome	VDUs and repetitive strain syndrome	Office drinks
Smoking	Stationery and other consumables	Fixtures, fittings and equipment
Energy use	The washroom	Teleworking

Figure 4.1: Environmental issues in the office. The company needs a corporate policy to cover office topics.

- **Carbon monoxide** comes from exhaust fumes vented via air intakes, through windows or from tobacco smoke. It can cause chest pain, impaired vision, headaches, dizziness, confusion and nausea. It can be reduced by proper venting and exhaust fans.
- **Solvents** such as benzene come from paints, varnishes and glues. They are also found in correction fluid, thinners and spray fixatives. They can cause breathing difficulties, and also pollution. Try to minimize their use.
- **Biological pollutants** include bacteria, mould, mildew viruses and pollen. They cause irritation of the eyes, nose and throat, shortness of breath, dizziness, fever, digestive problems and asthma. They can be resolved by thorough and regular vacuuming, and better ventilation.
- **Asbestos** is found in old insulation, fireproofing or acoustic tiles. It can also be found in roof claddings, gutters, ironing boards (and outside the office in car brakes). Long-term effects are chest and abdominal cancers, and lung disease. Asbestos must be removed by qualified contractors.
- **Lead** pipes are still found in older buildings and should be replaced. Lead-painted surfaces need to be covered up. Lead can cause headaches, tiredness and constipation among people exposed to it. It is also thought to reduce IQ in young children.
- Poorly maintained **air-conditioning** plant can cause Legionnaires' Disease. Check that the air-conditioning has a proper maintenance programme. Hot water should be above 50°C, and cold water below 20°C. Debris and rust should be collected from the bottom of the boiler, and dead pipework cleared. It is also worth noting that CFCs are often used as a coolant for such plants.

The best solution is to get rid of the toxic materials. If they cannot be changed, aim to boost the ventilation. This will improve the air, even if the pollutants only go elsewhere.

Companies seriously worried about the quality of the air in their buildings can have it tested. A multi-gas analyser will measure levels of benzene, formaldehyde, carbon monoxide, carbon dioxide and water vapour.

You can also buy equipment to reduce pollution. Ionizers displace pollutants, while air filters can trap dust and microbes and pass the air through a carbon filter, removing gas, smoke and odours.

Regular vacuuming will also reduce dust, harmful fibres, pollens and other irritants.

A more recent solution is to introduce house-plants. According to the American space agency (NASA), one house-plant will purify 100 sq ft of air. It will breathe in the carbon dioxide, and turn it back into oxygen. NASA researchers found that certain air pollutants are absorbed and detoxified by particular plants:

Substance	*absorbed by*
Formaldehyde:	Spider plants, Philodendron, mother-in-law's tongue, Rhapis, Dracaena.
Benzene:	Ivy, Dracaena and Spathiphyllum
Trichloroethylene: (found in varnishes, lacquers and glues)	Gerbera and chrysanthemum

AIR QUALITY CHECKLIST

◆ Analyse the air quality for substances that cause 'sick building syndrome'.

◆ Check furniture, furnishings and building construction for pollutants.

◆ Check that air-conditioning plant is properly maintained.

◆ Avoid thinners, correction fluid and spray mount that use solvents.

◆ Remove pollutants where possible.

◆ Ensure regular vacuuming.

◆ Reduce pollution through the use of ionizers, filters and house-plants.

◆ Ensure that there is a regular flow of fresh air.

Occasionally, headaches, tension and sickness can be ascribed to sick building syndrome, when they are simply due to office stress. Constant interruptions, conflicting tasks, no breaks and unsympathetic bosses can create similar symptoms to sick building syndrome. So can boring, dead-end jobs. They can be resolved by human resource solutions. The Personnel Manager should be able to advise.

VDUs

The radiation levels from VDUs are no longer thought high enough to pose a danger to health. But operators suffer from other symptoms, including headaches, stiffness and fatigue. This results from bad posture and visual strain, and can be prevented by improving the office ergonomics.

Office workers also suffer from Repetitive Strain Injury (RSI), which occurs as pain from overworked wrist and elbow muscles and tendons. This can be resolved by regular breaks and improved ergonomics.

The keyboard should be detached, so that the operator can reposition it. Key tops should be concave and should not reflect light. The operator should be able to tilt the screen in all directions, and the image should be free of flicker. A soundproof cover should muffle the sound of a noisy printer.

The operator's posture must be upright, with elbows at the same height as the desk top. Feet should be on the floor or on a footrest.

There should be no glare from windows or lights, and the screen should be free from reflections. To achieve this, it should be facing a continuous wall. Plants or pictures will provide visual relief centres for the eye.

The chair should be easily adjustable in height, and provide lumbar support. There must be room for the operator's thighs to go under the table. This will enable the operator to get close enough to the keyboard – many chairs have arms that prevent the operator from doing so. The operator should not be leaning forward – the small of the back should be fully supported.

The desk should have a matt surface, and there should be sufficient storage and filing facilities. A copyholder should be provided.

Operators should take a break every 60 minutes, and they should be given regular eye tests.

VDU CHECKLIST

- Check the posture of everyone who spends time at a VDU or computer.
- Check sickness records for signs of RSI (repetitive strain injury)
- Replace poorly designed computers, desks or chairs.
- Ensure that typists get proper breaks and work no more than the agreed number of hours.

OTHER OCCUPATIONAL HEALTH AND SAFETY MATTERS

Health and safety is closely connected with the environment. Smoking causes litter and cancer, for example. So it is worth thinking about office health and safety at this point. Consider the items in the following list:

○ **Electricity**: Are electrical cables safely routed, and trailing wires avoided?
○ **Lighting**: Are lighting levels adequate?
○ **Ventilation**: Can it be easily altered?
○ **Fire**: Are curtains or foams in office chairs a fire risk? Are safety exits marked, fire doors in place, and an evacuation plan organized? Are fire extinguishers handy?
○ **Maintenance**: Is shelving properly secured to the wall?
○ **Machinery**: Photocopiers and laser printers emit ozone. Because of this, they should not be near a work station, and should be placed in a well-ventilated area.
○ **Floors**: Are they kept dry and not slippery? Are obstructions removed?
○ **Glass**: Is safety glass used in doors?

SMOKING

Only one-quarter of office employees smoke, yet a non-smoker can breathe the equivalent of one cigarette for every 20 smoked in the same room. Non-smokers who live with smokers are 10–30 per cent more likely to get lung cancer than if they lived with non-smokers, according to a UK government advisory committee. These figures can easily be extrapolated to the office, where people spend as much time as they spend awake at home.

Environmental Health officials are now taking action on smoking. Following complaints from staff at an insurance company, officials in Birmingham, England, threatened the company with enforcement action over smoking. The company agreed to confine smoking to a few designated areas.

More companies are now restricting smoking at work because of the dangers to non-smokers, and the threat of legal action. Four out of five large companies in the UK impose restrictions on smoking, while total bans are becoming more common.

Companies who have researched the problem have found strong support for smoke-free areas, even from smokers. In a survey of 3 900 employees of British Gas Wales, more than half were worried about the long-term effects of passive smoking, while only 12 per cent wanted smoking to be allowed in all areas. The company has since phased in a complete ban in the offices. Smoking is only permitted between noon and 2pm in a designated area.

You may want to designate one room as a smoking room, and this should be away from dining or work areas. The smoking room should not be the only staff break room.

OFFICE HEALTH AND SAFETY CHECKLIST

◆ Ensure that lighting levels are adequate.
◆ Check for hazards, especially fire.

- Check that the office is properly maintained and ventilated.
- Are photocopiers placed away from work stations?
- Are photocopiers well ventilated by windows or air-conditioning vents?
- Carry out a survey of all employees, to discover whether they would like restrictions on smoking.
- Limit smoking to a specific place and time (for example 12–2pm in a staff smoking room away from dining or work areas).

OFFICE DRINKS

Across the world, office workers are sipping their coffee out of plastic cups that are promptly thrown into the bin. The plastic will clutter landfill sites for generations to come, and every day the pile of plastic cups mounts up.

One solution is to recycle the plastic cups. This calls for a bin beside every coffee machine. A better solution is to get staff to bring their own mugs. They work perfectly well with most drinks machines. A washing-up area is needed to clean the mugs after use – a washroom will suffice for this.

Another typical drink is water, whether in designer bottles or out of the tap. Water is essential for the body: it purifies us and replaces lost fluids. The big increase in sales of bottled water shows how concerned people are about the quality of our drinking water.

Drinking water is also better than excessive amounts of tea, coffee or alcohol, whose stimulants affect the body rather than purify it. Herbal teas could also be introduced at work.

Rather than pay for water to be transported hundreds of miles in bottles, it is environmentally better to provide clean supplies from the tap. This will also benefit the more junior staff who do not attend boardroom presentations and drink Perrier.

A filtered jug system is not appropriate for an office of any size – it is messy and laborious. A better idea is to fit an in-line filter system with a replaceable cartridge. This will clean the water of many impurities, leaving it clean and good to drink.

Some companies are now banning the use of alcohol in offices – on the grounds that what is not allowed on the factory floor should not be allowed to management. Apart from the damage that excessive alcohol can do to the body, it is not conducive to serious work.

CANS

Watch out for the disposal of aluminium cans. Friends of the Earth say that only 1 per cent are recycled, with 400 million soft drink cans being thrown away each year. Extracting the bauxite (from which aluminium is made) causes a major environmental impact. It is easy and cheap to recycle aluminium, and uses much less energy. Collect the cans and take them to an aluminium can bank. To check whether a can is made of aluminium, touch it with a magnet – aluminium is not attracted. All cans can be sent for recycling. With its large magnets, a well-organized local authority can easily separate aluminium from tin.

DRINKS CHECKLIST

◆ Avoid using plastic cups for coffee.

◆ Provide filtered water drinking taps on each floor.

◆ Encourage the introduction of herbal teas in preference to coffee.

◆ Consider an alcohol ban (but get staff input first).

◆ Collect aluminium soft drink cans, and take them to a can bank.

BUYING RECYCLED STATIONERY

Next we turn to consumables: the purchase of paper, envelopes and other short-life materials, and their recycling.

Office stationery should be made from recycled paper. This includes letterheads, continuation paper, envelopes, computer paper and notepads. The quality of recycled paper has improved so much as to be indistinguishable from virgin paper. Most printers and designers are now familiar with recycled paper, and high quality recycled card is ideal for full-colour brochures.

The only people who criticize recycled paper are paper companies with a fixed investment in plant that produces virgin paper. And if recycled paper is not quite so bright as virgin paper, that is not a bad sign: it suggests that the paper has not been bleached with chlorine.

Using paper 'made from sustainably managed forests' is not quite the same. Paper made from growing trees uses much more energy. Producing paper from waste instead of virgin pulp cuts energy by 50 per cent and pollution by even more. Paper factories also use chlorine to bleach virgin pulp, and this is a highly polluting substance.

Locally produced pulp comes from pine trees which have been planted across miles of countryside. The pine trees make a poor wildlife habitat, and they are often grown on environmentally important sites.

What happens if we do not recycle old paper? It will be added to the piles of rubbish being thrown into landfill sites. It costs British industry and the consumer £50–£100 million to dispose of waste products, and it is estimated that up to 4 million tonnes of good paper is wasted each year. So it is not enough simply to collect paper for recycling. If you do not buy recycled paper as well, there will be too much supply and not enough demand.

The recycling process is not without its problems. The waste ink forms a thick sludge that is dumped in landfill sites. But at least the valuable paper is reclaimed, and biodegradable non-toxic inks should soon become more common.

Make sure people know your paper is recycled. Use paper with a 'recycled' sign in the water mark. Or print '100 per cent recycled paper' or a recycled logo at the bottom of your letterhead.

ENVELOPES

Internal mail should be sent in purpose-designed envelopes that can be reused many times. External mail should be sent in envelopes made from recycled paper: brown envelopes are usually made from recycled paper.

You can also reuse incoming envelopes. Many charity shops sell envelope reuse labels, and should be happy to supply commercial quantities.

RECYCLING YOUR USED PAPER

Paper should be used to the maximum and then collected for recycling. This applies to letters, photocopies, documents and computer listing paper. Some papers are not suitable for recycling: they include fax paper, self seal and window envelopes, very glossy paper, and waxed drink cartons. Their plastics and varnishes interfere with the cleaning process.

Internal reuse

Ensure that paper is fully used before being discarded. The average report may go through several drafts, each one being printed out afresh before reaching its final form. That means using a lot of paper. When the old draft comes back with corrections and alterations, the used paper could be bound into pads for use as notes. Committee papers, often inches thick, last no longer than the meeting for which they were prepared. This paper should be photocopied on both sides.

External recycling

Offer the paper to a local community group or youth organization: they will make money from passing it to the paper merchant. Alternatively, ask a merchant to collect the paper from your premises. The money can go to a charity, to the staff welfare association, or into general funds.

There is an opportunity here for fraud: one company gave the proceeds from its recycled paper to the staff club. It later found staff dumping reams of unused paper in the collecting boxes. This could be countered by periodic checks of the boxes.

Some merchants will accept only plain white paper, including photocopies and computer paper. It will need to be free from clips, staples and glued backs. Other material such as envelopes, cardboard and magazines are more difficult to recycle and are worth less. More sophisticated recycling plants are coming on stream, but in the short term you may find some types of paper less acceptable than others. You will make more money by sorting the two types of paper. Mixed piles of paper are priced at the cheapest rate.

Ask a local paper merchant what his requirements are, how much he will pay, and whether he will collect regularly. Also bear in mind that the market will fluctuate. If other countries dump waste paper in Britain, or if collection temporarily exceeds demand, the price will fall. These temporary hiccups should not deter you. Even without substantial financial rewards in the short term, it is worth doing.

Set up two collection boxes in each department or on each floor. Plastic dustbins or large kitchen swing bins will do. Label one 'White non-gloss paper', and the other 'All other paper'.

If you use 'in' and 'out' trays, you can stack another tray on top labelled 'for recycling'. This will encourage executives and secretaries to store paper for recycling rather than throw it away.

People need to know that their efforts are achieving results. Keep them informed about progress with a graph on the notice board showing how much money has been earned, or the weight of paper recycled.

NEWSPAPERS

Many companies receive daily newspapers, both for the reception area and for management to read. Check what happens to the papers at the end of the day – the cleaning staff probably throw them into a black bin liner, which goes into a skip.

Instead, set up a newspaper collection point. This could be a box in a cleaning cupboard, but a visible bin will collect more papers. Arrange to have your newspapers recycled along with all the other waste paper.

DIRECT MAIL

Put all your direct mail into the recycling bin – having first removed the plastic and window envelopes and staples.

STAMPS

All postage stamps can be given to a charity. Try putting a collection box in the Export Department. You can also ask managers who travel abroad to donate their foreign coins.

CHRISTMAS CARDS

When you return to work after the Christmas break, gather up the old Christmas cards and give them to a playgroup or charity shop. Larger pieces of reusable card are highly sought after by schools.

TOWARDS THE PAPERLESS OFFICE

- Check where the most paper is used. See how the amount can be reduced. Ask executives whether they really want personal copies of the letters they send.
- Use computers to enter, store and retrieve data. Develop a system that allows staff to check information on the screen rather than consulting a print-out.
- Provide all executives with a PC linked in a network. Encourage executives to type information straight to the screen, rather than write it out longhand.
- Develop an electronic internal mail system that does not need paper. Provide an electronic bulletin board.
- Use computers that send and receive faxes to memory rather than to a printer.
- Use sticky labels that re-seal envelopes and serve as a label for reuse.
- Buy internal mail envelopes that are designed to be used at least ten times.
- Post organizational information on notice-boards, rather than sending every member of staff a memo.
- Discourage the memo-sending culture: much of it may be political. Get staff to see each other if they have something to say.
- Encourage one-page reports.
- Ensure that each department is charged for stationery as a cost centre.
- Budget for every department to use 10 per cent less paper each year, using this year as a baseline. Charge a department a 100 per cent premium for its paper when it has exceeded its budget. This tactic helped Galileo reduce its stationery bill by 50 per cent in four years, despite doubling staff numbers.
- Consider stopping the directors' newspapers. Many go unread, and clog up landfill sites. Stopping the papers will also reduce the amount of reading matter each executive has to plough through. One advertising agency director diligently takes home his office copy of the *Financial Times* each night — it tells him what is on television.

As well as helping the environment, these methods will save time and money, and make your organization more effective.

PAPER CHECKLIST

- Assess what paper is used, and what percentage is recycled.
- Agree a plan to change all office paper to recycled within a set period of time.
- Ensure office newspapers are recycled; or stop ordering them.
- Set up collection bins for high- and low-grade used paper.
- Agree who will collect the used paper, and at what price.
- Create a plan to reduce office paper.

OTHER CONSUMABLES AND RECYCLING

Check recent invoices to see what other consumables have been ordered for the office. Then assess what they were made of, how long they lasted, and how they were disposed of.

Some of these consumables can be recycled. The UK Charities Aid Foundation provides information about charities that make use of old materials. Remember, too, that it is better to reuse materials than recycle them. Save paper clips from incoming mail, and remove slide binders from old reports.

AEROSOLS

Aerosols containing air freshener, spray fixative or furniture polish are sometimes powered by CFC gases. These eat a hole in the ozone layer which protects us from skin cancer. Check for the words 'Contains no CFCs'. Better still, avoid aerosol cans. Their manufacture uses considerable energy, they pump out pollutants even without CFCs, and they are difficult to dispose of. Try glue sticks and trigger-action sprays.

BATTERIES

Conventional batteries use 50 times more energy in their manufacture than they ever supply. This makes them a wasteful method of generating power, but rechargeable batteries are more acceptable. Buy a recharging device for each department, and make someone responsible for it. Calculators and portable computers should be run off the mains whenever possible.

Also avoid buying batteries that contain lead or mercury, which are toxic. Some battery companies, notably Varta, have made efforts to produce more environmentally friendly batteries.

GLASS BOTTLES

The manufacture of glass bottles requires considerable energy (every tonne of glass needs half a tonne of coal). There is a 25 per cent energy saving when bottles are made from cullet (old glass).

Milk bottles should be collected daily by a dairy for reuse. Every milk bottle is used up to 20 times. All other glass bottles, including wine and beer bottles and glass jars, should be put in a bottle bank. But do not put window glass or windscreens into the bottle bank. Your local authority will have the address of the nearest site. Large quantities of glass may be sold to a recycler.

PLASTICS

Much stationery is plastic; see whether you can buy refillable pens, rather than the throw-away type.

Plastics are not easily recycled at present, unless you happen to live in a city where recycling facilities exist. PET bottles exemplify the problem – these are the large plastic bottles used for soft drinks. They are cheap to make, so recycling them does not save money. But they take up a lot of room in rubbish tips, and they do not biodegrade.

An increasing number of incinerators use PET and other types of plastic as a fuel to help them burn other less flammable materials. This means that their value is recovered in energy.

PHOTOCOPIER AND PRINTER MATERIALS

British industry spends £104 million on fabric printer ribbons and a similar amount on plastic ribbons. Most of these are used once and then thrown away, adding to the piles of rubbish. Now companies like Bristol-based Inkwell are offering a re-inking service. Fabric ribbons can be re-inked 20 times, and this reduces both cost and waste.

> BP Chemicals (Advanced Materials Division) uses several types of cloth ribbons and all are re-inked without difficulty. Significant cost-savings have been achieved, and the re-inking fits in well with BP's environmental policies.

For some service companies the printed word is their 'product'. Such companies may find the appearance of fabric ribbon output unsatisfactory (though re-inking often provides a denser image), and are converting to laser printers. Lasers, too, can be be made more green by using recycled cartridges.

In the UK, 100 000 spent laser cartridges are dumped each month. They are not biodegradable, cannot be incinerated and are filling up our landfill sites. Spent cartridges can now be recycled with a 60 per cent cost saving for the customer, says Tonertec, a laser toner business. In the USA, the recycled cartridge market is larger than the market for new ones.

Many photocopiers use one-shot cartridges, but recycling is more difficult than for laser cartridges as there are more than 20 types of photocopier toner on the market. This problem will ease in time, but you should consider using a photocopier that takes screw-in toner bottles rather than throw-away cartridges.

OFFICE CONSUMABLES CHECKLIST

♦ Check what materials other than paper are used in the office.
♦ Assess how they could be recycled.
♦ Avoid the use of 'disposable' items that are used only once.
♦ Send printer ribbons and laser cartridges for re-inking.
♦ Ensure that bottles, plastics and cans are recycled where possible.
♦ Recycle your printer ribbons, laser cartridges and photocopier cartridges.

FIXTURES, FITTINGS AND EQUIPMENT

Fixtures and fittings include desks, lights, cabinets, carpets and fire extinguishers. We next examine a few of these in detail, along with such equipment as computers and copiers.

OFFICE FURNITURE

When refurbishing the office, you can sell the old furniture to a second-hand furniture dealer, send it to a local auction house, or give it to a non-profit organization. This will extend its life considerably. You can offer old carpets to a local school or playgroup. Do not simply throw away worn chairs: see if the seats can be re-covered.

METAL OFFICE FURNITURE

Do not throw away metal filing cabinets and cupboards. Have them refurbished and repainted in co-ordinated colours by an office supplies company. This will add considerably to their life.

WOODEN DESKS, SHELVES AND CUPBOARDS

Wooden furniture is often made from chipboard, which uses formaldehyde (see 'The Sick Office', above). Try to buy wood products that are formaldehyde-free. More upmarket desks are sometimes made from tropical timbers. These contribute to the destruction of the rainforest unless they come from sustainably managed sources. Check the source of such products.

FIRE EXTINGUISHERS

Halon fire extinguishers can damage the ozone layer. Check whether your extinguishers are halon based. If they are, consider replacing them.

COMPUTER EQUIPMENT

Offer your old computer equipment to a skills training project, or to a charity that will give it to the Third World. IBM will remove its old computer equipment for recycling or safe disposal. There is a small charge for this.

PHOTOCOPIERS

Make sure that your photocopier can easily produce double-sided copies: this will substantially reduce the amount of paper you use. Ensure, too, that secretarial staff are briefed to produce double-sided copies unless instructed otherwise.

You should also ensure that any new photocopier will readily accept different types of recycled paper, and that it automatically changes to standby mode to reduce energy use.

ENERGY USE

Offices use electricity for all kinds of purposes – lights, heating and office equipment. It looks like clean power, but it is not. The power stations that generate the electricity are notorious polluters. Up their tall chimneys goes carbon dioxide, which heats the world and contributes to global warming. Also up the chimneys go sulphur dioxide and nitrogen oxides, which drift hundreds of miles to poison lakes and forests, and eat away statues.

The solution is to turn off unwanted lights and computers, to insulate the offices thoroughly, and to keep external doors closed. Using low-energy lights will also reduce the energy demand.

OFFICE EQUIPMENT AND ENERGY CHECKLIST

- Check all fixtures, fittings and equipment for environmental implications.
- Check whether existing furniture is formaldehyde-free.
- Check that new furniture is formaldehyde-free, does not contain material that emits other vapours, and does not damage the tropical rainforests.
- Recycle old office furniture and equipment.
- Check the energy efficiency and materials usage of new equipment before buying or signing a lease.
- Use photocopiers with an energy-saving standby mode.
- Introduce a policy of double-sided photocopying. Ensure all new copiers can handle this easily.

- Check whether there is a planned refurbishment or capital investment plan. Ensure that the environmental issues are considered.
- Reduce energy demand through insulation, turning off unwanted lights, and other measures. (See Chapter 7, Engineering.)
- Replace halon fire extinguishers.
- Check that office cleaning materials are environmentally friendly.

THE WASHROOM

Both in the office and the washroom, it is easy to become obsessed with cleanliness, to listen too closely to television advertising which preaches the virtues of a sterile germ-free world. Cleanliness is important, but excessive use of harsh chemicals is not good for the environment.

When cleaning chemicals are flushed into the sewage system they can interfere with the bacteria that are busy decomposing the waste. Bleach is also dangerous in that, if mixed with an acidic cleaner, chlorine gas can form – with potentially lethal effects.

You need not attack lavatory stains with unduly powerful cleaners. A build-up of lime can be cured by neutralizing it with vinegar, then brushing it off. This may take several repeated applications.

You should also be cautious about using too much detergent. Many brands contain phosphates, which damage water life. They also contain drying agents which can increase the body's absorption of pesticides in food.

As discussed earlier in this chapter, aerosols should be avoided. The worst type of aerosols contain CFCs which damage the ozone layer; and all aerosols are over-packaged and non-recyclable.

Air fresheners are best avoided. A synthetic smell is not healthy, nor is it a sign of cleanliness or purity. Any strip or cake that gives off fumes is likely to damage health. Lavatory smells can be avoided by opening a window, while effective cleaning will rid the air of impure smells. Simple and regular vacuuming, sweeping and washing of floors and other surfaces will keep them free of germs.

Toilet tissue made from recycled paper is also essential. The quality has improved immeasurably, and some paper is now cheaper than ordinary paper. Roller towels are thought to be more environmentally attractive than disposable paper towels or hot air driers.

Many offices and washrooms are cleaned and serviced by contractors. In such cases, find out what materials they are using. Often these are in the cleaner's cupboard. Go and investigate. Then set up a discussion with the cleaning firm's management. Specify what you want used. Remember that the cost of changing to environmentally friendly materials will be negligible. If the cleaning company does not respond positively, find another supplier.

You should also try to minimize water use. The washroom consumes a lot of water, which requires more pumping, more electricity, and more greenhouse gases. Each time you flush the toilet, 20 litres goes down the drain.

You can reduce the amount of water by putting a brick in the cistern. A better solution is to convert the existing cistern to dual-flush. This can save 50 litres of water a day per person – amounting to a billion cubic metres of fresh water a year. Urinal flushing can also be controlled by movement detectors that operate the flush only when someone approaches the urinals. Regulators can also reduce the amount of water flowing from the tap, from an excessive 20 litres per minute to a more desirable 8 litres.

> At the University of Durham, ozone-friendly aerosols have been in use for a number of years, but these are gradually being phased out in favour of hand-triggered sprays. A minimum amount of bleach is used, and toilet freshener blocks that contain PDCBs (Paradichlorobenzenes) have been rejected: the chemicals may prove to be toxic in the long term.
>
> The university relies on recycled paper products, such as toilet rolls, hand towels and bulk packs, and has switched to unbleached versions of these products.

WASHROOM CHECKLIST

- Use recycled lavatory paper and hand towels.
- Avoid using powerful bleaches or detergents in cleaning.
- Avoid the use of synthetic fresheners.
- Reduce the amount of water held in the cisterns and produced by taps.
- Check for leaking taps.

TELEWORKING

Centralized offices create traffic jams, rush hours and pollution. They produce a poorer standard of living for everyone – the people who commute to the cities, those who live there, and everyone else who suffers from the pollution fall-out.

Telecommuting (or teleworking) is one solution to crowded commuter trains. It means working from home, while being connected to the office by computers and telephone. Teleworking saves time and money, reduces city centre traffic, and allows people to work even when they are caring for small children or invalids. It also allows people to work in a more peaceful and attractive environment, and to spend more time in their own community.

Some jobs can easily be done at home. They include data analysis, data preparation and report writing. People who benefit from home working include salesmen, account handlers and computer programmers.

Prerequisites for teleworking include a standard computer format, a fax machine at home and a procedure for regularly communicating with the office. Electronic mail and a time sheet system will also be helpful.

The technology still lags behind human needs: integrated speech and data networks (ISDN) allow people's faces to be shown on the telephone, and for text and data to be sent at the same time. But though this technology exists, it remains to be introduced. When this happens, it should considerably facilitate teleworking.

Even with the best technology, telecommuting poses problems for the employer:

○ **Control**: are people actually working, or are they really watching television?
○ **Flexibility**: it is not easy for telecommuters to start a different piece of work; they cannot reach for a file if it is at the office.
○ **Communications**: how do you explain a complicated new procedure over the phone?

Moreover, many tasks are best performed in a group. Creative activity (deciding what price to put in a quotation) benefits from a face-to-face discussion.

One solution is partial teleworking, a mid-way point between working solely from the office and being based completely at home. This will allow executives to spend a certain amount of time working from home, carrying out tasks such as proposal writing.

TELEWORKING CHECKLIST

◆ Analyse the jobs that could be either wholly or partly home based.

◆ Create a plan that allows staff to spend at least some time working from home.

◆ Create systems to measure and control this work.

5
BUYING

◆

At one time, the main function of the purchasing manager was to keep costs down. Today, raw materials need to be 'green', and legislation has made the workforce more aware of the dangers of hazardous substances.

Many purchasing managers are unsure what importance should be given to environmental issues. How much extra should they be prepared to spend on 'green' products? And will this extra spending be criticized by the Board?

Two things will help to prevent this uncertainty: a buying policy, and better information.

A BUYING POLICY

The simplest way of drawing up a buying policy is to adapt the corporate environmental policy, if one exists. This will ensure that buying department practice matches corporate policy.

In drawing up a buying department policy, several factors need to be decided. Which issues are important? How will supplier standards be checked? Will you give existing suppliers time to reach the right standard?

Figure 5.1 shows how a buying policy evolves out of corporate strategy and information, and how the whole process is continuous.

CRITERIA FOR PURCHASING

Where alternatives are available, a purchasing department should avoid buying products that seriously damage the environment (for example, CFCs would not be used as a refrigerant).

Where alternatives are not available, the department should advise the supplier about its concerns. It should discuss with the line manager whether the product can be avoided. It should also monitor the trade press for substitutes.

Over the next decade products that seriously damage the environment will

A GREEN BUYING POLICY

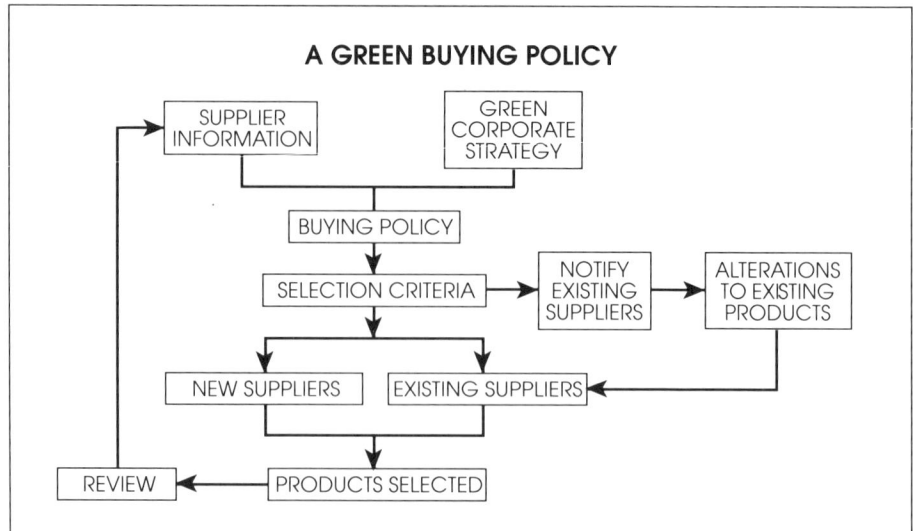

```
SUPPLIER INFORMATION     GREEN CORPORATE STRATEGY
            ↓                   ↓
         BUYING POLICY
                ↓
         SELECTION CRITERIA → NOTIFY EXISTING SUPPLIERS → ALTERATIONS TO EXISTING PRODUCTS
                ↓                                              ↓
         NEW SUPPLIERS    EXISTING SUPPLIERS ←─────────────────┘
                ↓              ↓
         REVIEW ← PRODUCTS SELECTED
```

Figure 5.1: A green buying policy. This green buying policy supports existing suppliers but not to the detriment of the business. Product selection is a continuous process.

become less common. So where there is a choice of environmentally satisfactory products, the department will be able to consider more traditional criteria, such as price, performance and supplier reliability.

If the department finds it lacks an environmentally friendly product in certain categories, it will need to be proactive. It should tell its suppliers the type of products it is seeking. Perhaps their products can be modified – by using less packaging, fewer raw materials, or greater concentration?

The buying policy can be presented as a charter, which will be given to suppliers as well as other departments in the company. In the box below is a specimen Buying Department Charter.

BUYING DEPARTMENT CHARTER

We will not use environmentally damaging products where an alternative is available.

Within financial reason, we will use the least environmentally damaging products.

We will aim to use 100 per cent recycled or environmentally friendly products by the year _____. This figure excludes products which by their nature are not recyclable.

We expect suppliers to meet the same standards we set ourselves for environmental protection.

Suppliers will be notified which standards are mandatory, and which are simply preferable.

An existing supplier who fails to meet environmental criteria will not be dropped immediately. A timescale will be set for the achievement of standards.

The company will from time to time expect to visit suppliers' sites, to check health, safety and environmental controls.

The company also expects an environmental policy statement and information about operating standards from all companies supplying in excess of £_____ a year.

The company expects environmental information about all products it purchases over an annual value of £_____. This information will include country of origin, ingredients or content, methods of testing used, method of manufacture, use of non-renewable resources, degree of hazard, handling instructions, disposal instructions, and any other relevant environmental information.

The company is pleased to offer its suppliers technical advice and assistance to help them bring their products up to standard. In cases involving considerable work, a charge will be made.

This charter sets out clearly how the department plans to operate, and what it expects from suppliers. It will also guide more junior buyers, and will inform line managers about the department's intentions.

BETTER INFORMATION

The buying department should determine what environmental factors are important or relevant. These will include packaging, recyclability and biodegradability. It will then rank products according to these criteria.

The simplest report format is to classify purchases according to the percentage that are 'recycled or environment friendly'. Each product category will have its own definition. Paper products might need to contain at least 50 per cent recycled fibre. Cleaning products might need to avoid chlorine.

BUYING DEPARTMENT ENVIRONMENTAL TRACKING

	Total Spend (£000)	Spend on Environmentally Friendly products (£000)	Criterion	% Spend on Recycled or Friendly products
Refuse sacks	49	49	100 per cent recycled	100

Paper towels Toilet rolls	78	78	100 per cent recycled	100
Cleansing materials	142	14	No toxic ingredients, CFC free	10
Liquid fuels	432	216	Unleaded, Diesel	50
Cut and flat paper	263	13	100 per cent recycled	5

The chart should be totalled, providing an overall figure for environmentally friendly purchases. Each year's percentage can be recorded, with the ultimate objective of reaching 100 per cent.

More complex analyses can also be performed. The department may categorize environmental factors as 'essential' and 'preferred'. This will provide a two-pass filter, in which some brands will be deleted in the first analysis, leaving others to go into the second screening. With paper products, 100 per cent recycled fibre might be regarded as 'essential', while a recycled watermark might be 'preferred'.

A stage beyond this is to construct a matrix that lists all relevant environmental factors (such as those listed in the box below).

A SUPPLIES MATRIX

- What is it made of?
- Is it a scarce or non-renewable resource? Is it suitably managed?
- Is the product made from recycled raw materials?
- Who made it?
- Where was it made? (Was it made locally – to avoid transport costs?)
- How much environmental damage was caused by its production (was bleaching used)?
- Is it non-toxic?
- Is it cruelty-free?
- How much waste was created in the process (none/minimal, some/substantial)?
- How long will it last?
- How much waste is produced in our process? Is the waste recyclable?

- ○ Can components be recycled?
- ○ Is the product biodegradable?
- ○ Is it energy efficient?
- ○ How hazardous is the product?
- ○ Is the packaging excessive?
- ○ How carefully does the supplier abide by environmental regulations?
- ○ Who wins from the purchase? Could we buy from a socially worthwhile organization?
- ○ Is there a better alternative?
- ○ Is it essential? Could we do without it?

Other considerations: _____

_____

_____

_____

It is particularly important to analyse your purchases from the Third World. Here your choices will have a disproportionate impact. In buying from the Third World, take into account the following factors:

- ○ Buy products where value has been added in the country of origin. This provides extra income for the country and reduces its dependence on fluctuating raw material prices. This means buying doors rather than raw timber.
- ○ Buy from countries and suppliers which provide good social and working conditions. Your purchases will be less exploitative.
- ○ Develop a long-term relationship with Third World suppliers. Help them acquire skills and equipment.
- ○ Buy products that lessen the country's over-reliance on cash crops. Many Third World countries need to diversify their exports.
- ○ Source products from local communities where the profits stay within the area.

By taking these steps you will be helping to reduce Third World poverty, and this in turn will reduce the damage to the environment. In the coming decades, the greatest abuse to the environment will take place in the poorest communities. If nothing is done, these people will be forced to exploit their dwindling natural reserves, and will themselves be vulnerable to exploitation.

Whichever criteria you select, use the matrix to score each product you use. Score 1 to indicate a problem, and 0 to indicate no problem. In a table with ten dimensions, products that seriously harmed the environment will score highest (from 7 to 10). Others with a lower priority will score in the middle range (4–6). A third group will pose no real threat to the environment (those scoring 0–3).

The department may develop a still more sophisticated model, which weighs each of the dimensions according to their importance. For example, 'Waste produced' could have a weight of 10, whereas 'environmental labelling' could have a weight of 2.

A computer spreadsheet can perform useful analyses. Purchased items can be ranked in order of annual cost. This will show where changes will have the greatest effect. The spreadsheet can then rank the items in order of their environmental score. This will reveal the most damaging products used by the company.

This matrix can be adopted to suit specific projects. For example, when deciding which of several competing brands to use, the department could compare their ingredients in a matrix format.

ASSESSING COMPETING ARGUMENTS

Environmental arguments are never simple. Imagine the purchasing manager is thinking of changing from ordinary paper to recycled paper. Two salespeople are sitting in front of him. One is from the existing paper company. The other is from a recycled supplies company. Their arguments go something like this:

Existing supplier:	We're 10 per cent cheaper.
Recycled company:	But we're better for the environment.
Existing supplier:	We've been your supplier for a long time. You shouldn't drop us after such good service. Besides, will the other firm be so reliable? And the quality of their product is much poorer.
Recycled company:	That's because we don't use harmful bleaches.
Non-recycled company	Recycled paper causes sludge which has to be disposed of. And besides, our paper is made from sustainably managed forests.
Recycled company:	That still destroys the countryside and uses more energy.
Non-recycled company:	Ours is a sensible middle of the road approach. You have your image to think about. Their paper is much less white.

	Customers will think your quality is slipping. Besides, you don't want to be associated with hippies.
Recycled company:	We're a perfectly respectable limited company, with major customers and a range of products.
Non-recycled company:	But not a complete range. You can buy *all* your stationery from us. Changing will make your life much more complicated. You have more things to do than worry about this minor issue.
Recycled company:	It's a good thing to have more than one supplier – it keeps both on their toes.
Purchasing Manager:	If I could interrupt for one moment . . .

The arguments are never as clear as they first seem. Environmental issues sometimes conflict with business practice. It is always worth asking a competing supplier what he thinks about a subject: he may have an opposing and equally logical viewpoint. If this happens, you may need to allocate plus and minus points for each brand. By totalling them you may more easily reach a conclusion.

Avoid rushing into a decision. Gather all the information. Ask questions. Find out whether an environmental claim is simply a badge, an irrelevant piece of marketing. Check whether a green product creates more problems than it solves. Be tough on suppliers who attempt to deceive with green claims – you may help to prevent another customer from being taken in.

PURCHASING SYSTEM CHECKLIST

- Draw up a charter, and send it to all major suppliers.
- Obtain environmental information on all main products and services.
- Revise computer systems to allow for environmental data analysis.
- Analyse what products are available.
- Screen products to determine which are least damaging to the environment.
- Set targets for buying environmentally friendly products in each purchasing category.
- Revise purchase orders to include environmental requirements or to make reference to environmental standards.
- Set up a system to verify that purchased products conform to specifications. This will include visits to suppliers' premises.

PACKAGING

Packaging provides an essential function – it prevents waste by protecting products from being damaged or broken. But if a product is over-packaged, it will add to the company's costs and contribute to the growing mountains of waste.

Many people see plastic packaging as bad, and paper as good. The reality is not that simple. All types of packaging have advantages and disadvantages, and no one type of packaging is inherently superior to any other.

Paper, for example, though cheap and biodegradable, is not rigid or impermeable enough to protect certain products. Used inappropriately, it will lead to product losses that substantially outweigh any environmental gains. Moreover, when paper is buried in a landfill site, it will not rot in the absence of air. The same applies to all other types of 'biodegradable' materials.

Likewise, glass is easy to recycle, but it uses substantial raw materials and its weight adds to transport costs. Plastic is ubiquitous – light, tough, cheap and waterproof. But being of low value and bulky, it is difficult to recycle profitably. Recyclers have to collect huge quantities of PET bottles to obtain even a small amount of recycled plastic, and the cost of collecting PET bottles can be more expensive than making new bottles.

> Carello Lighting in Staffordshire makes car lights, which it used to package in cardboard. Now it delivers its products in returnable plastic trays. The lorry takes full trays to the customer and returns with the empties. This has saved Carello the cost of the cardboard, and reduced its environmental impact.

Most packaging has evolved over time, with companies selecting the most appropriate one for their products. Here is a checklist with guidelines for selecting packaging.

PACKAGING CHECKLIST

- Avoid excessive packaging – check how many layers and types of packaging each product uses. Decide how much packaging the product really needs.
- Use packaging made from recycled materials.
- Use biodegradable packaging wherever possible.
- Avoid products sold in composite packaging (for example card and foil laminate) – this cannot be recycled.
- Avoid aerosols, even those that are CFC free. Hand-trigger bottles are just as effective, and use less energy in their manufacture. They can also be disposed of more safely.
- Rationalize the types of plastic you buy. Recycling single polymers is easier.

- Try to buy loose or bulk products.
- Look favourably upon suppliers who will take back their packaging for reuse.
- See whether packaging could be reused within the company.
- Check whether line management could use an environmentally friendlier packaging system for the products the company sells.

TIMBER

Buying timber and wood products has become a problem for environmentally conscious people. Everyone knows that cutting down tropical forests is destroying plant and animal species, and turning indigenous peoples off their land.

'Sustainably managed tropical hardwoods' have now arrived on the market. Unfortunately some of these claims have been revealed as untrue. And it is difficult to investigate the truth of a claim.

Only use hardwood whose stocks you are convinced are genuinely renewed. Alternatively, use softwood that is commercially cultivated and replaced.

Softwood too is not without blame. Conservationists have criticized the blanket planting of pine trees across the British countryside. Being of little use to birds and insects, it can turn whole hillsides into an environmental wasteland.

Check that the timber has not been sprayed with pesticides during growth, and that it has not been treated with any form of preservative after felling.

As regards wood products, some chipboard contains formaldehyde resin, which gives off fumes and may injure health. Chipboard can be found in worktops, floorboards, and other wood surfaces.

PAPER

Kodak has long worked with recycled papers, and 20 per cent of its copier customers are now using recycled paper, a figure that has jumped from 7 per cent in 1989. Rank Xerox now endorses the use of recycled paper in its machines, a reversal of its previous policy. On the other hand, IBM specifically excludes recycled paper from some of its machines on principle.

Society benefits hugely from the use of recycled paper, and these benefits were discussed in Chapter 4, The Office. For the buying department, there need be no added cost; in fact, it is possible to save money using recycled paper. Islington Borough Council saves £2 500 a year from using recycled paper.

We have already seen some of the arguments about virgin versus recycled paper. There is also a debate about the different types of recycled paper. Some mills whiten their recycled paper with bleach or optical brighteners, an action that is frowned on by some conservationists.

Much of the necessary brightness can be achieved by ordinary recycled paper, sometimes with a percentage of virgin white paper added. Some companies simply decide to 'downshade' their white papers, while others use tinted recycled paper.

Other mills pulp virgin paper, and call that 'recycled'. Therefore, it is worth asking exactly what the paper is made from. It could come from various sources:

A   Virgin paper offcuts from paper mills
B   Unprinted virgin paper, including printers' and converters' offcuts
C   High-grade office waste and printed virgin paper
D   Newsprint and low-grade waste

You might find that a certain paper was made with 30 per cent B, 30 per cent C and 40 per cent D.

MATERIALS TO AVOID

To list all the materials that could be dangerous would take another book. A better strategy is for the purchasing department to know the contents of each product bought, and to know the effects of each ingredient. It is unwise to accept at face value a supplier's statement on safety – he is bound to underestimate the product's toxicity. The fact that a product has been on the market for 20 years is not in itself a safeguard. Only now are products coming under real scrutiny. Get an unbiased opinion from an expert.

- Look outside your own country. If a product has been banned in Canada, the US or Germany, it was probably with good reason.
- Check the government's Red List of dangerous substances, and the equivalent EC lists (see Appendix II).
- Be wary of poisons (whether fungicides, pesticides or herbicides).
- Be wary of chemicals whose usage instructions indicate they are dangerous.
- Be wary of products that should not be used in an enclosed space
- Be wary of chemicals which warn against contact with bare skin.

Using such products may create health hazards for the workforce; they may cause dangerous by-products; and they may create extra problems for the factory in waste disposal. They may also create health risks for the customer, and cause problems when disposed of after use.

If in doubt, choose ingredients that:

- Have a gentle or simple action
- Match nature's products
- Do not cause violence in their production (to land, air, water or living things).

The substances listed below are comparatively easy to check. Less easy are the apparently harmless products that come from non-renewable sources, that have been made with a dangerous process, or whose disposal is hazardous. Learning to recognize these products will become one of the buyer's essential skills.

HAZARDOUS SUBSTANCES

2,4,5-T is a pesticide which is banned in nine countries, including the USA. A suspected carcinogen.

Additives in food can cause a variety of complaints ranging from hyperactivity in children to cancer. Additives include colourants, anti-oxidants, preservatives and processing aids.

Asbestos is used in brake linings and a few imported products. It is a carcinogen.

Benzene is a solvent that can cause leukaemia.

Bricks and building stone can cause environmental damage through quarrying and transport operations. Buy reused materials. Use secondary and recycled aggregates for concrete when applicable.

Cadmium is a heavy metal used in paint to provide orange and yellow colours. It is also used in rust proofing.

Carbamates are used in pesticides, and can harm the nervous system.

Carbon tetrachloride is a hazardous solvent which damages the ozone layer.

Chlordane is a poison that is thought to be a carcinogen.

Chlorine is a bleach whose use in paper (for example) creates toxic dioxins, which pollute water and air.

CFCs are used as aerosol propellants and as refrigerants. They damage the ozone layer.

DDT is a toxic insecticide.

Endrin, aldrin and dieldrin are three related pesticides, which the World Bank has advised against using.

Formaldehyde is found in some foam insulating material, wood treatments, carpets and other products. It can cause eye, nose and throat irritation, headaches and asthma, and is linked to increased cancer risk. Urea formaldehyde foam insulation is banned in the USA.

Glass fibre may be a health hazard if inhaled.

Halons damage the ozone layer. They are used as fire fighting agents.

Hexachlorophane is used in certain soaps and can be dangerous to small children and babies.

Lead can reduce children's IQ.

Lindane is a commonly used and dangerous insecticide found in timber preservatives and pesticides. Banned in the USA.

Manufactured Mineral Fibres or MMFs are fibrous substances used as thermal and acoustic insulators in loft and cavity wall insulation and for lagging pipes and tanks.

They are irritants and are suspected carcinogens. They include glasswool, rockwool and ceramic fibres.

Mercury is a dangerous heavy metal.

Nitrates are used in fertilizers. They leach into the water supply and may be a carcinogen.

Nitrites are used for preserving food. They are thought to be carcinogens.

Organochlorines are found in many pesticides, paints, solvents and plastics. Acute exposure causes nausea, dizziness and other symptoms, while long-term exposure can damage organs and cause cancer. The pesticides are by definition toxic. Cleaning solvents can accumulate and damage liver and kidneys. Vinylchloride and PCB (polychlorinated biphenyls) are carcinogens.

Organophosphates in pesticides can harm the liver.

Paraquat is a poisonous weedkiller which is highly toxic and can even be absorbed through the skin.

PCP (pentachlorophenol) is a fungicide found in some wood preservatives. It is a health hazard.

Perchloroethylene is a solvent that can lead to nervous disorders.

Phenols are found in disinfectants, glues and wood preservatives, and are highly toxic. PCP (pentachlorophenol) is banned in Germany.

Phosphates are used in detergents, and can cause eutrophication (when excessive algae growth clogs up the waterways and removes the oxygen from the water, suffocating the fish).

Titanium dioxide is used in paint. Its manufacture creates dangerous wastes which pollute the waterways.

Toluene is a dangerous petrochemical product.

Trichloroethane is an ozone-damaging solvent used in industrial cleaning. It is due to be withdrawn.

Volatile Organic Compounds or VOCs include benzene, toluene, propane, butane etc., and come from petrochemicals. They cause dizziness, and some are carcinogens while others are depressants. They are found in paints, cleaning solvents, polishes and perfumes.

Wood preservatives or wood treated with harmful preservatives should be considered carefully before purchase. In particular, avoid wood preservatives that contain tetrachlorophenol, lindane or tributynoxide.

Use this list as a starting point. The number of hazardous materials is endless; and the purchasing department will have to decide which materials to accept and which to reject. The aim should be to make a balanced and informed assessment of each product.

6
PRODUCTION

◆

Protecting the environment is similar to what most production managers have been doing in recent years. In introducing Total Quality Management and ISO 9000 (BS 5750 in Britain), managers have being seeking to reduce scrap, to introduce control systems, to check materials as they enter the system, and to get staff to take responsibility for their work.

Such principles are also at the heart of an environmental management system. So much so that the British Standards Institution (BSI) Environmental Standard looks strikingly familiar to managers used to BS 5750.

Manufacturing activities can be analysed into three categories, inputs, process and outputs. In Figure 6.1, by way of example, the inputs are feedstock, process chemicals, manpower and power. The process is seen here as a black box: it produces various outputs, wanted and unwanted.

In the past, managements have concentrated on three outputs: products,

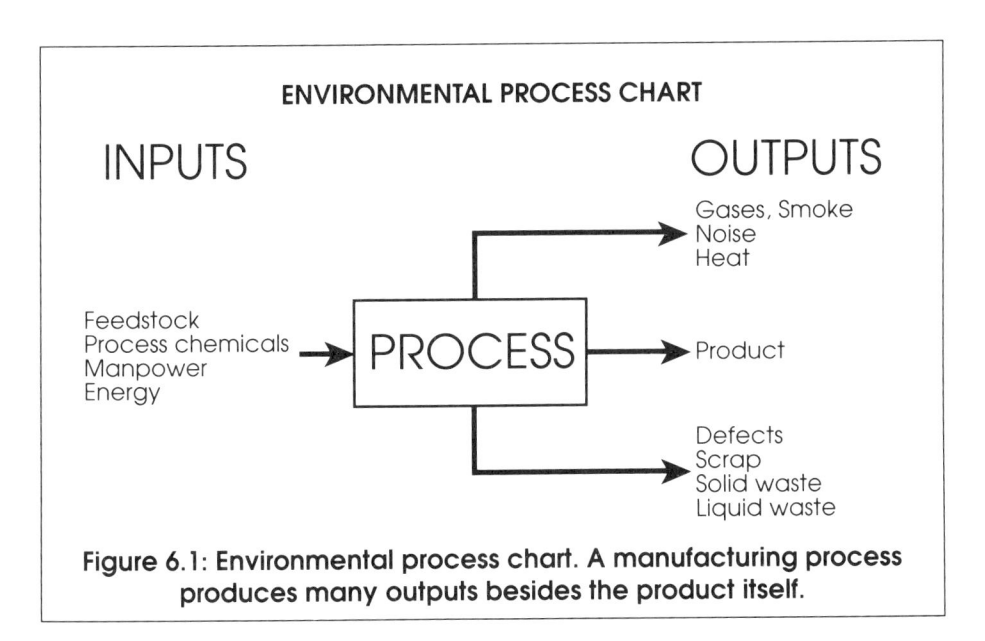

ENVIRONMENTAL PROCESS CHART

INPUTS

Feedstock
Process chemicals
Manpower
Energy

→ PROCESS →

OUTPUTS

Gases, Smoke
Noise
Heat

Product

Defects
Scrap
Solid waste
Liquid waste

Figure 6.1: Environmental process chart. A manufacturing process produces many outputs besides the product itself.

defects and scrap. Now managements are having to concern themselves with the other, usually unintended, outputs (shown here as noise; gases; heat; and solid and liquid waste). In this chapter, we look at the environmental impact of these unintended outputs, to see how they can be minimized.

ATTITUDES TO POLLUTION

Most factory managers think their own plant is in good order while everyone else's is not. In a survey by *Works Management* magazine in July 1990, 90 per cent thought that companies do not do enough to minimize environmental pollution. But 83 per cent said their own companies were taking positive steps to reduce environmental damage.

There is little evidence to back their assertion that they are acting against pollution: only 41 per cent have a budget for environmental control and 65 per cent admit that pollution control is not regularly discussed at senior management meetings.

About half the sites say that cost is a limiting factor in overcoming pollution, yet 72 per cent think technology is sufficiently advanced for industry to counter environmental threats created by their industries. So although most managers admit that the means to tackle pollution are available, there is a marked reluctance to use them. The reason is cost and a fear of losing a competitive edge.

One manager is brutally honest in saying, 'Reduction of pollution costs money and in most cases is not commercially viable.' Another sums up the feeling of many: 'The entire area is very dependent on cost. Everyone would like to do something about it, but when you are struggling to compete and make a profit in a tight market place, environmental issues have to take a back seat.'

HOW FACTORY MANAGERS SEE POLLUTION

What is the most threatening environmental issue?

	%
Airborne pollution	32
Toxic waste disposal	26
Wasteful use of resources	23
River pollution	17
Noise	2

Source: *Works Management*, July 1990

First we look at the question of pollution, whether of air, land or water. Then we consider the various hazards that are found in the plant. We also consider other important factors such as noise and safety.

WHAT IS ACID RAIN?

Acid rain is produced when sulphur dioxide, nitrogen oxide or other pollutants are emitted from a power station or other source, and later fall on land or buildings. It does not necessarily fall as rain – it can also fall as dry deposits or gas.

The results are varied. Some Scandinavian lakes have become so acidic that nothing can live in them – they are dead. The German government has calculated that 50 per cent of West German forests contain damaged trees. And historic monuments are being eaten away by the acid deposits.

Power stations are the main producers of sulphur dioxide and nitrogen oxide. Cleaner power stations and reduced output are the best ways of halting the damage.

Companies can help by reducing the energy they use. Less energy means less output from power stations, which means less pollution.

THE NEW LEGISLATION

In the past, air and water pollution and waste disposal were treated separately, and were handled by different regulatory authorities. Now the UK government has brought all types of pollution under one roof. It has also defined the industries and processes with the greatest potential to pollute. They include power stations, waste disposal incinerators, petrochemical works, iron and steel works, and paper manufacturing. Rubber, timber, dyes and glass processes are also included.

Companies that operate processes listed in the UK's Environmental Protection Act 1990 must apply for a licence. The only exceptions are where the process does not involve emissions or where the emissions are in trivial amounts.

Applications for a licence must be advertised in the local press, and objections will be considered. Public registers are to be kept, and the public may inspect the registers free of charge.

The registers will include authorizations, any prohibition notices issued, appeals, convictions and full monitoring data. The register is a new feature of the legislation: far-sighted companies will want to clean up their act before journalists and environmentalists start turning the pages.

Local and national inspectors have 'extensive powers' (in the DoE's words) of entry, inspection, sampling, investigation and seizure of articles. The regulatory authority can serve enforcement notices and prohibition orders on any company that contravenes the regulations. In the case of a prohibition notice, operators can appeal but they must stop operating until the appeal has been decided.

Companies can be prosecuted in the magistrates' courts or even the High Court; company directors and managers may be held personally responsible.

To make the system self-financing and to make pollution a cost to business, companies will have to pay for their licences. This will consist of an application fee and an annual charge. This concept of charging conforms to 'The polluter pays' principle.

BATNEEC

Licence holders will have to use 'best available techniques not entailing excessive cost' (BATNEEC). What this means for each industry is described in a series of government guidance notes. Existing plants will have to be upgraded if necessary, and new plants will have to conform to BATNEEC before they start operating.

'Best available techniques' include both the process plant and management's control of it. It covers the numbers and qualifications of staff, working methods, training and supervision, and also the design, construction layout and maintenance of buildings.

'Not entailing excessive cost' modifies the words 'best available techniques' to ensure that the costs will not be excessive. Existing plants will be required to upgrade to current technology, but the length of the plant's life and the extent of the pollution will be taken into account.

The regulatory authority will normally express BATNEEC as a performance standard; that is, a level of emissions which the plant should not exceed.

AIR POLLUTION

Clean air has long been a contentious issue. Now global warming, acid rain and depletion of the ozone layer have added to people's concern. These factors have caused new legislation to be introduced all over the world.

From the business perspective, air pollution is a waste. As Figure 6.2 shows, lost gases can be reduced, processed or reused. Anything that escapes could make trouble for management, in the form of expensive consents and local hostility.

Air pollution has both short- and long-term effects, ranging from headaches to lung cancer. The pollution comes from several sources:

○ **Carbon dioxide** results when any organic matter is burnt. It is not a

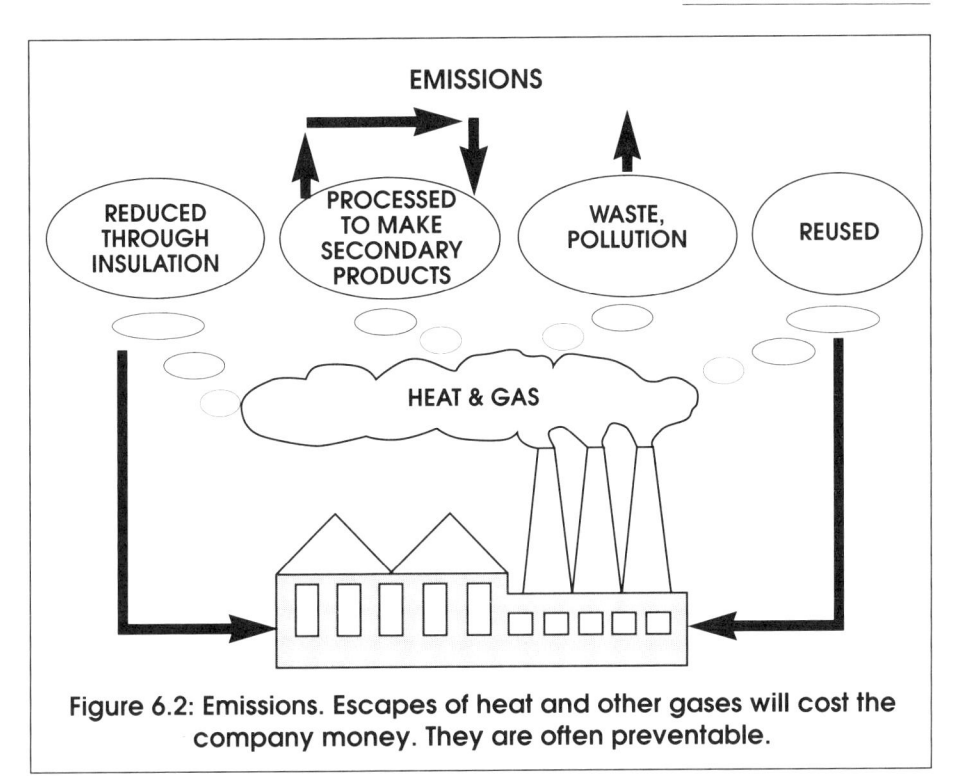

Figure 6.2: Emissions. Escapes of heat and other gases will cost the company money. They are often preventable.

pollutant, and trees actually need it, but it adds to the greenhouse effect by warming the earth.

○ **Carbon monoxide** comes from burning fossil fuels. Of the total 88 per cent comes from car exhausts, with the rest coming from cigarette smoking and faulty or unvented heating equipment. In the short term it causes headaches and breathing difficulties, and in the long term it can kill.

○ **Hydrocarbons** include petrol, diesel, gas and some solvents. Emissions come from unburnt matter in car exhausts, and through fuel evaporation. They react with nitrogen oxide to produce ozone (see below).

○ **Lead** comes from the exhausts of cars using leaded petrol, and from lead-using industries. Lead is thought to impair IQ in children, and it can damage the nervous system. Following a 60 per cent reduction in the lead content of petrol in 1986, air lead levels have fallen by 50 per cent. Leadworks and scrapyards can have high lead levels.

○ **Ozone**, as in the stratospheric ozone layer, is essential for protection against the sun's rays, but ground level ozone is an unwelcome pollutant. Ozone is formed by the reaction of nitrogen oxides and hydrocarbons. It contributes to acid rain and to the greenhouse effect.

○ **Nitrogen oxides** are emitted by car exhausts, power stations and industrial processes. Nitrogen dioxide can cause throat and eye

irritation, and photochemical smog. Cars are responsible for 48 per cent of nitrogen oxide, which also contributes to acid rain.
- **Particulates** are tiny solids or liquids that come from partly burnt fuel, and are found in coal and diesel smoke. Particulates can enter the lungs and may cause cancer.
- **Radiation** can derive from radon, an invisible gas that seeps from the ground, and is found in high concentrations in certain parts of Britain, especially the South West. In the long term it can cause lung cancer. Other forms of radiation come from the ground, from food and from medical X rays. Discharges from the nuclear industry contribute only one-thousandth of our total radiation. However, 2.2 million tonnes of low level radioactive waste have been pumped daily into the Irish Sea for 30 years, and nuclear workers have been discouraged from having children.
- **Sulphur dioxide** is an acidic gas that comes from burning coal and gas, and 85 per cent emanates from power stations. It corrodes stonework and irritates eyes and nose.
- **Volatile organic compounds** (VOCs) are substances like benzene and formaldehyde which evaporate easily. They are found in exhaust fumes, cigarette smoke, synthetic materials and household chemicals. They can cause eye and skin irritation, and some are carcinogenic.

Reducing air pollution is discussed elsewhere in this book (see especially Chapters 4, 7 and 8).

WHAT IS GLOBAL WARMING?

The world's temperature has been gradually increasing. Scientists now believe that global temperatures will have risen about 1.1 per cent above the present day average by the year 2030, and 3.3 per cent by 2090.

Although the increases seem tiny, they will cause havoc to the sensitive ecosystem. Severe reductions in food production in different parts of the world will be one outcome, with a much smaller increase in production in other areas. Flooding, storms and drought are also forecast.

A total of 55 per cent of the cause of greenhouse effect is caused by carbon dioxide emissions (from cars, power stations and other sources), 24 per cent from CFCs (in aerosols, foam blowing agents and fridges), and 15 per cent is due to methane (caused by rice production and cattle rearing). The ploughing of fields and use of nitrogen fertilizers is creating nitrous oxide, which contributes 6 per cent of greenhouse gases.

Even if greenhouse gas emissions were curtailed immediately, the atmosphere would continue to warm by 1 per cent over the next 50 years, due to the slow warming of the oceans.

As an integral part of society, business must try to do all it can to minimize the increase in global warming. The best solution lies in energy efficiency and conservation. This will reduce the amount of fossil fuels burnt in power stations. Reduction in energy demand saves companies money — so there is a strong reason to investigate it. We discuss energy saving strategies in Engineering (Chapter 7) and Land and Buildings (Chapter 3).

Another solution is to reduce vehicle emissions — a subject we discuss when we reach the Transport Department (Chapter 8). Reduced spending on petrol will also save companies money.

A third solution is the replacement of CFCs with more environmentally friendly coolants and propellants.

AIR POLLUTION CHECKLIST

- Sample air quality regularly, and analyse results.
- Check for escapes of gas or heat.
- Take steps to reduce air pollution.
- Consider using an alternative process which avoids the use of solvents or other pollutants.
- Enclose the process to stop escapes of dust or gas.
- Introduce dust and fume extraction.
- Plan to eliminate CFC usage.
- Reduce energy use to reduce pollution from power stations (see Chapter 7, the Engineering Department).

LANDFILL

Land pollution takes place when waste products are disposed of in a landfill site. This means putting waste in holes in the ground.

At one time landfill was considered standard practice. Now as the sites ooze methane gas and the piles of rubbish grow, other methods are being sought.

Under the UK's Environmental Protection Act 1990, companies now have a 'duty of care' to ensure that waste is safely disposed of. There are now unlimited fines for unsafe disposal of waste, and offenders are liable to up to two years' imprisonment.

Companies must find out what is happening to their waste — their responsibility no longer ends as the contractor's lorry leaves the factory gates. This will benefit the professional waste disposal companies who can offer greater peace of mind than cowboy operators, albeit at a higher price.

One-third of manufacturers and 17 per cent of chemical companies do not know the disposal method for their waste, according to research by the waste management business Effluents Services. The survey showed that many companies are unprepared for 'the duty of care' requirement. It also found a vast array of job titles for those responsible for waste disposal: 36 different titles were discovered among 60 companies, suggesting that waste disposal is tacked on to other jobs as a secondary responsibility.

Landfill sites are made safer if their bottom is lined before use with non-porous material to prevent contamination of the water supply. After the dump is finished it can be covered to prevent leaching by rainwater. Dumps are also made safer if the waste (especially hazardous waste) is placed in sealed containers.

One of the main problems comes from old sites. In the past toxic materials have been dumped in landfill sites by people who did not realize the problems that would be caused.

> At Helsby in Cheshire, a disused industrial dump is leaking polychlorinated biphenyls (PCBs). Stopping the seepage would cost several hundred thousand pounds. But the owner (who acquired it only recently) cannot afford it. The solution would be to cap the 10 acre dump with an impermeable clay layer. This would stop rainwater trickling down from the surface, though it would not stop the toxic material leaking from the base of the tip.

In future, the energy potential of landfill sites are likely to be harnessed, with methane being used as an energy source. At the Shanks & McEwan Stewartby landfill site, the gas powers four generators: 73 per cent of the electricity goes to a local brickworks, 14 per cent is exported to the national grid, and 13 per cent is used for internal consumption.

Another solution is to turn municipal solid waste (MSW) into compost. Greek glasshouse trials have shown that ornamental pot plants can be successfully grown in a mixture of peat and 20 per cent MSW. Meanwhile in Newcastle upon Tyne, the Byker reclamation plant produces refuse derived fuel pellets which save 5 000 tons of coal a year.

INCINERATION

3M decided to stop landfilling liquid hazardous wastes in 1969. It achieved that by constructing an advanced incinerator in 1972 at the company's Chemolite Center in St Paul. Though more than 15 years old, the incinerator remains state-of-the-art, the result of continual upgrading.

The incinerator has reduced the total volume of hazardous waste by 95 per cent and its toxicity by 99 per cent. The heat energy is recovered and used in Chemolite production facilities.

Ciba Geigy also decided to switch away from landfill, and this has cost the company an extra £1m a year. This happened despite the fact that almost all the company's 8 000 tonnes of organic waste could legitimately be landfilled.

Incineration is especially suitable for hazardous waste. By burning it at high temperatures, the toxicity of the waste is greatly reduced. Incineration reduces the bulk of the waste and it also can provide a useful energy source. The 27 million tonnes of domestic and commercial rubbish that is sent to landfill in the UK each year has the energy equivalent of 9 million tonnes of coal. For business, however, it is expensive: incineration costs can be 50 times higher than landfill.

Incineration is not a panacea, however. The British protest group Communities against Toxics has called for cleaner production rather than waste disposal. It points out that 'if the UK doesn't develop the clean techniques used in the US and elsewhere, we'll lose out'.

Greenpeace toxics campaigner Tim Birch calls incineration 'landfill in the sky'. Toxic materials have to be burnt at very high temperatures to reduce pollution, and strict procedures must be followed if escapes are not to take place. If the experiences of the nuclear power industry are anything to go by, many incinerators will not be as clean as the regulatory authorities would require.

A select committee survey of incinerators in Wales found that only two of 36 health authority incinerators used any form of air cleaning equipment, and only ten burnt the waste at sufficiently high temperatures. The National Association of Waste Disposal Contractors (NAWDC) believes that most of the 800 plants used by health authorities in Britain are polluting the air with heavy metals, dioxins, acids, dust and sulphur.

The best solution to land pollution is to reduce the amount of waste produced, and to make the waste biodegradable. We consider this in the Engineering Department chapter (Chapter 7). But first a checklist which focuses on waste disposal.

WASTE DISPOSAL CHECKLIST

- Check how much material is being dumped, and analyse its contents.
- Find out where it is going.
- Check the routes used, standards employed and documentation used.
- Review the insurance cover.
- Assess the facilities, equipment and methods, technical skills and permits of the company used for waste disposal.
- Evaluate the contractor's size and financial standing.
- Ensure the cost of waste disposal is high enough to ensure safe methods.
- Check the policies and attitudes of the contractor's personnel.
- Investigate alternatives to landfill (incineration or a waste reduction programme).

- Assess what would happen to your costs if waste disposal costs rocketed (as they might)?
- Determine how you could avoid such problems by reducing the production of waste.
- If you own a landfill site, check what safety systems are in place.
- Check whether you have old dumps that could contain toxic materials. If so, investigate what steps are being taken to resolve this problem.
- Have you acquired any companies which disposed of rubbish in dumps? What material was dumped? What steps have been taken to investigate the dumps?
- If you are acquiring a business, check whether it has any old or existing dumps.

WATER POLLUTION

At one time, generous 'consents' and public indifference meant that British companies could legally discharge polluted waste water into the rivers without worry. Now water pollution has become a more expensive, visible and embarrassing affair than it used to be. Companies are being taken to court for infringing consents, and are having to invest in water treatment plant.

Yet senior managers do not always know exactly what is being poured down drains or into the nearby river. Ignorance is never a defence in law, and today fishermen, householders and public officials are actively watching for pollution.

Most industrial discharges have to have public consent, and registers of consent are available to the public. Under the Water Act, companies can be fined £20 000 in magistrates' courts, with unlimited fines and prison sentences in the Crown Court.

Discharges into sewers are granted under a different act (the Public Health Act 1937) by the water companies in Britain. When in turn their water reaches rivers or the sea, they become liable to the regulatory authority.

The water companies are also tightening standards, and there has been a noticeable increase in enquiries from companies facing prosecution since water privatization. This is despite no apparent change in the quality of their effluents.

Water pollution comes from a variety of sources, including discharges from industry, agriculture and sewage treatment. Other sources include rainfall run-off from urban areas, and chemical sprays from local authorities.

Some solutions to water pollution are less than perfect. SCM Chemicals, a Hanson subsidiary which makes titanium oxide, extended its outfall pipe further into the Humber estuary. Its wastes are carried further from the shore and are diluted in a larger volume of water. But Greenpeace's Tim Birch says that building longer outfall pipes is like building higher chimney stacks. It does not deal with the problem: it just makes it someone else's problem.

SCM's effluents include mercury, cadmium, DDT and lindane, all of which appear on the government's Red List of dangerous substances. SCM is legally entitled to discharge 200 microgrammes of arsenic in every litre of effluent. But in future such consents could be tightened.

ICI has ten plants around the Mersey basin, which between them discharge billions of litres of effluent a year through its 50 pipes. In the 1970s, ICI spent the current equivalent of £25 million building plant to reduce the volume of mercury washed into the Mersey. The plant costs £1.5 million a year to run.

Norsochem, fined £800 for illegally discharging effluent into the River Mersey, has begun a large scale investment programme. A holding tank which intercepts and balances effluent on its way to the river has been built at a cost of £1.75 million. The company is also reviewing the process to try to stop problems at source.

On the River Humber, Ciba Geigy discharges quantities of organic compounds through extended pipes. The Swiss-owned company is now spending £30 million over 3 years to reduce the discharge of organic carbons into the estuary by 90 per cent. The plant has a team of 16 people to monitor environmental performance.

Coalite is entitled to put 18kg of cyanide into a tributary of the Rother every year. The company monitors 15 parameters through random sampling of the feed into the treatment system and the outflow. And Rhone Poulenc's 180 acre Staveley site, also on the Rother, produces an environmental index which measures performance of key environmental criteria. The index fell by a third between 1988 and 1990. To achieve further improvements, the company is spending £1–£2 million a year on environmental matters.

WATER POLLUTION CHECKLIST

- Find out whether any liquid is discharged from your plant into the sewers, rivers or sea.
- Analyse its contents. Keep records.
- Analyse what processes are causing pollution.
- Set targets for reducing pollution.
- Aim to clean used water before it enters the drains.
- Seek to reduce the problem at source, rather than at 'end of pipe'.
- Make a study of site history, to assess whether groundwater could have been contaminated over the years.
- Install groundwater monitoring wells.
- Assess the nature and source of any identified contaminants, and take appropriate action.

NOISE

Noise can affect employees' health and the peace of the local community. It can also lead to industrial accidents, which can in turn lead to more pollution. So noise is an important environmental concern. In the UK, 1.7 million workers are exposed to noise levels above the lowest legally recognized threshold. Now employers are facing union-backed claims for compensation. Ford Motors has paid out £6 million plus costs to its workers at Dagenham, and its Halewood plant could pay as much again.

Despite legislation, many shop floors still operate at excessive noise levels and without ear protection. The company should take steps to protect its workers from noise. Between 85 and 90 decibels (dBA), noise can cause hearing damage; and even below 85 dBA there is a small risk.

If you have a noisy work environment, carry out a noise assessment. Noise assessments are usually needed when people have difficulty being heard by someone two metres away, or when they have to shout. There are three thresholds:

- A daily personal noise exposure of 85dBA. Employers must provide suitable protection if employees ask for it.
- A daily personal noise exposure of 90dBA. At this level, an employer must identify, mark and restrict entry to 'ear protection zones'. Noise must be reduced by engineering levels, protection must be provided, and management must ensure it is used.
- Peak sound level pressure of 200 pascals. This happens where there are sudden loud noises, such as cartridge operated tools. Here the same action applies as for 90dBA.

Noise levels need to be monitored (say once a year) or if changes take place, such as when new machinery is introduced or old machinery is modified. Noise can also increase when machine speeds are increased, when machine layouts are changed and as machines get older.

A record of each assessment should be kept, showing:

- Workplace or job assessed
- Date of assessment
- Noise levels
- Action to be taken.

The noise assessment will:

- Identify the source of the noise
- Identify measures to reduce noise levels
- Identify priorities
- Take appropriate action
- Monitor future noise levels.

Priority should be given to the areas of greatest noise, areas affecting most people, and alterations that achieve the greatest effect. Reducing noise can be done by fitting silencers, using a quieter process, buying quieter machinery, providing ear protectors.

NOISE CHECKLIST

◆ Analyse noise levels in each area of the plant.
◆ Determine whether noise levels exceed safety limits.
◆ Agree action to reduce noise.
◆ Monitor noise levels and compliance with safety regulations.

HAZARDOUS SUBSTANCES

The COSHH (Control of Substances Hazardous to Health) Regulations have given British employers new responsibilities for protecting employees from hazards. The regulations deal with substances that can harm people or animals, or damage the environment, so they have a place in this book.

Some hazardous substances are obvious: they come in a tanker with a big HAZCHEM label on it. Others are more difficult to spot. Flour, cement and shampoo are three ordinary substances that can cause health hazards. Hazardous substances affect people in many different ways. They include:

○ Dust that people breathe
○ Chemicals that irritate the skin
○ Vapours that cause breathing difficulties
○ Poisonous plant material
○ Micro-organisms that can be swallowed
○ Substances injected into the body through sharp objects or by high pressure equipment

The effects of hazardous substances can be instant or can build up slowly over several years. Some may affect only people with allergies. Others may be harmful only when mixed with another substance (a chemical cocktail).

Using the checklist below, analyse whether hazardous substances are used in your company. If they are, you will need to implement COSHH regulations. Apart from being required by law, they make for a greener company.

HOW TO TELL IF YOU SHOULD UNDERTAKE COSHH ASSESSMENTS

	Yes	No
Do you use toxic substances?		
Do you use substances that cause asthma?		
Do you use substances that cause severe dermatitis?		
Do your staff suffer similar related ailments?		
Is your industry known to cause certain ailments?		
Do you use chrome solutions?		
Do you use substances that cause cancer?		
Do you use substances used for fumigation?		
Do suppliers provide raw materials which contain dangerous substances?		

If you answer 'yes' to any of these questions, you should implement COSHH controls.

STEPS TO TAKE IN IMPLEMENTING COSHH REGULATIONS

Depending on the substances you handle, you will need to:

- Assess workplace risks
- Replace hazardous materials or processes with safer alternatives where possible
- Implement safety precautions, starting by enclosing the substance or process to minimize human contact
- Provide exhaust ventilation to remove fumes or gas
- Reduce the number of people exposed to the hazards, and the duration of their exposure
- Provide protective clothing
- Consult employees, and ensure they are aware of all dangers
- Collect regular data (by checking employees' health or skin)
- Analyse the information for ailments, report any found, and take action to stop the ailments.

> Kirk Precision Ltd manufactures high-tech magnesium bicycles, and the company's hydraulics system used phosphate ester hydraulic fluid. This had many advantages for the machine, but was unsafe to handle. So Kirk changed to water glycol; this enables standard seals to be used for the hydraulic system and is safe to handle. In future, spillage and leaks will not pose a health problem.

HAZARDS CHECKLIST

- What hazardous substances are bought in?
- Are they fully labelled?
- How are records kept and updated?
- What dangers does each substance present?
- Where are the substances stored?
- Where are they used?
- How are they transported into your site?
- How are they moved around the site? Could this be done more safely?
- What hazardous substances are produced in production?
- Are finished products hazardous? In what way?
- What hazardous substances are used in maintenance, cleaning, research or testing? Can safer substitutes be used?
- What substances are disposed of? How are they disposed of? Can they be rendered safer?
- Are any one-off activities happening (for example, removal of asbestos)? Is this being done safely?
- Describe the activities, substances and processes that are found in each main area. Is more information needed on any of these?
- What hazards are faced by ancillary staff (cleaners, maintenance staff, researchers, contractors, fitters etc.)?
- How do people use each substance? How often are they in contact with it?
- Are any staff more at risk (pregnant women, those with breathing difficulties)?
- How long are people exposed to the hazard? Can this be reduced?
- In what way do they come in contact? Can this be avoided?
- In what way could accidents occur? Who would be affected, and to what extent?
- How are health checks carried out (blood or urine samples, checking of hands and forearms etc.)?
- Can less dangerous alternatives be introduced?

◆ Has a safety plan for dealing with emergencies been prepared? Has it been lodged with HSE and the emergency services?

Golden Sea Produce (GSP), a salmon farming business based in Scotland, uses an organophosphorus compound, dichlorvos, to rid the salmon of parasites. Dichlorvos can be harmful to crab and lobster larvae. So GSP has introduced a small fish species called wrasse into its salmon cages. The wrasse graze on the salmon lice, obviating the need for chemical treatment.

HOW TO MINIMIZE THE RISK

The following steps should be taken to reduce the risk to health among employees and other people.

○ Do not introduce new material on site until full documentation is available and is understood.
○ Store hazardous substances carefully in locked rooms with adequate ventilation, away from the workplace.
○ Label all substances prominently.
○ Do not decant hazardous substances into other containers.
○ Provide adequate washing facilities.
○ Ensure that all production processes are carried out in a safe manner.
○ Ensure management supervision to maintain standards.
○ Use robots or mechanical handling systems to reduce human contact.
○ Ensure safe working practices.
○ Provide regular training – in handling and using substances, in reducing risk, and in identifying symptoms.
○ Provide first aid training appropriate to the substances handled.
○ Introduce less harmful alternatives where possible.
○ Appoint a suitable person to carry out regular health checks of all staff. His or her skills and qualifications will depend on the nature of the substances.
○ Appoint safety representatives, and liaise with trades unions. This will aid information gathering.
○ Inform staff of the dangers of all chemicals they normally use.
○ Maintain proper records.
○ Report any symptoms immediately to a doctor.
○ Provide a written code of practice and put it prominently on display.
○ Agree a spillage procedure, and communicate it to staff.

Smiths Industries has reduced the amount of hazardous work on its aerospace site by sub-contracting the plating operation to a specialist company. Smiths Industries has recognized that it does not have to be expert in every single aspect of manufacturing, and that certain operations can be carried out more safely by specialists.

The net result is a reduction in environmental impact, because the chosen contractor has the equipment, systems and staff that let it carry out the operation more effectively. The policy change also makes the Smiths site safer.

OTHER ASPECTS OF SAFETY

With the advent of COSHH, it is easy to overlook the importance of other types of safety that do not involve hazardous substances. Fire has major environmental implications. A factory or warehouse fire can kill people and animals, and release toxic fumes into the air.

- **Prevent fires**: use less flammable substances, store flammable material safely, and do not have naked flames near flammable materials.
- **Minimize the effect of fire**: have plenty of fire extinguishers around, keep fire doors closed, and do not leave flammable rubbish lying around the site. Ensure that fire exits are marked and operative.
- **Take special care with pressure systems**: ensure that safety procedures are used.
- **Train staff**: hold fire drills, and display fire action instructions.

7
ENGINEERING

◆

According to the CBI, trade and industry in Britain produce 50 million tonnes of waste each year, of which 3.5 million tonnes are hazardous. Though this is only 10 per cent of the national volume of waste, the levels of waste are beginning to swamp local authorities. Moreover the problem of landfill pollution is only now beginning to emerge.

This means that business will be increasingly expected to reduce its factory waste, to minimize the amount of packaging it uses, and to recover packaging from its consumers.

In future the regulatory authorities will more strictly restrict the dumping of waste (whether on the land, into the air or into water), and they will charge more for the privilege of polluting. So, unlike previously, there will be a financial incentive for companies to reduce their waste.

Figure 7.1 shows how to control waste. Companies can alter the raw materials, the process and the product design, and reuse the waste itself.

REDUCING WASTE AND POLLUTION

It is better to stop pollution at its source – to prevent it from occurring rather than handle it once it has been produced. This can mean tighter management control or better maintenance. It can also mean redesigning the product, using better raw materials or introducing a better process.

Failing that, the company can clean the waste. Liquids can be treated and air can be filtered.

Finally, the waste can be reused by being put back into the process, or it can be recycled – usually by selling it to someone else. We examine all these options in turn, starting with the need for improved information.

OBTAIN REGULAR INFORMATION

It is important to know exactly what emissions are taking place, and what physical waste is being disposed of. Establishing your own laboratory will

WASTE REDUCTION OPTIONS

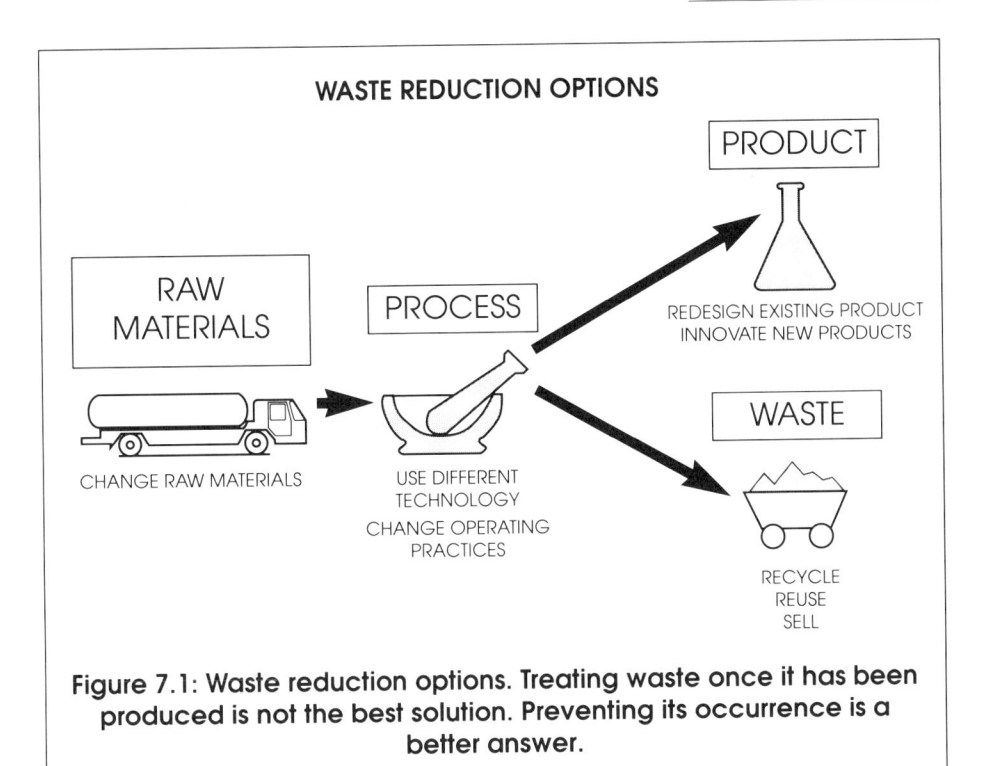

Figure 7.1: Waste reduction options. Treating waste once it has been produced is not the best solution. Preventing its occurrence is a better answer.

enable you to analyse emissions regularly. Regular readings are a vital first step.

> At Ciba Geigy's plastics division in Duxford, Cambridge, the company has placed pollutant-sensitive plants in tubs at five locations around the site. The company takes fortnightly observations on plant growth and leaf damage. Other companies have installed boreholes to monitor ground water quality.

Improved electronic monitoring systems will also help. This may involve automated sensing devices which shut down processes if they exceed predetermined limits. A gas analyser, for example, will monitor air quality. Sensors should be automatic or linked to human action: the site manager must be required to shut down the plant if pollution reaches a certain level.

Hartlepool Council in Cleveland has installed a computer-based continuous warning system to provide early warning of potential accidents. The £20 000 system monitors pollution levels around the large chemical plants in the area.

The system consists of a PC linked to outstations fitted with measuring and monitoring devices. The central PC polls the outstations hourly. The system monitors hydrochloric acid, and a range of gases, including sulphur dioxide, hydrogen sulphides and nitrogen oxides. If pre-set safety levels are breached, the system alerts environmental health officers.

SET STANDARDS AND TARGETS

Assess whether there are relevant standards – in water cleanliness, for example. Then set targets for achieving those standards. In the absence of recognized standards, you may need to set your own, or use an international standard.

> AH Marks, one of the largest manufacturers of phenoxy weedkillers is aiming to reduce emissions from its factory to zero. In 1990, the company spent £6 million (25 per cent of its total capital expenditure) on environmentally orientated work. It now has mechanical handling techniques to reduce the risk of spills and emissions, and has introduced water reuse technology.

INTRODUCE BETTER MANAGEMENT CONTROLS AND SYSTEMS

Improved training, better reporting systems, the allocation of responsibilities, quality circles and other techniques can all help to reduce waste. A greater number of quality inspectors, and improved process control can also reduce emissions and scrap.

Better standards of maintenance can reduce leaks and energy losses, and lessen the output of scrap. Improved movement of materials through the factory can reduce spills.

A waste audit team could be set up. This would identify where waste is occurring, and define solutions. Waste disposal costs should be allocated to the departments which generate them.

> At the Forbo Nairn floorcovering plant in Kirkcaldy, Scotland, up to 5 per cent of material disappeared during the production process. The workforce was actually hiding faulty sheets by using them as factory floorcovering and later throwing them into skips.

DESIGN A BETTER PRODUCT

Designing a better product prevents hazardous waste being created in the first place and eliminates the problems associated with handling hazardous substances. Johnson Wax, for example, stopped using CFCs back in 1975.

Changing from solvent-based paints or inks to water-based ones will stop the escape of solvents during manufacture and cleaning. For the customer it also means a change for the better, because he will not discharge solvents when using the product.

MODIFY THE PROCESS

Designing a better product usually involves modifying the process. By introducing cleaner technology, the company can reduce pollution and reduce the creation of by-products.

At a pharmaceutical plant in Northbridge, California, a solvent coating for medicine tablets has been replaced with a water-based coating. Changes to the spraying system cost $60 000 but this eliminated solvent purchases of $15 000 a year and the need for $180 000 in emission control equipment. The company reckons this has prevented the escape of 24 tonnes of airborne pollution every year.

Sometimes new machinery can do the same job in a more efficient and cleaner way. And when updating your tool room, pause before putting an old machine on a skip. The Third World needs old equipment. Charities can arrange for the equipment to be overhauled and sent to Africa or India, where it will help a village to acquire new skills and earn money. Early-numerically controlled equipment will, in any case, be more suited to the type of intermediate technology relevant to Third World societies.

Pause, too, before discarding hand tools. They are needed in the Third World. All kinds of tools are needed, including woodworking, engineering and tailors' tools. Charity addresses are at the back of the book.

CLEAN THE WASTE

Pollution escape can be tackled by means of filters and scrubbers. This will contain the pollution that the process is creating.

Waste liquids can be passed through a pre-filter to sieve out solid particles. The liquid can then be gradually filtered using reverse osmosis. Water is pressurized to push it through a very fine membrane which filters out molecules larger than water.

During the filtration process, the liquid can be acidified to kill bacteria. The acidic water can then be neutralized to an agreed pH and sterilized. It can also be oxidized to destroy potentially harmful organic compounds.

Liquid effluent can be treated with a flocculent which coagulates suspended material. The coagulate can be brought to the surface using air bubbles, and can then be skimmed off.

Micro-organisms can be used to feed on the waste and convert it. Evaporation or incineration can also be used to condense and solidify residues.

> At Sterling Organics, the company is checking the possibility of distilling waste methanol to a quality which could be reused in the chemical industry or else as boiler fuel. It is also investigating the reuse of acetic acid and sodium sulphate. The latter could be purified for sale, or converted through electrolysis into sodium hydroxide and sulphuric acid.

Some solutions can bring added disadvantages. Wet scrubbers can lead to a problem of disposing of the contaminated liquid. A thermal oxidizer to incinerate solvent vapours will use substantial energy (thereby adding to the greenhouse effect). In the latter case, one answer is to incorporate heat exchangers. DRG Kwikseal Ltd, an adhesives company, adopted this solution, and now captures enough heat to power all its ovens.

Many companies now treat liquid effluent with bacterial cultures, rather than simply pouring it down the drain. Oil contamination in soil or water can be treated biologically, as can various forms of industrial effluent. Waste oil can be captured and either cleaned or sent for treatment, after which it can be reused. Ford has a trade effluent plant that takes spent coolant and detergents from its manufacturing operation, and separates out the oil to produce hydraulic oil.

REDESIGN THE EQUIPMENT

The green company will modify equipment so that it performs better. Or it may modify equipment to take advantage of available resources (such as by-product steam from another process).

The Office Systems Division of 3M is saving 137 tonnes of scrap each year. Start-up temperatures in the coating and drying process were too low after down-time. This was causing inferior production of the division's photographic paper, which had to be discarded. From an investment of only $16 000 in computer control, the company achieved correct temperature faster, saving the waste in silver, paper, solvents and labour.

PREVENT ESCAPE

It is wise to have a second line of defence: a fail-safe system will prevent toxic material escaping. Chemical companies are building containment basins or retaining walls around their chemical stores; site drains are re-routed to the containment basins. When sprinkler systems in chemical warehouses switch on, automatic block-off valves also come on to prevent sprinkler water from entering drains.

SCRAP AND WASTE CHECKLIST

- Maintain records of scrap, re-work and waste.
- What does this cost in terms of lost revenue, treatment, distribution and disposal?
- How is the scrap caused?
- Analyse what steps could be taken to reduce the scrap.
- Introduce new systems and procedures to prevent scrap.
- Arrange regular meetings on scrap and re-work.
- Provide written standards for each process.
- Ensure these standards are regularly updated.
- Ensure that processes are monitored and controlled during production.
- Improve materials usage.
- Other than scrap, what other waste is produced?

- What happens to the waste?
- Redesign products which produce waste.
- Redesign production processes to reduce waste.
- Use raw materials which involve less pollution.
- Treat waste before it reaches the outside air or public water.
- Brief R&D people to produce a 'no waste' product.

RECYCLING THE WASTE

Recycling recovers value from waste materials. In the words of the old saying, 'Where there's muck, there's money'. There are also substantial environmental advantages in recycling. The extraction of metals from their raw materials uses huge amounts of energy. Mining operations scar the environment, create noise and dust, and disturb wildlife habitats. The heavy lorries add to pollution and road congestion. Recycling metal requires only a fraction of the energy cost, and avoids the depletion of non-renewable resources.

Creative thinking about wastes could lead to reduction in waste and even another income. What looks like rubbish to you could be valuable to someone else.

One company grinds waste glass and uses it in abrasive papers. Another reclaims silver from used film. A third takes lignin from pulp wastes. The most commonly recycled materials are:

Paper waste	Scrap metal
Plastic waste	Used textiles
Old batteries	Old tyres
Used catalysts	Effluents

These wastes may need further modification or processing. They can then be used in various ways:

- In the same process (reuse)
- To make a secondary product
- As imperfect products
- As fuel
- As a gift

REUSE IN THE EXISTING PROCESS

Raw materials can often be recovered and reused. An Acid Purification Plant will reclaim acid. In so doing, it will reduce waste disposal, and minimize the cost of purchasing fresh acid.

Water, too, can be recycled. One Volkswagen plant reuses water seven times before purifying it and returning it to the River Aller nearby. The waste water is actually cleaner than the rest of the river.

At an aluminium plant, the dross (a mix of oxides and non-metallic materials) is collected by a contractor who extracts the residual aluminium and returns it to the company for reuse.

SECONDARY PRODUCTS

Scrap metal can be sorted into type and then sold to a scrap metal dealer. Certain types of swarf produced in machining operations can be degreased and sold for recycling.

Hydro Fertilisers Ltd sells its plastic trimmings from packaging for reuse; some two tonnes of plastic per week are recycled in this way.

ICI Katalco has developed a catalytic technology for preventing chlorinated caustic effluent. The system converts the waste into reusable oxygen and brine. The new method is easily integrated into a modern chemical plant and has potential applications worldwide.

At 3M's Chemolite Center the company has halted the annual pollution of 677 tonnes of waste water. Thanks to an evaporation process it now recovers diluted ammonia from waste water created in the manufacture of magnetic oxides. The ammonia is concentrated into a 40 per cent solution and sold to farmers as a liquid fertilizer. The evaporator cost $1.5m but eliminated the need for $1m in water pollution control equipment.

At Grimsby, Tioxide makes titanium dioxide, the white pigment used in paint. The company used to discharge sulphur into the Humber, as part of the process. Now Tioxide neutralizes the sulphuric acid with limestone to create gypsum. Tioxide sells this to a nearby factory for making plasterboard. In so doing, it reduces its discharge costs and generates cash.

SELL IMPERFECT MATERIAL

Quality is an admirable goal, but its pursuit should not sidetrack us into believing that imperfect products must be thrown away. Sometimes imperfect materials can be melted down and put back into the process. But often the finished imperfect product cannot easily be recycled. If this happens, the product could be sold as second quality.

Pottery, glassware and textile companies divide their output into first and second quality, and there is a strong demand for 'seconds'. The same applies to clothing companies, who simply rip out the label before selling it to a retailer that sells 'seconds'. Shoe manufacturers and many other industries do the same thing.

Decide whether there could be a market for your second quality goods, and how this could be implemented. If necessary, they can be sold in an export market.

Waste sometimes occurs at a packaging stage. If perfect goods are imperfectly wrapped, the whole product is scrapped. A New Jersey film products company, Imaging Systems, now sends its imperfectly wrapped products to a sheltered workshop, where they are dismantled and recycled.

FUEL

According to the UK Department of Trade and Industry, John and E Sturge Ltd now gets 10 per cent of its energy requirements from methane produced on site. The methane comes from an anaerobic digester which was primarily installed to treat the effluent from its citric acid process.

Another digester is used by Bishops Castle Meat, an abattoir. The digester is fed with abattoir waste – blood, stomach contents, straw and muck – products that were costing the company large sums to dispose of. Now the methane satisfies 75 per cent of the company's energy requirements.

IF ALL ELSE FAILS, GIVE IT AWAY

Some waste may be scrap to you, but would be welcomed by other people:

> Around 400 businesses in Avon donate 520 tonnes of waste materials a year to a charity called Children's Scrapstore. The charity has 900 member groups which take their pick from the stockpile, taking it away by the trolley load. Over 150 000 local children benefit by putting their fertile imaginations to work on materials of all shapes, sizes and colours, in a wide range of art, craft, science and play projects.
>
> The variety of commercial and industrial waste would otherwise be destined for landfill.
>
> There are other scrapstores around the country; but you can offer your material directly to playgroups and schools. They especially like paper, card, fabrics, wallpaper, leather, wool, tubes, clothes for costumes, netting and thread.

USING OTHER PEOPLE'S SCRAP

You may be able to buy waste material for use in your own products. Newcastle householders are saving their plastic containers, which are then used by Proctor and Gamble in the manufacture of its fabric conditioner bottles.

West Midlands-based Robinson Brothers take another company's waste metal plating solution, and use it as a raw material in the manufacture of organic metal salts. They also use waste hydrochloric acid, which contains dissolved iron, to treat their own dithiocarbamate waste.

Various waste exchange schemes operate around the UK. They serve to put waste producers in touch with companies which could use the waste. The DTI Environmental Programme may be able to help.

RECYCLING METAL

Up to 40 per cent of total aluminium consumption in the UK is supplied from recycled material: some 200 000 tonnes a year. The source of this material is the aluminium works themselves, merchants and 'bottle banks'. Reusable aluminium is a valuable material, priced at several hundreds of pounds per tonne.

Recycling aluminium needs only 5 per cent of the energy needed to produce primary metal from ore. Over 30 per cent of European consumption is recycled, and in the USA 50 per cent of all aluminium drink cans are recycled, producing 1 million tonnes of metal per year.

> IBM has introduced a recycling and disposal service for computer equipment in the UK. The company provides the service on a non-profit-making basis, typically charging £15 for collecting and disposing of a visual display unit. The returned equipment is sorted, and components reused or recycled where viable.
>
> IBM has introduced the service so that it can offer a 'cradle to grave' support service for all its products, including those deemed by their owners to have reached the end of their productive lives.

British Steel Tinplate is also encouraging the recycling of steel cans or 'tins'. Steel is easy to recycle: the waste disposal company only needs a magnet. Steel is the only common metal that is attracted to magnets, so sorting (a key problem in many recycling schemes) is cheap and simple. The material is then sold back to British Steel which uses it to make new steel products. Unlike other recycling schemes, the value of the metal is greater than the cost of extraction, so no subsidies are required.

Steel recycling also requires no effort on the part of individuals or companies – any steel thrown away can be reclaimed by the local authority. In the UK, 1 billion steel cans are being recycled every year, and the number is growing.

Scrap merchants are another valuable recycling outlet: Steptoe and Son were around long before bottle banks. Scrap merchants will take many types of metals – including cables, lead, copper, brass and aluminium. Batteries, cast iron, stainless steel and zinc are also collected.

RECYCLING PLASTIC

Less than 1 per cent of process plastics are thrown away at the manufacturing stage. As with most materials, the problem is what to do with it after it has served its purpose. Only 10 per cent of polyethylene film and 7 per cent of polypropylene is recycled in Britain. Check with your suppliers whether they can use spent raw materials or packaging.

> At its Hayes warehouse, Marks and Spencer has cut the amount of waste it sends to landfill by 80 per cent. The rest is now recycled and earns money for the firm, with the result that the cost of waste disposal has dropped by half.
>
> The M&S lorries that deliver merchandise to the stores used to come back empty. Now they bring back packaging materials, stored in a manageable way. One major item is the polyethylene used for protecting clothes. As a

nation, we use ten times more polyethylene film in packaging than PET bottles.

Recycling mixed plastics is more difficult and less efficient than recycling a single polymer material. It is therefore important to separate plastics into their respective types before reprocessing. So Marks and Spencer is standardizing the plastic used for the trays that are put straight on to shelves. This simplifies the recycling process.

For plastics, recycling is only one solution. Another answer is to use them as an energy source. Burning plastics in an incinerator can produce power for the national grid. A kilo of polymers commonly found in household waste produces 38 megajoules, whereas a similar weight of coal produces only 31 megajoules.

Another solution is degradable plastics, several of which have been launched — to a mixed reception. Some are photodegradable (they break down by exposure to sunlight), and retailers fear they may have an uncertain shelf-life. Others are biodegradable (they break down in soil), and there are fears about their cost and their slow degradation.

Finally, it is worth remembering the other benefits that plastic brings. In the West, only 2 per cent of food is wasted before consumption, thanks in part to plastic packaging. In developing countries 30 per cent to 50 per cent of food is wasted, due to inadequate storage, packaging and distribution.

RECYCLING GLASS

Glass-making uses a large amount of energy and raw materials. Every tonne uses 1.2 tonnes of sand and limestone; and this has to be quarried, a process that scars the landscape and disrupts the peace of the countryside with noise and heavy lorries.

When recycled, however, glass becomes an environmentally friendly form of packaging. The British doorstep delivery system ensures that milk bottles are reused up to 30 times, and this system can be adopted by any business that supplies glass containers to major customers or to a few delivery points.

For each tonne of glass that is recycled, there is an energy saving equivalent to 30 gallons of oil. In 1989 Britain saved the equivalent of 9 million gallons of oil this way, even though it recycled only 17 per cent of its glass compared with a European average of 39 per cent.

RECYCLING CHECKLIST

- Analyse the components of your waste. Is any of it potentially useful?
- See whether waste material could be reused within the company.
- Analyse whether waste products could be processed into useful material.
- See if any waste products have a commercial value.

- Check whether waste could be used by a charity or other organization.
- Check what factors inhibit recycling (for example, use of composite packaging materials). How could this problem be overcome?
- Could you offer to take old products back at the end of their life?

ENERGY USE

In Britain some two-thirds of the energy used by business goes to heat buildings; and up to 40 per cent of this could be saved by simple conservation methods. Best available technology in building design and equipment can reduce energy consumption in specific uses by a factor of ten. Apart from the cost savings, there would be a reduction in greenhouse gases, and a reduction in the demand for fossil fuels.

Reducing energy use has numerous environmental benefits. It reduces global warming, and decreases the loss of fossil fuels. It saves the company money, and employees benefit from a temperate, draught-free environment.

Energy is a variable cost which can be controlled, unlike other building costs such as rent or rates. And from the company's point of view, saving energy can produce a sizeable reduction in costs. Companies can expect to reduce their energy costs by between 10 per cent and 30 per cent. Outside energy-intensive industries like steel production, energy sometimes accounts for only 5 per cent of total costs, so the level of resources and investment put into this area needs a careful cost/benefit analysis.

But first, we need to consider how to introduce energy conservation into a business. We start with the appointment of an Energy Manager.

THE ENERGY MANAGER

The most important task is the appointment of an Energy Manager who will be responsible for monitoring and controlling energy. In a large firm, the function will take 100 per cent of the individual's time, while in a small firm it may be just one of several duties.

Like every other function, the work needs a job description. This should define the scope of the work and should state who the person reports to. The support of top management will also be needed in introducing change.

In appointing a manager, you should not overlook the need for involving all the other people in the company. Line managers need to be given responsibility for their department's energy use, and all staff need to be aware of the importance of energy conservation.

SURVEY USE, SET TARGETS, MONITOR PROGRESS

Facts and figures are essential. To gather the data, you will need to conduct an energy audit. This will assess where the most power is being used. Metering

BREAKING DOWN ENERGY USE

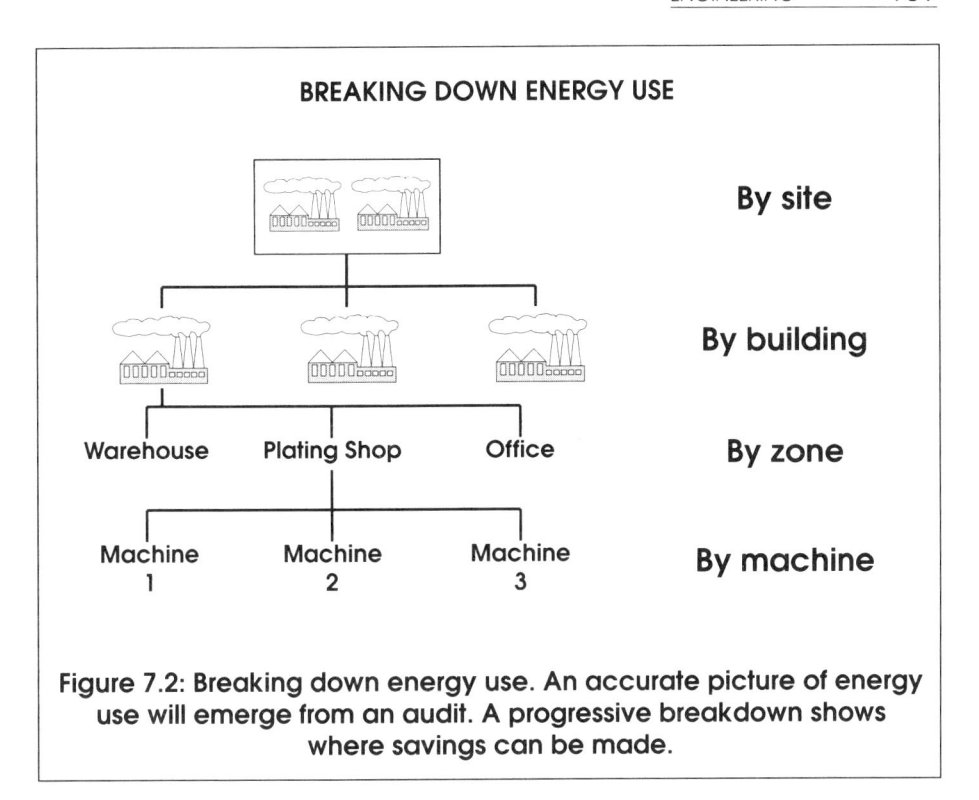

- By site
- By building
- By zone (Warehouse, Plating Shop, Office)
- By machine (Machine 1, Machine 2, Machine 3)

Figure 7.2: Breaking down energy use. An accurate picture of energy use will emerge from an audit. A progressive breakdown shows where savings can be made.

specific plant and equipment (as shown in Figure 7.2) will provide a breakdown of energy use. It will also allow the company to evaluate different buildings and machines.

You can compare your building's energy use with government figures for comparable buildings. This is done by measuring kilowatt hours per cubic metre. The Energy Efficiency Office has information on how to produce a 'Normalized Performance Indicator'. If your energy use is in the Fair or Poor category, there will be an opportunity for considerable cost saving.

After establishing the level of consumption, set goals for reducing energy use. In 1985 IBM UK set a target to reduce energy consumption by 20 per cent by the end of 1989. By 1989, these savings amounted to £2.6 million. This was achieved by numerous initiatives – from simple things such as switching off lights to complex energy management systems.

After the goals have been set, progress should be monitored and corrective action taken. For smaller companies, monthly monitoring can be time-consuming, so annual audits and an automatic control system may be more cost-effective.

ENERGY USE STRATEGIES

Look at each area of energy use in turn. Savings will be achieved by tackling the following issues:

Item	Activity
The building	Reduce draughts
	Improve insulation
Lighting	Use energy-efficient lighting
	Avoid unnecessary lights
Space and water heating	Avoid over heating
	Shorten heating times
	Reduce losses
	Maximize boiler efficiency
Ventilation	Reduce use
Air-conditioning	Reduce use
	Avoid excessive cooling
Machinery	Use energy-efficient machinery
	Prevent energy losses

Some of these solutions are free, others are cheap, and a third category is expensive. We look briefly at each in turn.

No-cost improvements

The cheapest way to reduce energy costs is to make people aware of the opportunities for saving energy. Turning off lights, turning down radiators and shutting windows can produce immediate savings. This requires action from all staff. Keep them aware of progress by displaying graphs showing year-on-year changes in energy use. You can also make use of free government videos and literature on energy efficiency.

> At the UB frozen pasta factory in Fakenham, Norfolk, the energy bill represented a third of the direct labour cost. Therefore any savings would be substantial. In 12 months, the company succeeded in reducing electricity use by 9 per cent and fuel oil by 22 per cent.

The management consultants' secret: go into the building at a weekend or in the evening. Run your hand over machinery. Is it still on? Is it hot? Look up: are lights still on? Stop and listen: is the air-conditioning still humming? Can you hear motors still whirring?

Low-cost improvements

Draught-proofing leaky windows and insulating boilers will bring dramatic savings at low cost. Insulating roof and wall spaces are also cheap options.

A thermal imaging camera will detect heat losses. Infra-red photography will identify areas that need insulation.

Higher-cost measures

Some other measures will involve higher costs, notably the replacement of old and inefficient heating systems. It is important to conduct a cost benefit analysis on the competing projects before selecting the most cost-effective ones.

> The energy bill at St. Thomas's Hospital, London, has fallen by £70 000 since the introduction of a new Energy Management System. The system monitors electricity, gas and oil use, water consumption, lighting and room temperatures, and provides information about outside weather conditions.

ENERGY STRATEGY CHECKLIST

- Appoint an Energy Manager.
- Meter consumption.
- Carry out an energy audit.
- Determine where greatest savings can be made.
- Set up an energy reduction programme.
- Set targets, and monitor progress.
- Introduce good housekeeping measures.
- Insulate and draughtproof.
- Formulate a capital investment plan.
- Give line managers responsibility for energy use.
- Train staff to conserve energy.

Next we look in more detail at four key areas for energy conservation: insulation, lighting, heating and machinery.

INSULATION AND DRAUGHTS

Up to 50 per cent of a building's heat is lost through external walls – more in a detached building. So good wall insulation is essential.

Roof spaces should be insulated to prevent heat from escaping. Make sure the layers of insulation meet government standards.

You can also use mineral fibre under-floor insulation. Concrete floors can be insulated with layers of cork and other insulating materials including CFC-free polystyrene.

Transparent plastic door curtains reduce the amount of heat lost through warehouse and factory entrances, while allowing people and fork lift trucks to pass without delay.

> At Alupres, an aluminium extruder, floating plastic balls restrict heat losses from the anodizing line.

Double glazed windows need an 18–20mm gap between the two window surfaces to minimize heat loss. Bigger gaps reduce noise – another pollutant for companies with buildings in a city centre or beside a busy road.

One way to identify heat losses at a large or complex site is by an aerial infrared survey.

INSULATION CHECKLIST

- Insulate walls and roof spaces, boilers and pipes.
- Use heat reflective foil behind wall mounted radiators to reflect the heat back into the room.
- Double glaze windows.
- Check for draughts around doors and windows, and draughtproof. Introduce draughtproof lobbies and draughtproof doors.
- Install automatic door closures.

LIGHTING

Introducing more efficient lighting can cut fuel bills by up to 40 per cent. This can be done by using energy-efficient lights, by not having lights on when they are not needed, by good maintenance, and by making use of daylight.

LIGHTING CHECKLIST

- Change to low-energy fluorescent or sodium lights. Although they can initially cost more to buy, they save money in the long term. Fluorescent lights use only one-fifth of the energy of tungsten filament.
- Install the right type of lights for each work activity.
- Switch off lights when not in use. Consider automatic lighting controls. After work, ensure that only sufficient lights needed for security purposes are left on. A microprocessor system will turn off lights at the end of the day.
- Paint walls and ceilings in a light colour – this will require less wattage to light and will reduce the need for artificial light.
- Make maximum use of daylight. Site work benches next to windows, and keep the windows clean to allow maximum daylight.
- Keep lights clean – this will reduce the need for extra lights.

SPACE AND WATER HEATING

It is important to fit boilers appropriate to your needs, and to use a cost-effective fuel. Select the right size boiler: one that is too large will be unnecessarily expensive to run. Fitting point-of-use immersion heaters for hot water will allow the boiler to be switched off in summer.

It is also important to prevent excessive use of air-conditioning plant. Some systems are set at too low a temperature, and thereby use excessive energy. Air-conditioning plant needs a proper maintenance programme to prevent Legionnaires' Disease.

HEATING CHECKLIST

- Fit thermostats to heaters.
- Fit timers to lights and heaters.
- Fit visible thermometers around the building.
- Install automatic cut-off switches.

Management measures

- Ensure doors and windows are kept closed during periods of cold.
- Reduce unnecessary ventilation.
- Turn down radiators.
- Ensure that power is switched off at night and weekends.
- Improve boiler maintenance.

More advanced heating measures

- Reduce areas of glazing in stores and warehouses – the extra lighting costs will be small in comparison with the reduction in heating.
- Reuse waste heat.
- Use combustible waste as a fuel.
- Check the suitability of the heating system.
- Introduce a microprocessor-controlled energy management system with zoned heating.
- Recycle process energy by using heat recovery from industrial processes for space or water heating.

  British Home Stores has achieved savings of £4 million since 1981 when it started training local store staff in energy efficiency. To achieve this level of profit at the tills, the compnay would have to have sold an additional £20 million worth of merchandise.

MACHINERY AND EQUIPMENT

Equipment should be set to correct speeds or temperatures. This will not only use less energy but will help prolong the life of the equipment. When not in use, equipment should be turned off.

EQUIPMENT CHECKLIST

- Compare the energy use of competing makes before buying or leasing equipment.
- Introduce new equipment that uses less energy.
- Prevent leaks of compressed air or steam.
- Add meters.
- Buy electricity at the most advantageous tariff. Consider using off-peak electricity.

    At Hydro Fertilisers Ltd (formerly Fisons) the company harnesses the process heat generated from the reaction of nitric acid. The steam is used to generate electricity so that the site is nearly self-sufficient in energy.

COMBINED HEAT AND POWER

Rather than buying power from the national grid, you may want to generate your own. One of the most efficient ways to do this is with a combined heat and power (CHP) plant.

A CHP system provides both heat and electricity, and does so extremely effectively. All energy generation has transmission and heat losses, and grid electricity only achieves up to 35 per cent efficiency. But CHP captures the heat it produces, and uses it to provide process heat, space heating and hot water. Excess electricity can also be sold back to the national grid.

But an organization needs a base electrical load of 40kWh, which should run for at least 4 500 hours a year. It should also have a large requirement for heating. And, with typical installation costs of over £2 million, it needs a generous bank balance.

RENEWABLE ENERGY

There has been a surge of interest in renewable fuels. In 1989, ETSU (the Energy Technology Support Unit), run by the British Department of Energy, was handling 200 enquiries a month about renewable energy. By 1991, the number of enquiries had risen to 800 a month. The department handed out

214 000 items of literature in response to enquiries from government bodies, companies, schools, children and private individuals. Only the press was not interested.

ACTIVE SOLAR ENERGY

Solar-powered products are now widely available and perform a variety of tasks. However, the traditional complaint about active solar energy is its mismatch between demand and supply: supply is greatest in the summer, when demand is lowest.

In the past, too, installation costs have outweighed the energy savings. As a result, the British Department of Energy has halted its research, even though one firm, Thermomax, won a Design Award in 1986 and a Queens Award for Export in 1987.

Even in the temperate British climate, solar heating is an option for water heating because radiation comes to us in the form of electromagnetic waves, most of which are invisible. Today's more efficient solar panels work even in cold, windy or cloudy conditions. Once the unit has been installed, the power is free.

Solar heating can complement conventional heating systems (which may be used as a back-up), and solar heating is also useful where large amounts of tepid water are needed, such as in agriculture.

Mounted on the roof and requiring no extra construction skills, solar panels consist of flat plates through which water or glycol is pumped. The panels can absorb enough heat to meet about 50 per cent of typical domestic hot water and space heating requirements, though information on commercial users is still sketchy. Solar panels may do a specific job, such as supply hot water for hand washing. This will allow the company to contribute to energy conservation.

By metering its hot water usage, a company can estimate its annual solar energy requirements. According to Greenslade Solar Systems, a solar system can collect 600 kWh per square metre of panel (more in the south and less in the north). Thus if a business used 6 000 kWh a year, it would need collecting panels 10 square metres in size. Different proprietary systems will have different efficiency rates.

Solar energy can also be used to power outside lights. These store daytime solar power in Ni-Cad energy cells, and switch on at dusk, providing security, walkway and decorative lighting. Some early devices produced very little light and were flimsy in construction, and these have hindered the development of the market.

WIND ENERGY

The power of the wind can be harnessed in many ways. The smallest wind turbines will power 12V batteries, which in turn can run lights, telecommunications equipment or alarms. Medium-sized wind turbines have maximum power outputs of 500 kilowatts. They are used by farmers, businesses and hospitals to reduce their demand for electricity imported from the national grid, and they can supply energy back to the grid.

Much larger wind turbines can generate up to 4 megawatts, and are used to supply electricity to the grid. A wind farm is a real possibility for companies with large sites.

> When steel production ceased at Consett, County Durham, the town was left with a 700 acre void. Now that space is being filled by the Genesis project, a green development which includes a wind farm, country park, industry, leisure centre, housing and offices.
>
> Being 900 feet above sea level, the prospects for the wind farm are good, and it is eventually expected to produce 8 megawatt of electricity as well as being a tourist attraction.
>
> The site is being developed as a partnership between the local council and a number of companies including the Halifax Building Society and Lovell.

Wind turbines are a clean source of energy. They do not produce any pollutants, and are safe to run. There are no risks of fuel cost inflation, since the wind is free. In contrast to traditional large power stations, wind turbines can be constructed quickly and in batches. This allows more flexibility in planning. The capital invested starts producing a return much more quickly.

Enthusiasts see turbines as graceful machines, and local populations do not seem to resent them, especially if local people are given a proportion of their earnings. However, there is an obvious visual impact, and varying amounts of noise depending on the site. Some conservation groups are opposed to them for these reasons.

There have been few cases of injury to birds, livestock or wildlife. Research by the RSPCA suggests that there is no measurable effect on birds which, it says, seem oblivious to the large wind turbine blades.

WATER POWER

British-made hydroelectric plants now power tea plantations in Sri Lanka and are in common use in Nepal and Peru. A 1 megawatt computer-controlled version installed in Ireland supplies power to the national grid. These river-based systems have a 5 year payback, and are competitive with diesels. Simpler versions are also available for use on farms.

Energy from tidal power is likely to grow, and will take the form of estuary barriers. These have commercial value to the construction firms who build them, as well as to consumers who benefit from a non-polluting form of energy. Conservationists, however, are deeply concerned about their impact on estuarine wildlife, especially birds.

OTHER RENEWABLE ENERGY SOURCES

Other renewable sources of energy are worth considering. Biofuels are becoming more widely used. They involve organic matter taken from plants or animal waste, landfill gas, or refuse derived fuel. For example, shredded and screened refuse provides 20 per cent of the energy used in the cement kilns at Blue Circle cement works at Westbury, Wiltshire.

Energy from landfill gas will also become more prevalent over the next decade. Britain is second only to the USA in the exploitation of landfill gas. Purists point out that landfill gas is not truly green, in that it depends on the production of rubbish; pragmatists say that the energy is the highest value use of landfill waste.

Another biofuel is 'energy forestry', whereby the trees are coppiced and the cuttings cleanly incinerated. This shows real promise as a new 'crop'.

Other renewable energy sources cannot be so easily bought off the peg, though they could be developed as a partnership between government and business. Water power is one such example with wave power being strangely under-developed for an island nation.

Power from the earth is also being considered. In some parts of the world, hot springs or aquifers (underground water) are used to generate power. There is one such scheme in Southampton. An investment in hot dry rock (from which the earth's heat is tapped) is being made at Rosemanowes, Cornwall, and elsewhere in the world.

The British government spends pitiful amounts of money on renewable energy. It spent £15 million on all renewable energy research in 1988, compared with £145 million into nuclear research alone. The government has also located its renewable energy research inside the Atomic Energy Research Establishment at Harwell, an organization not known for its benign support of alternative energy.

PASSIVE SOLAR HEATING

As we have seen in Land and Buildings, passive solar energy is the art of using the sun's warmth to heat a building, while avoiding excessive glare or overheating. Typical strategies are:

○ Effective siting of the building – protected from winds and making maximum use of the south aspect.
○ Careful choice of windows to capture maximum light and warmth without excessive solar gain. Large south-facing windows and small north-facing windows are used.
○ Use of glazed roofing.

This is usually coupled with other energy saving strategies, such as:

○ Effective insulation to prevent heat losses.
○ Heater thermostats which maintain a constant internal temperature.
○ Use of a ventilation system to draw air from warm parts of the building to the colder areas.

Ventilation systems can also extract the heat from used air, and use it to warm the incoming fresh air. The same applies to used water. A heat exchanger takes heat from used 'grey' water, and transfers it to clean water which is about to be used.

RENEWABLE ENERGY CHECKLIST

- Evaluate the possibility of installing solar panels.
- Consider introducing solar-powered lights.
- Check the possibility of using wind power.
- Examine other sources of renewable energy.
- Make use of passive solar heating.

REDUCING WATER USE

If your water is not metered, it is easy to believe that it is a free resource. In fact water is a scarce resource, and not just in the Third World where countries like Ethiopia suffer repeated droughts. In many parts of the west, water is scarce. Hose pipe bans are increasingly common in Britain, and it costs money to collect, purify and deliver water to businesses and households.

It is all too easy to tip oil down the drain, to pour chlorine bleach into the lavatories daily, and to leave taps running or dripping. It is easy to use water in manufacturing processes, and then expel the polluted water back into the river. But all these actions pollute the water supply or make excessive demands on it. It is important to treat water as a valuable resource.

WATER USE CHECKLIST

- Repair leaking pipes.
- Repair dripping taps.
- Reduce the amount of water held in lavatory cisterns (by putting a brick in the cistern).
- Reduce the quantity of water used in rinsing baths.
- Use flow restrictors to reduce the flow of water in taps.
- Recycle waste water.
- Separate different types of water – drinking and service.
- Meter water usage by plant or type of machine.
- Choose water-efficient machinery.

8
TRANSPORT

◆

Contrary to what many fleet managers think, having cars that run on unleaded petrol or diesel does not in itself make a green car policy. A genuinely green company will go much further than this. Yet fleet managers do not usually see that green issues are especially relevant to company cars. They recognize that cars pollute, but they cannot see what alternatives exist.

No one wants to pollute the world, but people cannot easily do without their car. Nor are they keen to make sacrifices. According to MORI, two-thirds of people in Britain want the government to cut exhaust fumes, but only 17 per cent are prepared to use public transport to reduce pollution.

Cars give us unparalleled personal convenience and efficiency. But they also pollute the environment and cause destruction. Road transport accounts for 85 per cent of carbon monoxide, 45 per cent of nitrous oxides and 30 per cent of hydrocarbon atmospheric emissions in Britain.

We are defensive about the car. In a survey by the British Automobile Association, people blamed pedestrians involved in accidents in 71 per cent of cases, and children were said to be 'at fault' in 80 per cent. There was little criticism of the motorists' speed or driving manner.

Yet things are improving. New cars emit half the fumes and use up to 30 per cent less fuel compared with vehicles built a decade ago. Three of today's cars are together no noisier than a single one of ten years ago, and this reduces another source of pollution.

PURCHASE FACTORS

When acquiring company cars, the fleet manager would traditionally have considered:

- Method of purchase (lease, contract hire or outright purchase).
- Length of time that vehicles are kept (itself a function of depreciation).
- Value of car (set according to seniority or job grade).

THE GREEN CAR AGENDA

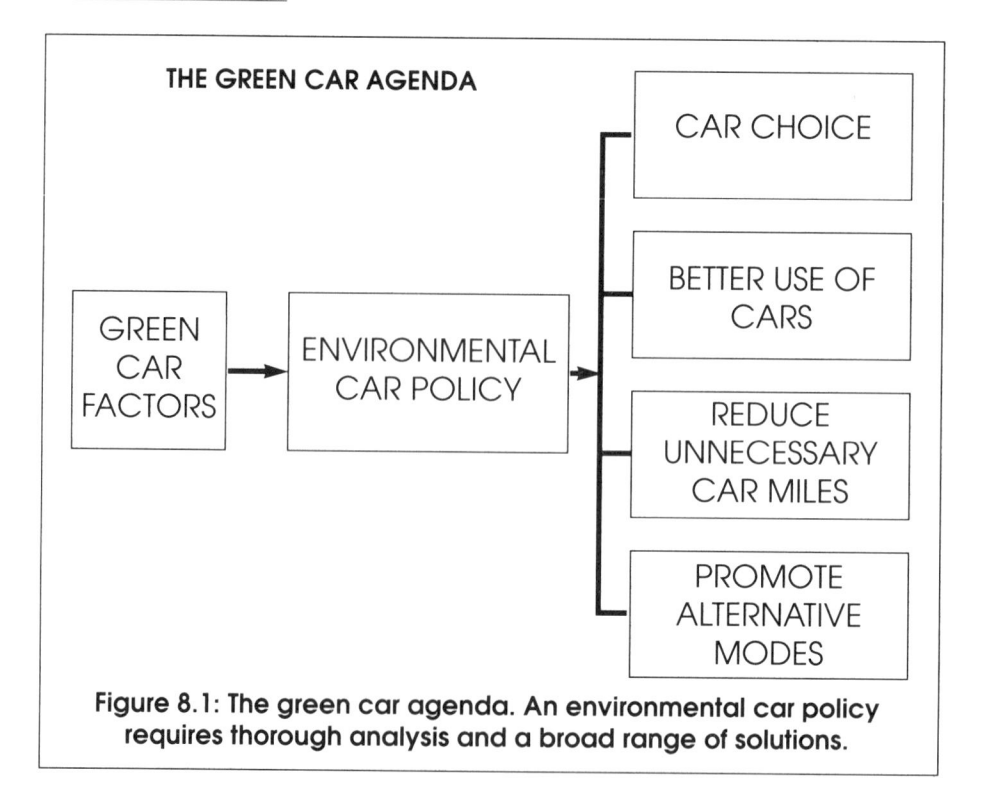

```
GREEN          ENVIRONMENTAL    ┌── CAR CHOICE
CAR      ──►   CAR POLICY    ──►├── BETTER USE OF CARS
FACTORS                          ├── REDUCE UNNECESSARY CAR MILES
                                 └── PROMOTE ALTERNATIVE MODES
```

Figure 8.1: The green car agenda. An environmental car policy requires thorough analysis and a broad range of solutions.

○ Country of manufacture (whether staff are allowed only locally produced cars or any car). This factor is based on the company's attitude towards supporting local industry and its concern about corporate image.

Today, environmental issues must be added to this list, and these are less clear-cut than they were once thought to be. The general issues involve fuel economy, recyclability, drag coefficient, safety and distance from point of manufacture. There is also an important discussion about the relative merits of petrol versus diesel engines. Among petrol-engined cars, the key issues cover unleaded petrol, catalytic converters and lean-burn engines.

As can be seen in Figure 8.1, an environmental policy stems from an analysis of green factors. First we shall discuss the factors that will lead to an improved choice of cars. Then we go on to consider how we can improve and reduce their use.

GREEN CAR FACTORS – GENERAL ISSUES

The following are the major environmental factors to be considered in choosing a company car.

Fuel economy and engine size

Fuel-efficient cars use fewer non-renewable resources, and are also likely to be less polluting. Mpg is greatly affected by engine size, as well as car driving style (which we discuss later).

The company should encourage its executives to drive cars with smaller engines. Every 100cc reduction in engine size gives roughly a 3 per cent reduction in carbon dioxide emissions. That means a 1.4 litre engine causes 33 per cent less pollution than a 2.5 litre engine.

Attempts to persuade staff to drive smaller cars will be stoutly resisted, especially among the sales force whose cars are their sole status symbol. More than any other possession, a car is considered to tell the world how much a person is valued. This matter needs to be handled sympathetically.

Consider banning the purchase of any company car over 2.5 litres or whose mpg is below a certain figure. This would leave most staff unaffected, and would show that the directors, who will be most affected, are committed to a green policy. Many prestigious cars come in a smaller-engined variant, and the smaller car will give the employee a tax advantage.

Another solution is to add the cost of the car to the salary, and let people buy their own cars. People generally buy a smaller car and pocket the difference.

Car life

Longer-lasting cars are better for the environment because they reduce the amount of scrap in the world, and extend the life of valuable materials. Some cars, like Volvo, have a longer life than their competitors.

Recyclability

German car manufacturers are leading the way with bumpers made from recycled material, and coded plastic parts to ease recycling.

Drag coefficient

Streamlined vehicle design helps to cut fuel consumption. Most vehicles today have been designed with the help of a wind tunnel. Provide executives with information on the drag coefficient of models before they buy.

Safety features

The government now releases figures showing the number of injuries in accident by make of car. These figures have been disputed because they do not take driver lifestyle into account, but they suggest that some cars are safer than others.

Country of origin

It makes more sense to buy a car made in your own country than to ship one all the way from abroad.

DIESEL VERSUS THE PETROL ENGINE

Many have hailed the diesel engine as environmentally superior. It is simpler in design, so it has fewer breakdowns and lasts longer. It also consumes 20 per cent to 30 per cent less fuel, and doesn't pump out CO_2. As a result, UK sales have risen from 6 000 to 123 000 in ten years.

Recent improvements in petrol engines have evened the balance between diesel and petrol engines, and attention has focused on the diesel's emission of particulates (see under Production), which are thought to be carcinogenic. Diesels have also improved, and now are less noisy.

PETROL-ENGINED CARS

Today all leading marques use unleaded fuel, so this is no longer really an issue. Cars that drive on unleaded petrol are so common that companies cannot point to their unleaded fleet to prove their green credentials.

There have been fears that using unleaded petrol causes a drop in performance and economy, and wears the engine out. However, this problem does not apply to vehicles specifically designed to run on unleaded petrol.

A catalytic converter reduces the emission of carbon monoxide and hydrocarbons, while a three-way converter also reduces nitrogen oxide. By the year 2005, says the British RAC, all cars will be fitted with a 'cat', and toxic emissions will have fallen to much lower levels. A 'cat' does not, however, get rid of the CO_2, which contributes to global warming. Catalytic converters are also said to consume more fuel, thus increasing CO_2 emissions. They also use rare and non-renewable metals, have to be replaced during the lifetime of the car, and are an 'end of pipe' solution.

> Johnson Matthey entered the catalytic converter market 20 years ago when the environment was not even on the agenda. Now it has a big share of the fast-growing catalytic market, and has manufacturing plants in the UK, Belgium and the US.

A lean-burn petrol engine burns nearly all the fuel, and produces few pollutants. However, some designs are not able to meet the new EC standards for emission.

NEW TYPES OF CAR

Various new fuels are being considered. 'Bio-diesel' can now be produced from oilseed rape, but the prospect of even more glowing yellow fields is not necessarily an attractive one.

The best solution will come from a car that does not use the internal combustion engine. Electric cars have long been seen as the answer because they are silent and do not emit pollution. Some critics say that electric cars merely push pollution upstream to the power stations (which provide power for the batteries). However, the net result is likely to be less polluting.

In enacting clean-up legislation to free the 12 million inhabitants of Los

Angeles from smog, California has decreed that 10 per cent of all cars, vans and light trucks sold in the state by 2003 must be zero emission vehicles (ZEVs). To meet the legislation, 150 000 such vehicles will have to be sold annually by 2003.

As always, legislation provides an impetus for business, and this is expected to have a major impact on the manufacture of battery-powered vehicles. General Motors plans to put into production an electric car, the Impact. This will have a range of 120 miles and be capable of travelling at 100mph. Peugeot has launched an electric 205 in France, and Ford and Fiat have prototypes.

With the advent of the electric car, substantial R&D effort is being put into battery design. Dr Roger Billings, who previously invented the computer disc drive, has now invented a car that runs on water. The car splits the water into hydrogen and oxygen, and the hydrogen generates electricity to propel the car. Almost silent, the car is pollution-free and its exhaust emits just water vapour. It costs only 1p a mile to run; and the oil companies are said to be nervous.

CAR CHOICE CHECKLIST

- Revise the car purchase policy. Buy cars which:
    - Are made locally. This avoids unnecessary distribution costs.
    - Last longest.
    - Have a low drag coefficient.
    - Have the greatest safety features according to *Which?* magazine, or according to government accident statistics.
    - Have the highest mpg.
    - Use recycled material and which can be recycled after use.
    - Are not advertised for their speed.
    - Have diesel engines or environmentally-friendly petrol engines (for example, are equipped with catalytic converters).

Having considered the issues involved in a green car purchase policy, we now examine how companies can encourage their staff to use the car to better effect.

BETTER CAR USE

Cars are a sensitive issue. As Figure 8.2 shows, companies can apply a range of tactics to change behaviour. One of the most important issues is training, which we consider next.

Encourage staff to drive carefully, avoiding unnecessary braking and stop-start driving. Arrange seminars on improved driving techniques, such as driving in the highest gear for the speed.

Discourage excessive speeding. Some executives routinely travel on motorways at speeds in excess of 100mph. This wastes fuel. Cars travelling at

CAR TACTICS

The carrot...

- Training/education
- Flexi-time
- Car pooling scheme
- Office pool cars
- Season ticket loans/subsidies
- Prominent timetables
- Transport to station/city centre
- Free bicycles/bike pools

and the stick

- Reduced mileage allowance
- Obligatory city-to-city rail journeys
- Car allowance rather than a company car

Figure 8.2: Car tactics. Changing drivers' behaviour may involve a number of factors.

70mph uses 30 per cent more fuel than those going at 50mph; and of course in many countries there are speed limits. Companies should discourage employees from breaking the law.

Set an expected minimum journey time for known journeys. You might set 45 minutes as the minimum time between two factories if many executives do it in 30 minutes. Show staff that there are no prizes for fast travel.

Adopt flexible working hours, so that employees do not have to travel in the morning and evening rush hours, which waste fuel. You could instigate a core period of 10.00am to 4.00pm, with employees choosing their own extra hours from 8.00am to 10.00am and 4.00pm to 6.30pm. This may call for a punch card system, but employees may appreciate the extra freedom it gives them.

Avoid driving in congested areas, where stationary cars pour out pollution. Avoiding this will require better timing of meetings or trips, or the use of public transport.

Keep your cars longer. As today's cars become increasingly more reliable, there is less need to replace them so often. Avoid the automatic response that because a car is three years old, or has done 40 000 miles, it should be dumped. All staff with company cars will need to know that your policy on replacing cars has become more flexible, with each car being judged on its own merits.

Encourage car-pooling. Try persuading staff to share cars, especially in the journey to work. Set aside space on a notice-board for car-sharing arrangements. A Royal Automobile Club survey showed that 81 per cent of people thought more could be done to encourage car pooling. And a Lex report showed that 80 per cent of drivers were willing to consider car-pooling.

Despite many attempts to set up car-pooling, most have failed. This is due to four main reasons:

○ More fuel-efficient cars have cut the financial need to share cars.
○ Car sharers are unreliable: they are unpunctual, fall ill and change jobs.
○ People need flexibility: they like to stop off to shop or play sport.
○ There are personal conflicts: smokers in non-smokers' cars, different attitudes to in-car music, and lack of privacy.

Check petrol consumption. A simple spreadsheet will allow the company to compare mileage and mpg for every driver. A monthly report should be sent to every departmental manager, comparing actual mpg with the manufacturer's predicted mpg. This will show up excessive fuel consumption as well as fraud. If the results are posted on a notice-board, the mpg will quickly improve and costs will decline, especially if linked to education.

Put a limit on the engine size of hire cars. This will save money as well as reducing pollution.

ENVIRONMENTAL ROADSIDE ASSISTANCE

The Environmental Transport Association is a green organization that provides roadside assistance in the UK. All calls are handled by a professional assistance firm GESA, and help is channelled via the 1 000 members of the National Breakdown Recovery Club. Subscription rates operate in a similar way to the AA and RAC, but there are discounts for cars with catalytic converters and the low-mileage motorist. The money is used to promote better public transport and less massive road building. Included in the cost is six issues of the ETA's magazine that brings you information on its transport campaigns.

REDUCING CAR MILEAGE

On some routes the car is the only sensible choice. This includes destinations which are far from a railway station or which involve several stops during the day (as sales staff might make).

But other routes are less suitable for going by car. They include city-to-city journeys, and long distance journeys. Some journeys are simply unnecessary. Car driving also prevents the executive from reading or writing. Time spent in the car is largely wasted, though the mobile phone has improved executives' productivity, albeit at some cost to their employers.

So how do you discourage executives from automatically leaping into their car at the first opportunity?

○ **Do not provide generous mileage allowances.** Over-generous allowances encourage staff to travel long distances. Reduce the

allowance after the first 50 miles per journey, or simply provide a single, low allowance for all cars. Do not provide higher rates for higher-engined cars. This will encourage the use of fuel-efficient cars.
- **Discourage staff from making unnecessary journeys**. Encourage the greater use of the telephone and fax. IBM saved 200 000 miles a year by encouraging its sales team to communicate more by fax and phone. Teleconferencing (holding distance meetings) saves time and money, but is not widely used by business.
- **Provide pool cars**. This will discourage people from feeling obliged to drive to work in case they need a car during the day. Lease modest-sized pool cars.

POSITIVELY PROMOTING RAIL

Encourage staff to use public transport where available, especially the train for medium- and long-distance routes. Public transport is safer, uses less land, causes less pollution, and costs less money than moving the same numbers by road. City-centre firms should encourage their employees to visit other city centres by rail.

Rail is less stressful, and staff can work on the train – so it is doubly efficient. Offer season ticket loans, and consider offering a subsidy on these loans. Provide company transport to the nearest rail station. Display bus and train maps on notice-boards, and make railway timetables readily accessible.

> P-E International, the management consultancy, provides a minibus that collects staff from the train station in the morning, and takes them back at the end of the day. This takes 15 cars off the road, twice a day. If more companies did this, the volume of traffic would be substantially reduced.

Rail is at a disadvantage compared with the company car, when it comes to the expenses claim, The company car is paid for each month, so for each trip the only bill is the cost of petrol. A rail fare will be higher, especially if the company permits first class travel.

Companies could give incentives to executives by allowing them to claim an extra 50 per cent when travelling by Standard Class. This would encourage executives to travel by Standard Class rail in order to claim the 50 per cent cash reward. All expenses would need to be accompanied by the tickets or receipts to prevent fraud.

The 'Standard Class plus X per cent' package would ensure that the cost of rail and road broadly matched, and would give the executive an incentive to travel by rail. Executives would still be able to travel by First Class, but the cash bonus would not apply.

Buses and other mass transit overground and underground systems are also a consideration. 'Park and ride' schemes now operate in many cities. Drivers park their cars at the city boundary and take a special bus into the centre. Encourage staff to make use of the scheme by paying part or all of the 'park and ride' fare.

Which is the best way to reduce congestion? According to a survey by Lex, drivers voted 'park-and-ride' and better public transport as the two top methods. They were well ahead of other suggestions such as 'build more roads'.

RAIL VS ROAD

For every billion passenger kilometres travelled in 1988 on the roads, there were 900 casualties. For British Rail it was under 70. The cost to the economy of road casualties was ten times that of rail (and these figures come from a particularly bad year for rail).

On any given rail corridor, up to 70 000 passengers can be carried every hour. To move the same number of people by road takes 13 times as much land.

According to a survey by Test, a transport consultancy, roads take 2 600 square kilometres, while rail occupies a mere 196 square kilometres.

There are no proposed rail routes which threaten sites of special scientific interest, but under the British government's latest road plans, 161 sites are threatened.

A total of 70 million birds and 47 000 badgers die each year on British roads. (Animals are also doubtless killed by trains, but the figures are likely to be lower.)

Unlike road, rail does not use polluting materials such as de-icing chemicals, bitumen and heavy metals.

Oil spilled on roads each year in the US amounts to 20 times that from the *Exxon Valdez* oil tanker spill in Alaska.

Transport consumes one-third of energy used world-wide.

The UK Treasury loses up to £3 billion a year on company car tax perks, yet pays out only £500 million a year in subsidy to British Rail. If the £3 billion was spent on rail, the country would have a better service.

The equivalent of a 267-lane motorway from London to Edinburgh would be needed to meet the Department of Transport's high traffic projections for 2025. An area the size of Berkshire would be needed at each end for parking.

TRANSPORT CHECKLIST

- Create a green car policy for the company. Publicize it among staff.
- Only provide a company car where it is essential for the job or necessary to attract or retain staff.
- Discourage fast or inconsiderate driving.
- Check the number of deaths, serious injuries and minor injuries caused

by accidents. Set a goal of reducing them by one-third in ten years' time.

- Produce regular reports on mpg achieved.
- Provide season ticket loans, deducted from the salary over the period of the ticket. Subsidize the loans.
- Encourage staff to use the train.
- Provide transport to the railway station.

THE BICYCLE OPTION

Bicycles cover 4 billion kilometres every year in Britain, with no pollution at all. Help to encourage bicycle use by buying bicycles for staff, providing interest-free loans or subsidies (deducted from the salary). If many staff live close to their work, they may be able to cycle to work.

You will need to supply secure storage for bicycles, with proper padlocks to prevent theft. Free marking may be another service you can offer. Offer a cycling mileage allowance (at the same rate as for cars), to encourage staff to use bikes. You can also set up a bike pool for local journeys.

> Oxford City Council has issued bicycles for staff to use on official business in the city. And at Exeter, 100 bicycles, painted lurid green and identity coded, have been provided at 10 bicycle parks. Cyclists may use them free of charge and are asked to return them to the nearest distribution point after use.
>
> The scheme, set up by the local police and probation service, is intended to reduce the theft of bikes in the city. The bikes have been obtained from police auctions of lost or stolen property, and have been renovated by young offenders.

Bikes are especially useful at large plants. At the 1 800 acre Shell refinery at Stanlow, near Ellesmere Port in Cheshire, workers are now allowed to ride the half a mile from the entrance gate to their work. This follows an attempted ban by management on the use of bikes on the site in favour of company vans.

People will not take to the saddle unless they have safe, fast and convenient routes to follow, both inside and outside the plant. Bike lanes should be set up within the plant boundary. You can also facilitate walking by providing wide pavements and zebra crossings within company land. Provide traffic calming measures such as speed limits, speed bumps and by avoiding long straight roads. Consider, too, the journey to work: lobby the local authority to set up cycle routes in the area.

BICYCLE AND PEDESTRIAN CHECKLIST

- Buy bicycles for staff.
- Provide bike sheds.

- Provide a bicycle pool.
- Provide bike paths on company premises.
- Provide a bicycle rate equivalent to the car rate.
- Lobby the local authority for better cycle path provision.
- Provide footpaths and zebra crossings.
- Lay speed bumps along your company roads to reduce speeding and increase pedestrian safety.

MAINTENANCE

Poorly tuned vehicles cause extra pollution. The RAC reckons that 1 per cent of all vehicles generate as much pollution as the cleanest 40 per cent. Company-owned cars are the newest and therefore cleanest vehicles on the road, but the age and condition of lorries vary considerably. Keep all vehicles properly tuned and serviced: this means observing the manufacturer's service intervals and watching out for faults.

Use asbestos-free brake pads. Every time a driver brakes on traditional pads, tiny grains of asbestos, a known carcinogen, are released into the air.

Also avoid the use of aerosols, especially those that use CFCs. Lubricants, cleaners, polishes and other materials are obtainable in non-aerosol containers.

Do not pour used oil down the drains. Old oil contains hydrocarbons, which are a carcinogen. Used oil also contains lead and other chemicals which will contaminate the rivers and possibly end up in the water supply. A total of 1.25 million tonnes of waste engine oil is unaccounted for, and probably ends up in the oceans each year.

Take used oil to a waste recycling centre. Here it will be cleaned and reused as heating oil. Some garages will also accept used oil for recycling – you should make enquiries.

Good maintenance applies to both company cars and lorries, a subject we turn to next.

LORRIES AND DISTRIBUTION

A logistics study is a useful starting point in analysing a company's distribution system. It will assess the warehousing and distribution pattern. It will take into account lorry sizes and drop sizes. It will check distances travelled, routings and the frequency of deliveries.

A logistics study provides data about distribution volume and costs, and the information is often broken down by post code. It will reveal the most efficient way of distributing goods, and should pay for itself by reducing costs. More efficient distribution means lower costs for the company, and less wear and tear on the environment.

> Chemical producer Albright and Wilson reduced the number of tanker movements by a quarter, simply by changing from 18 to 23 tonne vehicles.

> Tesco's new lorries have three variable-sized compartments. Each compartment can be set to a different temperature. Now only one vehicle is needed to supply a Tesco store with all product lines, compared with five vehicles that were previously required.

Once the logistics have been optimized, attention should focus on the vehicles themselves. Many things will improve their environmental performance. They can be fitted with aerodynamic enhancements to reduce drag. They can have transmission changes, and speed limiters can be added. This would reduce costs by 20 per cent.

A speed limiter will set the maximum speed of a lorry to 60mph, its legal limit. If all lorries were fitted with speed limiters, CO_2 output would be reduced by 500 000 tonnes a year, as well as achieving a 10 per cent saving in their fuel consumption.

If you make local deliveries, consider using electric vehicles. They are criticized by purists for moving pollution from the road to the power station (because electrical energy has to be generated in the first place). Nevertheless, they are a move in the right direction.

DRIVING WITH CONSIDERATION

Lorries should take care when driving in residential areas, especially if the business is located close to a school or shops. Routes should be chosen to avoid residential areas. In the interests of being a good neighbour, heavy lorries should not operate between 7.00pm and 6.00am in residential areas.

Drivers should be courteous on the road. They should drive at moderate speed, and leave space between themselves and the vehicle in front to let other drivers overtake. They should not drive near the middle of the road, nor use the size of their vehicles to intimidate other drivers. Lorries should be covered with a tarpaulin if they are carrying loose material such as soil, sand or coal.

If you use a contractor to distribute your products, check what standards the firm adopts. In Chapter 5, we discuss supplier contracts, and these are equally appropriate for distribution.

USING THE RAILWAY

Consider sending your goods by rail. The railway is considerably less polluting, and moving goods by rail reduces road congestion.

British Rail's Red Star service will deliver and collect door-to-door. It uses a simple consignment note system, and has 500 parcel points for companies that prefer to deliver their packages. By rail, goods travel at up to 125 miles an hour, so parcels can reach customers faster. Red Star has a same-day delivery service, and it also operates internationally. The Red Star guarantee provides a full refund for goods that are not delivered by the agreed time.

Even if you are committed to using a road haulier, it is worth checking whether he uses the train or would consider using it for part of the journey (especially the trunking section where it is especially wasteful to move goods by road).

If your premises are near a railway line, you might receive a grant for setting up a freight siding. More than 200 schemes have been assisted, receiving a total of £70 million. Together, these schemes have removed an estimated 3 million lorry journeys a year from the roads. For example, the Department of Transport gave Atochem £74 000 to help build a terminal at Stalybridge to send styrene monomer by rail.

Figure 8.3 indicates the topics for a green transport audit, many of which are discussed more fully in this chapter.

DISTRIBUTION STRATEGY CHECKLIST

- Conduct a logistics survey to establish the best routes and transport modes.
- Establish an environmental transport policy.
- Train drivers in energy efficient driving.
- Monitor fuel use by driver.
- Use the right vehicles for the job.
- Ensure that drivers take care in local communities.
- Maintain vehicles properly.
- Ensure that vehicles are optimally aerodynamic.
- Consider alternative, more environmentally friendly modes of transport.

DISPOSAL OF WASTE

We have looked at waste disposal in Chapter 3 under Engineering, but it is also worth considering waste from a distribution aspect. Whether it goes for incineration or landfill, company waste often has to make a road trip. So it is important to analyse the issue from the distribution perspective.

WASTE DISPOSAL – DISTRIBUTION CHECKLIST

- Who transports the company's wastes?
- To what extent are the wastes hazardous?

GREEN LOGISTICS AUDIT

MODE

- Rail
- Road
- Other

SYSTEMS

- Env. man. system
- Env. data collection
- Tachographs
- Controls
- Procedures
- Safety

TRAINING

- Courtesy
- Fuel economy

VEHICLES

- Number
- Size
- Design
- Drag coefficient
- Body kit
- Fuel consumption
- Speed
- Noise/fumes
- Spray
- Visual impact
- Hazchem

SCHEDULING

- Level of service
- Drop frequency
- Number of delivery points
- Route selection
- Timing
- Loading/capacity

WAREHOUSE

- Location
- Quantity
- Energy use
- Env. impact assess.
- Noise/fumes
- Local residents
- COSHH
- Health and safety

INVENTORY

- Size
- Nature
- Stock turn

PACKAGING

- Renewable
- Quantity
- Recyclable
- Biodegradable
- Returnable

Figure 8.3: Green logistics audit. The audit covers the warehouse and transport packaging, as well as the vehicles themselves.

- What precautions are used?
- Are the vehicles properly marked with HAZCHEM signs?
- What routes are used?
- Are there better solutions (such as waste reduction or distribution by rail)?

INLAND WATERS

You could consider using the inland waterways. This is not as fanciful as it might seem (at least in Britain): more and more miles of canal are being reopened, and many connect with the sea.

If you are near a port, you could also consider distributing products using coastal waters.

> Hydro Fertilisers distributes 1.2 million tonnes of packaged fertilizer a year. The amount carried by rail has grown from 100 000 tonnes in 1987 to 25 000 tonnes in 1990. Most raw materials arrive by sea, and are unloaded at the quayside adjacent to the factory. They are delivered by covered conveyor systems or pipeline to bulk solid and liquid storage facilities on site.

SEA TRANSPORT

A total of 71 per cent of the world's surface is covered with water, and the international movement of bulk goods is usually by sea. Britain's heavily used shipping lanes will always be at risk from collisions or accidents.

In 1989, three tankers in every 100 were involved in a serious casualty. The number of oil spills of more than 5 000 barrels has gone up to 36 a year. Norwegian government research shows that human error is responsible for 80 per cent of all marine accidents. Accidental spills are also related to the age of the tanker. Older ships lack the safety standards built into newer ones.

US studies show that 1.5 million tonnes of oil get into the sea each year as a result of shipping operations. 700 000 tonnes are from routine tanker operations, such as tank cleaning; 400 000 tonnes are from tanker accidents; 300 000 from the dumping of fuel and bilge oil; and the remainder from other causes.

However, the UN estimates that protection measures have prevented as much as 10 million tonnes of oil being disposed of into the sea each year from pumping out oil-contaminated tank-cleaning and ballast water.

The amount of oil entering the sea due to maritime accidents has also fallen in recent years, due to the development of improved standards, navigational aids, training and watchkeeping, and traffic separation schemes. Shell has an accreditation system which ensures that it only charters ships that meet high standards and operate a monitoring system.

To reduce fuel consumption, it is vital to keep the hull clean and coated; 60 per cent of total resistance results from hull friction.

SHIPPING CHECKLIST

- Train crew to be aware of the dangers of pollution and how to respond.
- Introduce newer, better-designed ships.
- Dispose of waste oils at port facilities.
- Do not discharge in prohibited zones.
- Dispose of oil from tank cleaning into a slop tank.
- Ensure that ships carry a fast response pollution plan.
- Clean the hull regularly.

OTHER TYPES OF SEA POLLUTION

In the past it was always assumed that the vastness of the oceans would disperse any pollutants. Now we are learning that the sea's capacity to absorb pollution is far from infinite. Man has been polluting the oceans in a big way for a century now. In 1915 a Dutchman out for a walk recorded 'On Wednesday, I found on the beach 18 guillemots, six gannets, two crows, one curlew and one diver, all but five covered with oil. It seems as if a ship with tar has been destroyed by a torpedo.'

It is not just oil that contaminates the oceans. Pollution also comes from:

- dumping of land based wastes
- dumping of ship rubbish

According to the UN, 10 per cent of marine pollution comes from the dumping of land-generated wastes.

Dumping at sea puts human health at risk due to pathogens; increased eutrophication from nutrients contained in wastes; the toxic effects of some substances on marine life; and the damaging effect of dumping on fishing, recreation and other activities.

The London Dumping Convention (LDC), which has been accepted by countries responsible for 65 per cent of the world's fleet, divides substances into three categories. The first is completed banned. They include organohalon compounds, persistent plastics, crude oil, high level radioactive waste, and materials produced for biological or chemical warfare.

A second category of substance may only be dumped after a special permit has been issued. The third category can be dumped after a general permit has been issued.

The dumping of sewage sludge and other wastes has decreased since the London Dumping Convention came into force. However, disposal or treatment of wastes on land is not necessarily less damaging to the environment, and sea-based dumping is likely to continue for some time, controlled by the LDC.

9
RESEARCH AND DEVELOPMENT

♦

It is easy to overlook the environmental disadvantages of the current product range, especially if they do not seem excessive, and if everyone else in the market is using the same raw materials or the same components.

It is also easy to ignore the environmental implications in a new product programme, especially when it is technology-led.

A third danger follows: it is a mistake to believe that the company has to work with existing technology, just because the business is using it.

For R&D departments, the public's interest in the environment represents an exciting opportunity. But time is limited.

R&D people should consider the environmental hazards of each aspect of the product, and substitute improvements. Some products that are currently satisfactory could be enhanced in a way that protects the environment, a process that will boost their attractiveness in the market-place. We are now seeing products being altered in ways that would have been unthinkable a decade ago. The changes apply to:

- raw materials
- product design
- processing requirements
- usage characteristics
- after-use and disposal

These factors are discussed in several chapters, especially those on Buying, Production, Engineering and Marketing. But there are some issues that are especially relevant to R&D. The first is the information-gathering process: R&D needs to be ahead of every other department in knowing what is going on in the world.

INFORMATION GATHERING

The company should set up an information-gathering system that incorporates environmental change, if one does not already exist. This will keep it abreast of changes in thinking, in raw materials, standards and markets. It will help the business stay in the forefront of change, and prevent it from being caught napping by a new entrant to the market.

In analysing the information, it is important to think outside your current products and markets. Hire, if necessary, an outside technical expert to review alternatives. Do not accept anything as inevitable.

> The market leader in vinyl flooring used to make the backing layer of the material from white asbestos. The firm believed this was the normal way of producing floorcovering, despite concern from consumers that it was dangerous to health, could shrink or expand, and would crack when being fitted.
>
> One day a rival firm launched a vinyl floorcovering that used a flexible sealed glass-fibre backing. The product was stable, easy to lay, and free from health risks. Overnight the market leader lost share, and was shamefacedly forced to follow suit a year later.
>
> For years the company had piled up thick volumes of market research which had failed to ask the right questions. It measured market share, distribution, and other factors. Yet it had entirely failed to ask, 'What do people dislike about the product, and how can we change it?'.

The moral of this story is: do not rule anything out. Treat the environment as a positive challenge. Environmental awareness is creating major opportunities in new products and markets for companies with foresight.

A GREEN R&D PROGRAMME

The next stage is to set up a green R&D programme. This will examine existing products and look for new ones.

It may be better to place the green programme under separate management, apart from normal company systems, and under the guidance of an enthusiast. Networking may also be important. You may need to set up or join an alliance of manufacturers to develop new products or systems.

You should not assume that the product has to be high tech. Consumers will increasingly see the value of intermediate technology.

> One controls company makes timers and controls which use a variety of technologies, old and new. The company knows that there is a place for simple technology, and concentrates on factors that are important to the consumer, such as styling and ease of use.

R&D STRATEGY CHECKLIST

- Set up a system for documenting, reviewing and acting upon environmental information.
- Plan an effective R&D programme, allocating responsibilities.
- Define relevant organizational and technical interfaces.

◆ Agree written product briefs. These should include acceptance criteria and meet regulatory criteria. The briefs should be agreed with relevant departments.

GROWTH MARKETS

Extensive new markets are opening up as a result of environmental pressure. The Centre for Exploitation of Science and Technology estimates that around £140 billion could be spent on cleaning up the UK environment over the next decade. For Europe it estimates the sum at £860 billion, and for the US £1 060 billion. Growth markets could include:

○	**Process control**	Electronic controls (for mixing, monitoring and warning)
○	**Pollution control**	Filtration equipment to improve water quality
		Gas filtration systems to reduce emissions of sulphur dioxide and carbon dioxide
		Environmental monitoring and control systems
○	**Waste management**	Treatment systems, including biotreatment and incinerators
○	**Cleaning systems**	This could include low and high tech solutions.
○	**Alternative energy**	Solar power, wind power, biofuels
○	**Energy reduction**	Insulation
		Improved building materials
		Lighting, heating, cooking etc.
○	**Transport**	New fuels
		Cleaner engines
		Public transport systems
○	**Recycled products**	This is appropriate to most markets
○	**Bio-friendly chemicals**	Biotechnology, gentle chemistry

○	Raw materials	Products and systems that minimize the use of non-renewable or damaging raw materials
○	Mind, body, spirit	Life enhancing products and systems
○	Natural materials	Cotton, wood, linen, linoleum
○	Recycling systems	In most raw materials and product categories
○	Nature conservation	Products that aid nature
○	Information	Publications, exhibitions
○	Consultancy services	In waste reduction, emission control, recycling and environmental protection.

Virtually every existing product has a green alternative. Green tourism, for example, is likely to grow in the 1990s. Broadleaved forestry is likely to take some of the land now used for intensive farming. However, it is important to know about the markets you are entering, as this case history shows:

> Concerned about defence cuts, a major British defence contractor decided to develop civilian products. It invested in a system for dumping waste in the sea off the US. Only when the system was ready for launch did the company realize that sea dumping was no longer welcomed in the US. The project had to be abandoned.

FACTORS BEHIND THE GROWTH

Various factors contribute to the demand for new products and markets. In particular, they stem from:

○ Environmental pressure groups
○ Consumer attitudes
○ Tax changes (for example, a carbon tax)
○ Legislation on waste control and pollution charges, or deposit refund systems (Sweden and Norway has a system for car hulks)
○ Energy awareness and cost-reduction programmes by business.

It is worth analysing the likely changes that could occur in the future (for example, impending EC legislation), and assessing the impact they will have on your markets and those you are interested in. The problems created in those markets will lead to a demand for solutions. For example, growing restrictions on today's synthetic pesticides will create a demand for less persistent products and pesticides that are derived from nature.

BP Chemicals at Hull won a Better Environment Award for its runway de-icer. The new product, called Clearway 1, gets rid of ice on airport runways. It is biodegradable, creates no waste in manufacture, and is harmless to groundwater, plant and animal life. It is based on vinegar, and conforms to strict aerospace performance requirements and corrosion specifications.

PRODUCT IMPROVEMENT

New products could incorporate the following advantages:

- Use renewable raw materials
- Use recycled raw materials
- Use less energy to make
- Use renewable energy
- Contain serviceable parts
- Avoid in-built obsolescence
- Last longer, have increased capacity
- Have no damaging effect on the environment
- Have fewer side effects
- Are more nutritious or healthy
- Use less packaging
- Involve no harm to animals
- Are quieter in use
- Are easier to use, ergonomically sound
- Are easier to dispense or provide better portion control
- Use less energy, water or detergent in use
- Emit less pollution
- Have secondary uses to extend their life
- Are biodegradable
- Are recyclable

Product improvements will come from changing consumer attitudes, as we have seen. Take food products. Nearly one-quarter (23 per cent) of people surveyed by Mintel said they avoided 'factory farmed' food. Mintel points out that they may associate the term only with battery egg production and not with other intensive methods such as pig and poultry production.

But if realization grows (and it only takes one TV documentary), the population could swing against intensive farming. This has implications for both agriculture and food processors.

> People won't buy a product just because it is good for them or good for the world. There must be other benefits. Nestlé lost between $5m and $10m over an expensive US flop called New Cookery. The healthy, low-calorie food was backed by extensive market research which promised great results. But people won't buy food unless it tastes good, and New Cookery didn't.

Companies now have to ensure that their products are environmentally sound 'from the cradle to grave'. This responsibility does not end when the product is disposed of, for the act of disposal (as in leaking landfill sites) could create an environment hazard. This means that the R&D department needs to consider the impact each new product will have on the environment.

SUBSTITUTING NEW COMPONENTS

Substitutes are not always to the standard that environmentalists would like. For example, in aerosols, CFCs have often been replaced with butane or propane – highly inflammable and explosive petroleum by-products – and these could hardly be called environmentally friendly.

A substantial amount of energy and raw materials is needed to produce aerosols, which are then discarded after a few weeks or months. Pump action or refillable systems may become increasingly favoured by the consumer.

UNPOPULAR PRODUCTS

Some products become unpopular when the consumer becomes aware of an ingredient. Varta batteries, for example, achieved sales growth by producing 'green' batteries and focusing on the disadvantages of existing brands.

Another unpopular product is irradiated food. Though it is now legal in the UK, companies have been reluctant to seek a licence. Irradiated products must be clearly labelled as such, and following media and pressure group activity, this label is unlikely to boost the food's acceptance. According to *The Guardian*, neither the UK Home Office nor the Ministry of Defence intends to buy such food for prisoners or the armed forces.

Companies can also turn consumer concerns to their advantage:

> Iceland Frozen Foods collects old fridges and freezers when it delivers replacements. The CFC refrigerants are removed and returned to ICI for recycling. Iceland has developed a portable system for engineers to use when repairing fridges in the home. The costs have been small, but the environmental benefits are great.

ICI has developed a way to make ammonia that uses less energy and cuts air pollution. The process reduces nitrogen oxide emissions by 87 per cent, sulphur dioxide by 95 per cent, and carbon dioxide by 60 per cent. It also reduces the ammonia content of the liquid effluent by 75 per cent.

If all the world's ammonia production used this process, it would be equivalent, in terms of nitrogen oxide reduction, to taking five million cars off the road.

New developments come from unlikely sources. Britain's offal industry is hoping to set up a power station fuelled by dead cattle, their intestines and other glands and organs. And the government is backing the research. This opportunity arises from the banning of cattle organs in pet food, which in turn followed the outbreak of bovine spongiform encephalopathy (mad cow disease). As a result 1 000 tonnes a week of animal matter which was once a useful by-product from abattoirs is now a liability. Because the dead cows are a renewable energy source, the power station would get more for its electricity.

> Nomix has developed a herbicide spraying system that solves the problems of excess application, spray drift, and employee safety. It consists of a sealed chemical container which is pushed on to the spraying device. There is no mixing of chemicals, and the specially designed nozzle ensures 40 per cent less waste. The system goes ten times further, but weighs one-sixth of conventional knapsack systems. It is therefore less tiring for the operator, and a greater area can be treated.
>
> Yet in the early days the company had such difficulties persuading manufacturers to develop the system that it had to go it alone.

TESTING TIMES

Laboratories are dangerous places which require protection for workers and the environment as a whole. Gloves and goggles should be worn, mouth pipetting banned, and bacteria handled according to strict procedures. A booklet called 'COSHH in laboratories' has been prepared by the Royal Society of Chemistry, and there are internationally recognized standards of Good Laboratory Practice (GLP).

Animal testing angers more people than any other ethical or environmental issue, according to a Mintel survey. The well-known British concern for animals exceeds its sympathy for people. MPs' postbags regularly contain more letters about the transportation of live animals than about starving Ethiopians, battered children, flooded Bangladeshis, or homeless Londoners. In 1990, Westminster received 25 000 letters about dog registration.

More than half the population refuses to buy products which have been tested on animals. This means that animal testing should be avoided on consumer products, especially for the cosmetics, toiletries and perfumes market.

Scientists have generally failed to put forward arguments in favour of animal testing, and as a result only the voice of the pressure groups have been heard. It would be a bold (even foolhardy) company that aimed to represent such an unpopular cause.

ANIMAL TESTING: HELP OR HINDRANCE?

Each year more than 3½ million animals die in British laboratories. Does animal testing benefit the human race? Is it necessary, or just needlessly cruel?

Testing shampoos and soaps on animals is a relatively simple issue. Many people today condemn animal testing by cosmetics companies. The Draize test (in which technicians drop substances on to rabbits' eyes and watch the effect) is widely condemned.

The same applies to food research: there are 3 254 colours or flavour modifiers already in existence. This seems quite enough; and if new foods are to be developed, animals should not be involved.

Psychological tests also involve animals. Many are reasonably harmless, while others that involve electric shocks, food deprivation or drowning seem increasingly undesirable.

But what about animal testing for drugs? In some cases, drugs are not the real solution. Cancers, heart disease and other illnesses are often related to the individual's lifestyle (for example, bad diet, lack of exercise and smoking). Pipe smokers get cancer of the lip, while radiologists risk getting skin cancer. Animal experiments have little to contribute here. In the last 100 years, according to the National Anti-Vivisection Society (NAVS), no animal study has ever led to any advance in the prevention of cancer.

Many of the world's worst killers can be solved by improved sanitation, better housing, a good diet and education. The spread of public drains in the UK coincided almost exactly with the decline of cholera, dysentery and typhoid. Animal testing and vaccination are not necessarily the most appropriate answers.

That said, drugs *are* necessary for countless purposes, not the least being for Aids sufferers. But are animal experiments helpful in developing drugs?

Not according to NAVS, which says that animals do not respond like people. Many drugs which were passed as safe in animals have since caused serious, often deadly side-effects in humans. These include Opren, Eraldrin and Osmosin.

The converse is also true. Corneal transplants were delayed for 90 years because of development work on animals. And Florey, who purified penicillin, admitted it was 'a lucky chance' that he had not tested the drug on guinea pigs, for it kills them.

Much of the research these days is for variants of existing proprietary drugs, rather than for new ones. The profit motive is at work here, the task being to get round other companies' patents.

There is a long list of medical advances from the study of people rather than the use of drugs: they include local anaesthetics, digitalis-based heart drugs, and Caesarian operations.

So while new drugs may be needed, there are many ways of developing them that do not involve animal experiments. Drugs can be tested using mass spectrometry, quantum pharmacology, computer modelling, and specially cultured human cells.

Finally, it is worth noting that we eat 400 million animals (cattle, pigs and poultry) each year in Britain. The RSPCA also kills large numbers of abandoned animals every year – far more than are used in UK laboratories. The issue is clouded by emotion, hypocrisy and inconsistency.

MAKING CLAIMS THAT CAN BE PROVED

Companies' claims will have to be more unassailable than before. Consumer organizations, pressure groups and local authorities are becoming more sophisticated when it comes to testing. A report by the Scientific Services Department of one British local authority mentions that:

- It can test products' 'green' claims.
- It has on-line computer facilities to a number of scientific databanks providing rapid information on standards of toxicity data.
- It has a monitoring unit which provides on site sampling and analysis – utilizing mobile equipment for atmospheric tests and noise monitoring as well as site investigations and sampling for laboratory analysis.

THE ROLE OF CHEMICALS

Business has often failed to promote the importance of its ingredients and activities. As a result, only the green activists' voices are heard. One such case is chemicals, which have always been used by man. Folk remedies depend on calming the patient with camomile, or boosting the heart with foxglove. For thousands of years, tannin, extracted from the bark of trees, has been used to turn animal hides into leather. Early peoples used chemicals to preserve food and make soap.

As the Chemical Industries Association has pointed out, the discovery of anaesthetics in the 1840s made operations painless for the first time. And in 1847, James Lister discovered the antiseptic qualities of carbolic acid, now called phenol. This was an important step in establishing the value of hygiene in medicine.

Next came the arrival of photography, with the discovery of light-sensitive chemicals. As a result, we have a permanent record of life gone by.

In the 1930s, polymer chemistry brought the discovery of polythene and polyurethane. These plastics were the forerunners of a whole range of artificial materials.

Man found that plastics could do the job of traditional materials, and could often do it cheaper and more effectively. They were light, hygienic and inexpensive to produce. Today, the chemical industry is a significant contributor to Britain's wealth, with export earnings over £12 000 million a year.

From the kitchen to the car, from the hospital to the farm, chemicals play an extensive role. They include life-saving drugs, lightweight packaging and compact discs. Clean water and the plastic squeezy bottle are two further examples of the benefits that chemicals bring.

But mistakes have been made. DDT was introduced to fight mosquitoes and similar disease-spreading insects, but it poisoned other creatures in the food chain. More selective pesticides were developed. For sixty years, CFCs were thought to be useful and harmless refrigerants, which helped food stay fresh. Now we know they damage the ozone layer, so alternatives have had to be found. And the factors that make modern packaging so effective (leak-proof, rot-proof and durable) have also made them difficult to dispose of.

> Some chemicals were simply too effective or powerful, such as chlorine bleaches. In other cases, chemicals have been used in excessive quantities. Spurred on by legislation and competition, farmers have spread extra fertilizer on their land, causing nitrates to seep into the water supply. Now reduced rates of application are being encouraged.
>
> In the 1990s the hunt will be on for chemicals with structures that more closely mirror nature. Improved disposal methods will also be important. Biodegradable plastics and incineration with heat recovery are two prime solutions. R&D people also need to explain more clearly to the general public the work they do.

PRODUCT DEVELOPMENT CHECKLIST

- Assess whether there are environmentally-orientated growth markets that you could enter.
- Consider whether legislation, pressure groups, tax changes and other effects could change your market. What response should you make?
- Evaluate whether you could make environmental improvements to your products or services.
- Ensure that product changes are a real improvement on the existing ingredients or components, and have no adverse impact on the world.
- Avoid unnecessary animal testing.
- Check that claims can be substantiated.
- Decide whether you can take advantage of unpopular or criticized products by introducing 'green' alternatives.

10
MARKETING

◆

The environment is just one of many factors which affect the customer's decision to purchase. Quality, price, availability, service, design and previous experience of the product may also be important.

Customers' attitudes towards the environment are constantly changing, so a marketing policy that is right today may be out of date in twelve months' time. A new piece of research or a product launch by competitors may change the market overnight. Technology and customers' attitudes need to be kept under review.

According to a Mintel survey, 39 per cent of British adults are 'dark green' – they buy environmentally friendly products wherever they can. A further 20 per cent are 'pale green' – they buy such products when they see them. A further 23 per cent are 'armchair greens' – though they profess concern about the environment, they have not changed their purchasing habits.

This means that nearly six out of ten adults actively buy products they perceive to be environmentally friendly.

For specific markets there are more detailed figures. In toiletries and cosmetics, 38 per cent of consumers want products that have not been tested on animals, and 32 per cent want products that have natural ingredients; 25 per cent want fragrance-free products, and 9 per cent want biodegradable packaging.

The same survey shows that 10 per cent of consumers now select stores because they stock environmentally friendly products.

These attitudes are not restricted to consumer markets. As we saw in the first chapter, business purchasers rate environmental protection highly.

> Mercedes Benz is asking its suppliers that they be capable of using recycled material. Guntram Huber, the company's Head of Engineering, told *The Times*, 'That is a yardstick for us whether we will continue to use them in the future.'

Many companies are now responding to these environmental pressures. According to research quoted in *Long Term Planning*, 92 per cent of multi-national companies are making some change to their existing portfolio, with new lines, concepts and additional product features. The changes do more than

THE GREEN MARKETING AGENDA

PROCESS	ISSUES
Information gathering	Defining audiences Market research Product analysis
Solution generating	Green products Ethical selling Green claims Advertising and promotion Labelling Packaging Distributors' standards

Figure 10.1: The green marketing agenda. The topics that green marketing needs to cover.

simply conform to legislation, for over 40 per cent of the respondents see them as providing new opportunities for their products and services.

However, we should treat this information with caution. Some new green products perform less well than the market leaders, and where performance is important the customer may revert to the old brand.

Moreover, customers' claims that they buy green products are not always borne out in practice. If the research was wholly accurate, green brands would have at least 40 per cent of each market. Yet even in toilet paper, an environmentally-sensitive market, recycled brands account for only 15 per cent. Andrex, the market leader in toilet tissue, only dropped from 35 per cent to 30 per cent between 1989 to 1991, though it lacked a green platform and though it faced intense pressure from recycled brands.

This should not lull marketers into complacency. Green brands will take an increasing share of every market. And customers will in future expect all products they buy to have green credentials. Moreover, greening a brand can give it a real competitive advantage.

In setting a green agenda (Figure 10.1), marketing people need to gather information and then generate solutions. We address these issues next.

THE AUDIENCES

INTERNAL	LOCAL	SALES	LEGISLATORS	OTHERS
STAFF	RESIDENTS	TRADE	MPs	GENERAL PUBLIC
TRADES UNIONS	ACTIVISTS	CUSTOMERS	CIVIL SERVICE	NATIONAL MEDIA
	MEDIA	TRADE PRESS	EC	INVESTORS
	AUTHORITIES	TRADE ASSOCIATION		PRESSURE GROUPS
	OPINION FORMERS	INTERNATIONAL		OPINION FORMERS

Figure 10.2: The audiences. The varied audiences a company must address.

DEFINING THE AUDIENCES AND THEIR ATTITUDES

As environmental issues become more important, the audiences grow wider, so it is worth listing all the people and organizations that the company should seek to influence. They are summarized in Figure 10.2.

Having defined the audience, find out what they think about your company. This can be done through surveys, which will provide information on which to base rational decisions. We look next at several types of research – aimed at revealing the attitudes and interests of local people, customers and the public at large.

LOCAL RESEARCH

A survey among local people will deal with issues such as noise and pollution. It can find out whether:

- The business is seen to be clean or dirty
- The business is seen as caring or uncaring
- It is improving or getting worse
- People have specific concerns or complaints

PRODUCT/SERVICE RESEARCH

Marketing research can examine customers' attitudes to green and ethical issues, and their perception of the company. It can also guide the company in the development of new products.

The research will identify what issues are important to the customer, whether packaging, ingredients or emissions. Customers can be asked to rate the company's products on a range of factors. This ranking system will measure the gap between what the customer expects and what he gets. It will also define the relative importance of different issues.

In other words, the customer may think that the packaging is inadequate, but he may not rate this an important issue. So it might be a waste of money to improve the packaging.

More sophisticated companies also monitor consumer attitudes to specific issues relevant to their market. If, for example, you use titanium dioxide, you can track customer awareness of this substance, and people's attitudes to it.

Regular research will allow the company to check levels of concern among different types of consumer. Respondents can be defined in terms of their use of the brand (whether loyal, promiscuous, lapsed, or a non-user). They can also be identified in terms of psycho-demographics: the views of today's opinion formers could in a few years' time be adopted by the population as a whole.

Marketing research can also analyse potential markets, assess the potential for new products, and get a response to specific communication strategies.

CORPORATE RESEARCH

Large companies, especially those in controversial markets such as petrochemicals, should track consumers' attitudes towards their image. This type of research will ask people about the industry and the companies within it. It will find out whether people think the company cares about the environment, and whether its activities protect or pollute the environment.

The questions can ask whether the company is doing enough, or should be doing more, to safeguard the future. It can evaluate awareness of the company's environmental communications – corporate advertising, sponsorship, sales promotion and educational materials.

This description of research is not intended to be complete, for there are many other targets. You can conduct research among city investors, shareholders, MPs or children. In Chapter 12, Personnel, we also discuss staff surveys.

MARKETING RESEARCH CHECKLIST

- Define your audiences.
- Carry out research to discover attitudes towards your market, your products, and your image.
- Decide what action should be taken in light of this research.

MARKETING ANALYSIS

Conduct an environmental product analysis on your products and those of your competitors. This lifecycle analysis (LCA) will assess their environmental impact 'from the cradle to grave' – in other words, from when raw materials arrive in the factory to when the customer finally disposes of the product. Some people now talk of 'cradle to cradle' or 'from conception to resurrection'. This implies that an old product should never die: it should be reborn as something new.

Minimizing the impact at each stage of the product's life is an important goal. In the checklist below, we consider how this can be achieved.

MARKETING ANALYSIS CHECKLIST

- What raw materials are used? Are any hazardous? Can any be substituted?
- How much energy is used? Can this be reduced?
- What hazards are involved in the manufacture of the products? Can these be reduced?
- What dangers are involved in transportation?
- Are any green threats posed to the retailer or distributor?
- What hazards do the products pose to the user?
- Describe the packaging. To what extent is it biodegradable or reusable?
- Describe how the product is disposed of. Can this be improved?
- Assess whether your products are environmentally superior to those of your competitors. In what way? Can this difference be quantified?
- Analyse whether competitors' products are environmentally superior in any way. Can you adopt these benefits?
- Do alternatives to your products exist? Can you adopt these alternatives?
- Can your products be made longer lasting, more natural, or provide fewer side-effects?
- Check for environmental developments in related markets. Can these be adapted?
- Discover whether there are any scientific developments which could be relevant.

Armed with the research data and the product analysis, you can assess what action should be taken. As we saw in Chapter 2, The Environmental Audit, this could be a SWOT or a NAP analysis.

The main variables are the product, promotion, and packaging/labelling. First we look at the product itself, in terms of creating a green brand.

DEVELOPING A GREEN BRAND

In some markets (such as paper products) new green brands have been highly successful. In other markets, green brands have failed to take any sizeable share. In the detergents market, sales of green brands peaked at 2 per cent in mid-1989 and slid down thereafter. Sales of the major existing brands were unaffected.

The key issue that determines the success or failure of new green brands are:

○ How important are environmental issues in the market?
○ To what extent do existing products damage the environment?
○ To what extent are consumers dissatisfied with the environmental performance of existing brands?
○ What advantages could a new 'green' brand bring the customer?

Take electrical plugs as an example. Environmental issues are not seen as important in the purchasing decision. Plugs do not obviously damage the environment; the consumer seems satisfied with their environmental performance; and new plugs are unlikely to be significantly better in environmental terms.

The situation could be different for, say, lavatory cleaners. Water pollution is an important issue, and consumers may begin to feel that lavatory cleaners damage the environment. If they become dissatisfied, the market becomes ripe for a different cleaner.

THE PROS AND CONS OF A GREEN BRAND

A green brand can offer many advantages. It could steal market share from the competitors. Or it could defend the company's overall share of the market.

But there are also disadvantages in launching a green brand. It could cannibalize the sales of the company's existing brands, reduce the efficiencies achieved by a major brand, and reposition the company's existing brands as undesirable.

On the other hand, doing nothing allows the competition to take the initiative. If green brands are inevitable in your market, you should launch yours first.

The key question is: to what extent is the company at risk from a green predator? Using the criteria above, a company should be able to decide whether to introduce a new brand.

> For many years the market leader in crisps avoided launching a low-fat brand of crisps. The company feared that a low-fat brand would alert consumers to the fact that its ordinary crisps were fattening. In response to consumer

pressure, supermarkets began to import their own low-fat crisps from abroad, depriving the market leader of sales.

In retrospect, there were several options for the company. These included reducing the fat content of its main brand or introducing a new low-fat brand.

While looking to the future, do not ignore the past. In an era when recycling is important, check for products and designs that the company sold in the past. Companies like Sanderson do good business from their William Morris patterns, and the same applies to Liberty the retailer and Stoddard the carpet manufacturer. Check, too, in museums for designs that can be resurrected.

New bodyshells for MG Midgets and Austin Healey Sprites are now being made by British Motor Heritage, a subsidiary of the Rover Group. The company uses original panel pressing tools it rescued and restored. As a result, owners of old British sports cars can give their vehicles a new lease of life.

REFORMULATING EXISTING PRODUCTS

Reformulation may be the simplest option. Do not rule out options too quickly, even if they initially seem unworkable. Take the cheap PET bottle: Spa Monopole has launched a returnable PET bottle in the Netherlands for a new range of fruit-flavoured soft drinks. The bottles are recycled into non-food bottles, electrical components and car parts.

AFTER-SALES SUPPORT

After-sales support may be increasingly important to environmentally aware customers. Engineers should be able to help customers reduce their energy use, extend the product's life, and dispose of the product safely. In some markets, an education programme may be needed, using newsletters, training schools or seminars.

MARKETING STRATEGY CHECKLIST

- Assess what a green competitor would offer in place of your products.
- Evaluate the extent to which your own green brands would cannibalize your existing products. What would be the net effect on the company's bottom line?
- Evaluate the effect of a successful launch by a green competitor if you did not have a green product.
- If appropriate, develop green products or reformulate existing ones.
- Test them through research.

◆ Evaluate after-sales servicing. See whether the customer can be helped to use the product more efficiently, or whether it can be reconditioned for longer life.

PACKAGING

Only a few years ago packaging raised no concern. Now it is an emotive issue. For example, 45 per cent of the population refuse to buy aerosols which contain CFCs; and in time consumers may come to prefer pump action packs to aerosols.

Other foreseeable events include legislation that would oblige retailers to put a deposit on recyclable packaging, and to collect packaging returned by consumers. So it is important for companies to examine their packaging.

One strategy is to reduce the size of the pack or its complexity. The simpler the pack, the less waste to be dumped. According to Friends of the Earth, just as anti-fur campaigns have made people regard animal fur as cruel, people will eventually see extravagant packaging as disgusting.

Companies can also offer refill packs. These packs can afford to be less robust than the original container, because their life is shorter – the consumer simply decants the contents into the original pack. Many fabric softeners now come in refill packs.

> After first defending polystyrene containers, McDonalds said it was abandoning foam packaging in its 11 000 restaurants. This followed pressure from its customers and the eco-group Environmental Defence Fund. Now McDonalds has gone back to blown foam packs. The continuing uncertainty has put the company in a spotlight from which other fast food restaurants can only benefit.
>
> On a different scale of packaging, Albright and Wilson has persuaded customers to take chemicals in bulk tanker loads instead of non-returnable drums which cause disposal problems.

Companies face a dilemma. After being encouraged to provide safe, hygienic, tamper-evident and child-proof packaging, they are now being asked to provide mimimal packaging. And while consumers may want green packaging, they will not accept damaged or contaminated goods.

Nor is it a straightforward issue of replacing plastic with paper. As well as being a less effective barrier, paper can also damage the environment. Paper mills are heavy consumers of energy, causing the release of sulphur dioxide and other pollutants. The chemicals used in bleaching paper are also toxic.

UK companies have been slow to introduce environmental packaging. In a survey of six major design consultancies, only one could provide an example of an environmental packaging brief. Yet by 1996 there could be a charge on anything that is not returnable or recyclable. *Marketing Week* believes that UK firms are five years behind Europe in their packaging.

The larger the company, the more visible it is. Marks and Spencer suffered a demonstration and public petition organized by the Women's Environmental Network for 'ignoring the issues of unnecessary packaging'. The store's response was not calculated to impress the activists: an M&S spokeswoman said 'We consider the level of packaging very carefully, to protect goods and make them pleasing to the eye.'

THE BODY SHOP AND PACKAGING

According to The Body Shop, most cosmetics packaging is designed simply to attract and seduce customers, convincing them that they need that particular product. This, says the company, is not The Body Shop's approach. Its packaging conforms to the following criteria:

- The packaging material must be compatible with the product.
- The container must be strong enough to contain the product from the time it is filled to the time it is empty.
- The packaging must provide an effective barrier to prevent contamination of the product. Safety is of prime importance.
- The company uses minimal packaging within the context of what is appropriate and practical. The company's gift baskets are more obviously packaged but they are designed to make attractive presents. The company also aims to make them as environmentally friendly as possible.

The Body Shop uses plastic packaging because it makes an effective barrier. It is durable, robust and light – this reduces fuel in transportation. The company's plastics are based on synthetic polymers which come from oil. But, claims the company, only 4 per cent of oil ends up as plastic. Moreover, The Body Shop encourages its customers to bring bottles back for refilling. Each shop has a refill bar, and there is a 20p reduction for every refilled bottle.

The company is also rationalizing the materials used in packaging, to increase the extent of recycling. Abbreviated codes on its packaging aid sorting and recycling.

The Body Shop aims to avoid glass jars because of their extra weight (and therefore added cost in transportation), and because if shattered, dangerous particles of glass could go unnoticed and cause damage to soft skin tissues around the eyes.

To carry away their purchases, customers are given a recycled paper bag, or a larger recycled plastic carrier bag. Staff ask customers whether they want a bag: many customers bring their own.

All cardboard boxes are returned from the shops to the warehouse. The company is now aiming to phase out cardboard boxes in favour of roller cages which are used over and over again.

PACK CHECKLIST

◆ Check how much packaging adds to the final cost of your product.

- Reduce the size or complexity of your pack, or use less material.
- See whether the packaging can be made biodegradable, recyclable, reusable or safer.
- Offer a returnable pack.
- Reduce the warehouse-to-retailer packaging.

LABELLING

Apart from the detailed green claims discussed above, labels need to carry a variety of environmental information, depending on the product and its market. They include:

- Recycled mark
- Potential for reuse
- Ingredients and their impact on the environment
- Disposal instructions
- Degradability
- Safety warnings
- Energy use
- Eco-label mark
- Other environmental information

Recycled mark

Recycled paper or card is indistinguishable from its virgin equivalent. Many customers now look to see if the product is wrapped in a recycled package, especially if the product boasts about its environmental friendliness. Did you look to see if this book was printed on recycled paper? People feel cheated if 'green' products fail the packaging test.

The recycled logo should be accompanied by a clarifying statement. This will vary according to the product. As we have seen in Buying (Chapter 5), some markets demand details about the origin of recycled material. The logo should not be used to mean 'recyclable'. This could mislead customers into thinking the product had been recycled.

Reuse

The customer may be able to reuse the packaging if you make useful suggestions about secondary uses which would extend its life.

> Blagden Packaging takes back its 210 litre steel drums once customers have used them. It then reconditions them for further use. The result is a drum that is as good as new, with a renewed life at a fraction of the original cost. Finally, when the drum has reached the end of its useful life, Blagden recovers the drum for further recycling as feedstock for the steel industry.

Ingredients

These should be listed even if this is not required by law. They should be listed in descending order, and in terms that the consumer will understand. It is not very helpful to say:

> Squezy contains amongst other ingredients
>
> 15% to 30% Anionic Surfactants
>
> Preservatives

It is useful to set consumers' mind at rest over controversial issues. John West tuna, for example, carries the message:

DOLPHIN FRIENDLY

> John West tuna is dolphin friendly. John West is totally committed to fishing methods which protect the marine environment and its species.

This message conveys two things: a statement of fact (the product is 'dolphin friendly' (whatever that vague term means) and a statement of policy (John West is committed. . .).

There may not be enough space on the label to include every detail of environmental information, and many consumers will not be interested anyway. It can be useful to include a statement that says 'For more environmental information, please write to. . .' Leaflets should be available for customers who write for the information. See Items to be Published box on page 169 in Chapter 11, Public Relations.

Disposal instructions

The consumer should be told how to dispose of the product safely. If a recycling scheme is in operation, the customer should be directed to it.

Degradability

Tell the customer if the product and its packaging will degrade harmlessly in the ground, and over what period of time. If it will not degrade, try redesigning it.

Safety warnings

Warn the customer if the product could be dangerous to babies or small children, if it is toxic, or if it should not be inhaled. 'Contra-indications' have long been included on medical products: they may also be useful for other products. The label on a heavy package might suggest that it should be lifted by fork-lift truck.

Energy use

The product should tell the customer if it uses less energy in manufacture or use, or if it uses fewer raw materials than similar products. The facts should be quantified.

Eco-label mark

If the product has been approved for inclusion in an eco-label scheme, include the logo on the pack. If it has not, consider submitting the product for approval.

Other environmental information

You might want to tell customers that the product uses less packaging. Again, this information should be quantified – what materials is the pack made from, and how much packaging is used?

COMMUNICATION AND ETHICAL MARKETING

As the consumer becomes more sophisticated and aware, marketing must become more stringently ethical. There are two main aspects to this: the product itself, and its promotion.

The product must not harm the world or the things that live on it. The consumer is conscious of this issue: more than four out of ten people in a Mintel survey said they avoided products which are 'irresponsibly marketed' so as to exploit or mislead consumers. The Mintel report highlights drug and baby food companies which sell inappropriate products to the Third World.

In terms of promotion, the company should avoid unethical selling techniques (the type that have given time-share a bad name). Companies must also be able to substantiate their claims, which is an issue we examine next.

AVOIDING FLAWED CLAIMS

Consumers are becoming more cynical about green claims. Seven out of ten people believe manufacturers use green claims to boost the price. Almost half want products to bear an official logo that ensures the green claims are genuine. And in the USA, where 25 per cent of new products are labelled 'green', a survey quoted by *Fortune* magazine shows that nearly one in two consumers see green labelling as 'mere gimmickry'. Madison Avenue calls it 'green-washing'.

Research by David Bellamy Associates shows that most companies are honourable in their attitude to green issues, and have no intention of making a 'fast buck'. But unchecked claims can sometimes slip into advertisements.

It is bad business practice to use **misleading claims**. The three-arrow recycling symbol has appeared on products that are not recycled – on the grounds that they 'can be recycled after use'. This is an unacceptable claim. Likewise, some plastic bags are labelled 'biodegradable', though they only degrade in sunlight and most will be dumped deep inside a landfill site.

GREEN CLAIMS CHECKLIST

Claims should not be:

- Misleading
- Inaccurate
- Irrelevant
- An infringement of green principles
- Vague
- General or absolute
- Unfairly implied by the brand name
- Debatable or unsubstantiated
- Out of date

It is also misleading for a washing-up liquid to say that it is 'phosphate free', if both it and all the other washing-up liquids never contained phosphate in the first place.

US environmental officials have served notice on several companies including Proctor and Gamble and Mobil for what the media term 'green collar fraud'.

Inaccurate claims should be avoided. BP was criticized for claiming that its unleaded petrol 'causes no pollution'. And the British Advertising Standards Authority (ASA) criticized Audi for claiming that 'catalytic converters convert dangerous gases to harmless CO_2', on the grounds that CO_2 is not environmentally harmless.

It is also wrong to make **irrelevant claims**. Rover said its unleaded cars were 'ozone friendly', when in fact leaded petrol does not damage the ozone layer.

Companies will be criticized for making **claims that infringe green principles**. One car manufacturer was taken to task for suggesting that its car was 'as hot as a vindaloo curry', and that it could reach 127 mph.

It is also important to avoid **general or absolute claims**. These are the claims that a product is 'green' or 'environmentally friendly'. An environmentalist could find something to criticize in most products, whether it be use of resources, pollution in manufacture, or difficulty in disposal. So unless you have convincing evidence, exclude such absolute claims.

> The makers of Coalite claim it was 'environmentally friendly' long before 'green' became an issue. In fact, the extraction and burning of coal products is by no means environmentally friendly.

Claims like 'farm fresh' are too **vague** to have any meaning. Consumers believe that such claims are inadequate and even misleading.

Tambrands, manufacturers of Tampax, have been censured for claiming that their product was 'environmentally friendly since 1937'. A women's group pointed out that the product contained rayon which has been bleached with chlorine.

Companies should also avoid brand names that imply greenness, such as 'Gardengreen' or 'Forestpure', unless the product is hyper-clean. Friends of the Earth criticized Monsanto for claiming that the name of its Greenscape weedkiller conveyed an image of gentleness, naturalness and kindness to the environment.

Such unguarded claims can bring a company unwelcome awards, such as Friends of the Earth's 'Green Con of the Year' award. Recent winners were Britain's Eastern Electricity for urging the public to use electricity rather than gas as a way of combating global warming. FoE also admonished the timber industry for its 'Forests Forever' campaign. The pressure group attacked Scott for claiming that its activities 'help counter the greenhouse effect'. Also BNFL won a prize for its Sellafield publicity campaign.

Beware of making claims to the trade that pressure groups could get hold of and use against you. You should assume that every claim you make, in a sales conference or trade advertisement, will be seen by an environmentalist with a grudge against your company.

It is dangerous to make **debatable or unsubstantiated assertions** such as:

○ 'Eutrophication is not a major problem in Britain.'
○ 'We have no evidence that . . . bleach will cause harm to the environment.'

It is also dangerous to use **out-of-date findings**. The Chemical Industry Association quotes a 14-year-old DoE statement that says:

> Very few documented cases of significant groundwater contamination due to landfill have occurred, thus indicating that the controlled disposal of wastes by landfill is acceptable. . . An ultra-cautious approach to landfill of hazardous . . . waste is unjustified.

In the light of constant media coverage about old dumps that leak deadly poisons, it might be safer not to use this old quote, even if the DoE were still to believe it.

In these days of environmental claim and counterclaim, some companies have set up a claims vetting section, which checks the validity of subsidiaries' claims before they can be issued. This prevents any subsidiary from getting into trouble with environmentalists, and prevents the corporate image from becoming tarnished.

ACCEPTABLE CLAIMS

The problems mentioned above are not intended to warn companies off making green claims, only to indicate which claims to avoid. Though rash claims should be precluded, it is equally important to be seen to be green. That means the company has to promote its green credentials. This can be done in two ways: on packaging, and in advertising and promotion.

'We haven't always been good at blowing our own trumpet (about environmental care)', says Lever Brothers Chairman Ronnie Gray. 'We believed that the massive continued use of our products over the years was proof enough that the consumer was well and safely served. Now we have to make sure, should anyone wish for information, that it is available in an understandable and helpful way.'

Claims should be checked against the checklist above. In particular, they should always be specific. A paper product could say 'Chlorine-free', while a shampoo could say 'Not tested on animals'.

USING THE ENVIRONMENT IN PROMOTION

More advertisers are seeing the advantages of using environmental friendliness as a selling proposition. Some companies have committed substantial sums to advertising their green credentials. BMW, a marque previously known for its engineering claims, ran a TV campaign pointing out that its cars were recyclable.

But to use the environment effectively in promotion, a company has to have taken green issues to heart. Companies with a vested interest in products that are not green should avoid the green arena.

The paper company Scott came under fire for a £3m TV commercial which told the world that the company uses wood from managed sources. The commercial was designed to defend Andrex, a non-recycled brand with 37 per cent of the market. The commercial's claims have been criticized by environmentalists as being faulty, and in retrospect the company might have been wiser to promote the brand's real strengths: its softness and quality.

Some companies use an environmental celebrity to communicate their message. The TSB has used David Bellamy to endorse a green investment fund. Other companies have obtained endorsement from the Soil Association, BUAV or the Vegetarian Society. The use of such logos can be a powerful sales factor.

The environment is also featuring in sales promotion, with green competitions and green sponsorship becoming common.

> Naylor, a clay drains company, has produced an informative colour wallchart on badgers. According to *Green* magazine, the company first became involved when it was asked to donate large pipes for baiter-proof artificial setts. The posters are free to schools.

Many companies have been attracted to WWF and its well-known panda logo. WWF has run promotions with such companies and products as Gales honey, NatWest, Cadbury's Wildlife Bar, Gillette, Proctor and Gamble (Pampers and Ariel), and business-to-business organizations like Jungheinrich fork trucks and OCS. Activities have included self-liquidating T-shirts, sponsorship of a Green Inheritance Banquet, sponsoring WWF brochures, and royalty payments for use of the logo.

The green movement is making itself felt even in the sign world. A.C. Edwards, a sign company, has produced a free-standing sign whose base is made from recycled plastic. The sign, which can stand outside shops, is made of just two interchangeable components and has no frame – so nothing gets in the way of the advertising message.

But the best campaigns stem from companies which have greened their products or services, and are communicating their knowledge and enthusiasm to their customers. The more that a company knows about green issues in its market, the more opportunities will unfold before it. Universal Office Supplies concentrated on providing green office materials, and published the Green Office Guide. This brought it substantial publicity.

SALES LITERATURE AND DIRECT MAIL

Sales literature should be modest in volume: green pressure groups are always looking for examples of waste. No company spends more than it has to on communications; but some corporate information can seem excessive to an outsider. Direct mail also needs close attention: the media enjoys stories about four-year olds being sent credit card mailings, so pruning the list will reduce cost as well as environmental waste. More judicious targeting, a reduction in the quantity of mailings, and slimmer mailers will all contribute to profit and a greener world.

A company that is conscious of its environmental image will ensure that all communications are printed on recycled paper. The quality is perfect these days: this can be a problem for companies wanting to demonstrate their green credentials. It is difficult to find rough-looking, poor quality, recycled paper that looks 'authentic'.

With this in mind, all communications should be labelled 'Printed on recycled paper'; or the effort involved in going green will be wasted.

GREEN INFORMATION CHECKLIST

- Check what green claims your products make, in labelling or advertising.
- Analyse whether any of these claims are vague, general or absolute. Assess whether they contain weasel words.
- See whether your brand names make implicit green claims. Is this justified?
- Check that all the company's environmental claims are specific and detailed.
- Can they be substantiated in front of an environmentalist who holds a Ph.D.?
- Can your product be endorsed by a green organization?

- Attain green expertise in your market, and then communicate that knowledge.
- Avoid waste in mailings or brochures.
- Ensure that promotional materials are produced on recycled paper or card.
- Add comprehensive environmental information to your labelling.
- Consider using the environment in advertising, sales promotion or sponsorship.
- Assess whether the company should enter its products or systems in a green competition.

SETTING STANDARDS FOR BUSINESS ASSOCIATES

If your goods are distributed by retailers or agents, ensure that they meet specified environmental standards. For example, a company that makes agricultural chemicals may want to ensure that spraying contractors avoid spray drift. This is in the company's own interest. If pressure groups find that the company's sprays are harming nature reserves or other protected areas, the manufacturer could be targeted for action.

Chapter 5 discussed in more detail a similar theme – suppliers' standards. It also contains a specimen charter suitable for business associates.

11
PUBLIC RELATIONS

◆

Companies can be curiously inactive when it comes to promoting their environmental successes. One chemical company is spending £10 million a year on environmental protection in the UK. Yet if asked for green information it can only offer three photocopied sheets taken from an ENDS report. 'This is the only published information we have on our environmental activities', writes the PR department.

A minority of companies have simply jumped on the bandwagon, adding an 'environmentally friendly' flash to their labels. This approach is equally unsatisfactory. Customers are deeply suspicious about products that take advantage of green concerns.

The PR department must manage the company's reputation, rather than simply conducting PR exercises. The difference is significant. One approach is thorough, the other superficial. One is based on reality, the other on appearances. One is based on marketing principles (satisfying customer needs), the other is opportunistic.

To win customers, to stay ahead of legislation and to avoid ugly news stories, the company must become environmentally friendly. Pollution will increasingly be unacceptable, waste will be frowned upon, and ethical marketing essential.

Consumers and the media now have access to companies' environmental records. Legislation is tougher than before. There are more watchdogs checking pollution. And consumers are becoming environmentally literate.

You must explain your policies to the trade and the consumer. There is no point grumbling that consumers are being taken in by competitors or environmentalists if you do not present your own side of the story.

> The US National Hardwood Lumber Association has produced a pocket-sized 'Fact Book'. Written in a question-and-answer format, each page tackles a specific issue, such as forestry stocks, hardwood use, the benefits of timber, biodiversity, and the greenhouse effect. The book also has a section on how to lobby public authorities.

When county structure plans are being drawn up or revised, the officials may decide to curtail the scope of your future operations, unless you can prove that they are not damaging the environment.

For all these reasons, the PR department has a big responsibility. In some companies it will be at the forefront of green thought, encouraging the rest of the company to clean up its act. In other companies, it will be the gatherer of information, finding out the many ways, large and small, in which the business is reducing its environmental impact.

> Godwins, one of Britain's biggest peat producers, faced criticism over its peat extraction activities in the environmentally sensitive Somerset wetlands, home to many rare species.
>
> Godwins decided to hand over worked-out peatlands to the Somerset Trust for Nature Conservation. These peatlands were to become a nature reserve, managed by the Trust. Godwins also provided earth moving equipment and manpower to help the Trust build banks and achieve the right conditions for nature.
>
> The company also started to introduce products that were based on peat substitutes. In this way Godwins showed its sensitivity to environmental issues.

DEFINING THE ENVIRONMENTAL IMPACT

Determine first how much the company's activities affect the local community. Any company that is close to houses, schools or hospitals will need to be extra conscientious. A company in a rural environment may have to be careful about its impact on wildlife, while a company in an architectural conservation area will have other concerns.

So much for the local community. Your focus should also include the company's products or services, and their impact. It will be the department's responsibility to tell the Board about the impact of the products on the company's reputation. Maybe some products need to be withdrawn, or others modified.

The PR department must also familiarize itself with the company's emissions, its raw materials, and other issues mentioned in this book.

> Over 20 years, one branch of Hartwells grew from being a small garage to a substantial Rover distributor. The local community viewed with concern the growth and its accompanying problems (extra noise and traffic, increased litter, and lorries parking in the roadway).
>
> The critics routinely complained that their comments were ignored. So when the company put up an important new Rover sign without planning permission, the council forced Hartwells to take it down. The locals had found a way of beating the company where it was vulnerable.
>
> At this point the company decided that it was time to sit down with the council, and work out some solutions.

PR STRATEGY CHECKLIST

- Determine the objective: to manage the company's reputation, rather than conducting short-term PR exercises.
- Define the company's audiences.
- Measure attitudes towards the company through a survey.
- Assess the key issues to be tackled – in the local community, the market and the population as a whole.
- Become familiar with environmental issues in the company.
- Measure factors that affect the local community. These will include air and water quality and noise levels at site boundaries.
- Assess whether floodlights or other nuisances disturb the local community.
- Analyse vehicle movements – their timing, route, noise and general impact.
- Develop a plan for resolving the issues.

TAKING ACTION

At this point the PR department can formulate a plan for improvement. A crucial part will relate to the local population. The next checklist suggests some ways of improving relationships with the local community.

LOCAL RESIDENTS CHECKLIST

- Reduce noise, air and water pollution through engineering solutions.
- Shield noise by relocating processes or surrounding them with other buildings or trees.
- Reduce the visual impact by landscaping, banks or trees.
- Shield floodlighting.
- Control the movement of lorries (see Chapter 8, Transport).
- Introduce Open Days to show local people how the plant operates.
- Set up a public meeting to expose new plans and minimize scaremongering or ill-informed comment.
- Set up a liaison committee. This could include representatives from local councillors, environmental health officers, regulatory officials, the Health and Safety Executive, conservation groups, and site

management. The committee could meet twice a year to review discharge levels and environmental complaints.

- Offer to improve the local environment – provide park benches, litter bins, trees and shrubs, painting or maintaining fences or communal buildings, or providing finance for local groups.
- Supply experts and officers for local committees.
- Offer company sites for community activities.
- Ensure that your sites look clean and well looked after.
- Consult the local community on proposed changes.
- Provide residents with information about the company's activities and plans. This could be in the form of letters, leaflets or newsletters.
- Produce a video.
- Publish an environmental impact statement for new projects (see Chapter 3, Land and Buildings).
- Keep the press informed.

At Motspur Park, south London, construction work on a new office development was causing as much noise and dust as such developments generally do. So Fairbriar, the developer, provided local residents with a series of newsletters to help them understand what was happening. The company used layman's language, talking about 'large corkscrews' (the piling rigs) and 'giant Meccano sets' (the steel frame). To add interest, the company publicly laid a time capsule under the foundation stone.

COMMUNITY INVOLVEMENT

Staff raise huge sums of money each year for many types of worthy causes. If they feel that green issues are important, they could devote some or all of the money to causes that protect the environment. Staff should be encouraged to undertake environmental activity outside the company. The business may find that employees' activity in the community gives it a better understanding of environmental and consumer issues, leads to better staff relations and an improved image in the community.

The firm may allocate a sum of money that employees can bid for. This money can go to help local green organizations, to fund research, or to facilitate other green activities.

COMPANY ASSETS AND SKILLS

Every company is a repository of important skills – managerial, scientific, technical, even physical; and these skills can be shared with the rest of the world in the form of staff time. The company should consider loaning selected members of staff who are motivated by the idea. The people could be loaned via Business in the Community, or via Voluntary Service Overseas.

The company can also lend or donate company assets (such as machinery, lorries or equipment).

WHO SHOULD BENEFIT?

Green dictionaries (such as Steve Elsworth's *Dictionary of the Environment*) record over 200 such organizations. They include:

- Campaigning organizations such as Greenpeace and Friends of the Earth.
- Animal charities such as WWF which prevent species extinction.
- UK-orientated wildlife charities such as The Woodland Trust or the Barn Owl Trust.
- Third World charities such as Oxfam and Christian Aid whose green activities involve digging wells, planting trees and preventing desertification. Wateraid, for example, is a charity set up by the British water industry. It helps Third World people help themselves to get safe water and basic sanitation. More than one in three of the world's people lack access to these essentials, and half the world's hospital beds are occupied by people suffering from waterborne diseases.

Third World countries need the skills that many western companies possess. Surveying, information technology, agriculture, bookkeeping and construction are vital skills. The same applies to inner city areas. Skills training and business expertise can help to regenerate run down areas.

COMMUNITY INVOLVEMENT CHECKLIST

- Set up a budget for employees' green activities.
- Encourage staff to be involved with or raise money for green charities.
- Loan staff or equipment to a relevant cause.
- Consider giving materials to a worthy cause.

BETTER PR COMMUNICATIONS

As we saw at the beginning of this chapter, some companies have very little PR information about the environment. Some fear that they have not reached a perfect state of 'greenness', and hesitate to talk about their 'light green' achievements.

It is an understandable feeling. Companies feel exposed to the wrath of environmentalists. Raising your head over the parapet makes it easier to be shot, even if you are waving a green flag.

But the same holds true for many business activities. Few companies have a perfect human resources policy, yet many are pleased to reveal in trade magazines how they are seeking to reduce staff turnover.

In future, companies will face more enquiries from genuine seekers after truth, and their PR departments will need to provide more information if the company is to remain credible.

Some companies have taken a positive approach. For example, 3M can supply a comprehensive dossier. It contains a card summarizing the company's environmental principles, a reprint from a trade journal, a sponsored guide to environmental policy making, and an externally written report for employees. Throughout, there is an emphasis on case studies, and facts and figures. It gives the impression of a successful company that knows what it is doing.

Other companies have less to say. One large food retailer sends enquirers a staff newsletter containing a green supplement, plus a badly photocopied environmental fact sheet. If slight on quantity, it shows that the company has at least thought about the issue.

> ICI's environmental literature contains graphs showing the reduction over 20 years in discharges of cyanide, phosphate and heavy metals at its Billingham plant. The charts also show the reductions in mercury per ton of chlorine at its Castner-Kellner works, and the chemical oxygen demand at ICI Francolor. These are expressed as an index, with the baseline year 1970 set at 100.

Many companies have undertaken an environmental audit, but most do not publicize the results. One well-known exception is Norsk Hydro, Norway's biggest industrial group, which has been praised for publishing the results of its audit.

One solution is to set a target date for publicizing a summary of audit findings. This date is likely to be five or ten years from the baseline – the year in which the company first started its environmental improvement programme and first started measuring environmental data.

> Having taken the decision to defend the use of phosphates in its Persil and Surf brands, Lever Brothers has issued leaflets and fact sheets about this and other issues.
>
> Its leaflets cover biodegradability, enzymes, and phosphates. There are also leaflets with tips about using the company's products more effectively, and an explanation on the company's labelling policy. For each product there is also a leaflet explaining the purpose of each ingredient.

Some organizations have produced material but fail to send it out. A packaging trade association is one such example: its staff are not sufficiently organized to send out the information.

This contrasts with companies that have a bias for action. Ring IBM for information and you can hear your address being hand-written on to an envelope; the material is almost guaranteed to arrive the following day.

One of the biggest failings is a lack of facts. Some firms provide a file containing speeches made by their Chief Executive over several years. Wading through the earnest but general statements gives the reader no sense of detail or of co-ordinated action. The box below contains suggestions for more effective communications.

ITEMS TO BE PUBLISHED

Environmental policy statement (see Chapter 2, The Environmental Audit).

Case histories on company successes. Note the examples dotted throughout this book. Most are simple, small-scale activities, but they give their companies environmental credibility, and they are easier to understand than pages of technical argument. For the press, these should be written as press releases and accompanied by photos.

Article reprints. These could be from a staff newsletter or a trade journal. If you have not gone into print on green issues, now is the time. Magazine articles have greater credibility because they are independent of the company.

Public information leaflets. Between them, Tesco and Sainsbury have issued 54 million nutritional leaflets since the mid-1980s, compared with 100 000 issued by the government. For the retailers this hard work represents a substantial defence against any future critic.

Notes on the company's processes, and how these are being managed. Describe what safety measures have been implemented.

Product ingredients. Their purpose, and their effect (or lack of it) on the environment. How safe are they? How long have they been in use? How have they been tested? Who has tested them? Are they biodegradable? Do they harm wildlife? Can they be recycled?

Fact sheet on the company's successes. These could cover:

- Reduction in waste (quantified achievements and target)
- Recycling introduced
- Energy conservation measures, reduction in energy use (quantified achievements and target)
- Noise abatement
- Reduction in air pollution, use of CFCs
- Other improvements made (quantified wherever possible)
- New expansion projects (for example, welcoming archaeologists before work starts)
- Community projects
- Scale of financial investment in environmental protection
- Use of sustainable raw materials
- For new projects – leaflets, letters or newsletters which apologise for disruption, explain the plan, describe progress and invite comment.

> ## ONE COMPANY'S FACT SHEET
>
> The active ingredients in our products have been biodegradable since the 1960s, long before this was required by law.
>
> In 1989 we launched a five-year, £8 million investment programme aiming to double environmental equipment in Lever factories.
>
> We believe that phosphate is the best researched, safest and most cost-effective water softener for washing powders and that there is no evidence of detergent harming the environment in this country.
>
> In concentrated formulation liquid brands we have cut our need for plastic packaging by 50 per cent.
>
> 80 per cent of the paper and board used for our cartons has been recycled. By increasing the density of Persil Automatic we have reduced the packaging used for the product by 20 per cent.
>
> Ways of recycling materials during the manufacturing process have been developed at Warrington. We no longer discharge any effluent directly into the Mersey and, over a three year period, have cut waste water discharge into the industrial trade effluent sewage system by 90 per cent.
>
> A new £1.5 million effluent plant at Port Sunlight removes detergent residues from the waste waters of our liquids operation.
>
> All our detergents are compatible with the environment, due to the stringent safety measures adopted over many years of successful manufacturing.
>
> All new company cars run on unleaded petrol and most cars in the existing fleet have been converted.
>
> A new communication programme to advise employees and consumers of the company's responsible attitude to environmental issues is under way.
>
> A confident record from Lever Brothers. It combines investment plans, packaging, wastes, discharges, biodegradability and car policy.

In the fact sheet above, we may distinguish between environmental benefits (cutting plastic packaging), opinions or assertions (phosphate is safe), and facts that are not really benefits (the company is communicating its responsible attitude to employees and consumers). The equivocal 'compatible with the environment' also raises more questions than it answers. This shows the importance of constructing an environmental fact sheet that cannot be criticized.

> When Safety-Kleen opened a £7 million solvent recycling centre at Sheffield, there was local opposition. As a result, the company organized a number of activities. It arranged a number of press visits; held a themed 'Olde English' Open Day; and hired Bill Oddie to act as a figurehead for the discussion of environmental issues and to draw the crowds.
> It also drew up a crisis plan to ensure the safety of visitors and to minimize disturbance in the event of protest action. It publicized the event in local

radio and press; and held two competitions: an environmental poster competition for schools and a 'Win a Helicopter Flight' in the local press.

As a result 600 people attended (twice the expected number). Media coverage included 22 minutes on local radio and 82 column inches of trade press coverage. Post-event research showed that people were happy to have Safety Kleen as part of the community.

HANDLING THE MEDIA

The press have distinct needs. The information they are seeking is:

- **Factual.** One fact is worth a thousand words. Journalists like detail, hate waffle. Do not write about generalized corporate policies: focus on concrete examples.
- **Photogenic.** The media adore interesting pictures.
- **Pre-written.** Being busy and understaffed, many publications appreciate press releases that they can slip straight into their publication.
- **Human.** The media like to write about people not factories. Even the highbrow newspapers will find a human angle if reporting a business story. That is one reason why celebrity openings work. Furry animals work even better than humans in winning coverage.
- **Controversial.** The media will not normally report a 'good news' story. To be used, a story has to have tension and drama. An environmental new product story should be couched in terms of 'protecting the population', 'safeguarding the factory's future' or 'protecting the world'. A story about investment in pollution control should be presented in terms of 'huge costs', or 'saving fish'.

There are countless ways to achieve coverage, from the simple press release to a journalist's tour of the business. A press pack on the company's environmental policies and action should always be available. Selected executives should be primed to answer questions on packaging, product safety, waste disposal, or other contentious issues.

Companies involved in hazardous activities should have a disaster plan ready, as should every company that operates machinery, uses toxic chemicals, or sells flammable or poisonous products. Most manufacturing companies come within these categories.

EDUCATION

Companies are keen to take their green claims to young people, but these activities need to be handled carefully. A report by the Food Commission showed that educational material supplied to schools contained over-strong branding and was in some cases misleading. One booklet issued by a leading breakfast cereal company showed the brand name or logo 40 times. Material from agricultural organizations left out information about factory farming or toxic pesticides.

The National Consumer Council has issued a set of guidelines, and the Health Education Authority is setting up an accreditation scheme for educational materials.

COMMUNICATIONS CHECKLIST

◆ Check what information could be sent out today.

◆ Analyse the procedures for issuing material. Laborious approvals, tailor-made letters and typed labels prevent material from being swiftly issued.

◆ Check that the information is factual, scrupulously honest and not open to criticism.

◆ Determine on what environmental issues the company can be attacked. What information is available on these issues?

◆ Decide what information should be given to schools or young people. Ensure it is accurate and restrained.

◆ Set a disaster plan in place.

◆ Prime executives to answer questions.

◆ Prepare standard environmental press information.

HANDLING CRITICS

Decide who are your most vociferous critics, and determine a plan for achieving a better understanding on both sides. The plan may involve:

○ Resolving difficulties for which solutions exist.
○ Minimizing the impact of problem areas that cannot be changed.
○ Involving the critics in the activities of the business.
○ Offering the critics meaningful benefits.

Critics should never be ignored. They will rarely go away. They should be invited on to the company's premises, treated courteously, and listened to. After due thought, the company should hold another meeting at which a set of solutions should be offered. These meetings should be publicized, and the company should be seen to be open and trying to solve problems.

Define the worst questions you could be asked. Prepare answers for these questions. Provide regular information for critics, and keep them informed.

> Toll-free calls allow customers to complain, demand information, ask questions or make comments. In the USA, Procter and Gamble receives 100 000 calls a year, including many new ideas for new products.

HOW TO RESOLVE COMPLAINTS

Complaints must be handled promptly and efficiently. Every complaint should be investigated and responded to. The complainant may need to be invited to discuss the issue with management. Solutions should be found where complaints are reasonable, and the information should be widely promoted. Sometimes complaints may result from another organization's activities, and this is why each complaint should be traced.

Sometimes local residents believe that the risk is much higher than the experts' judgements. This attitude has to be respected, not derided, and solutions must be found to reduce that perception of risk. Research suggests that if a landfill site smells, it is more likely to be perceived as dangerous. It may be that reducing a plant's odours or visible emissions will make the plant seem safer.

Evaluate the complaints, and decide how essential the offending activity is to your operations. Weigh up the financial advantage to the company against the impact on your image. Evaluate the impact if the issue should catch the national headlines, and your business is branded a polluter.

> Du Pont's licence to dump inert wastes into the Atlantic Ocean off New Jersey came up for renewal. The company had not been using ocean disposal for some time, and probably would not need to do so in future. But it decided to reapply for the licence despite public objections. After all, said the company, the materials being dumped did not harm marine life.
>
> With hindsight, the company says now, it was not sensitive enough to the views of the people living on the coast. They did not care about the technical data. They opposed ocean disposal of any sort, because their coastal region represented a valuable economic resource as well as a recreational area. Du Pont decided to withdraw its application.

A CODE OF CONDUCT FOR HANDLING COMPLAINTS

Person appointed to handle complaints: _____

In his/her absence, complaints will be handled by: _____

_____

Initial action to be taken on receiving a complaint:

- ○ Acknowledging receipt: _____
- ○ Logging complaint: _____ _____
- ○ Internal communication and action: _____

Person responsible for taking samples or visiting the source of complaint: _____

Methods of analysing or verifying complaint, by type of complaint: _____

People to whom findings will be distributed: _____

Person responsible for determining action to be taken, by type of complaint:

Method of communicating findings, conclusions and action taken to the complainant: _____

Method of collating complaints for statistical analysis: _____

Time limit for each activity (in other words, how soon should a complainant receive a response?): _____

COMPLAINTS CHECKLIST

- Determine who are the greatest critics.
- Evaluate their concerns and requirements.
- Draw up a plan for reducing their criticisms.
- Prepare a complaint-handling system.
- Devise a system for monitoring the effectiveness of corrective actions.

12
PERSONNEL

♦

Bringing environmental issues into an organization must be done with caution and foresight. Introducing green issues involves change, which can be seen as threatening.

Management attitudes to the environment span from altruism to hostility, as shown in Figure 12.1. Many managers start with an apathetic or defensive attitude. This is often because they have a concern which needs to be voiced. Once the objection has been discussed, and their fears allayed, the manager moves into the positive area of the chart. (Some corporate concerns are reviewed in Chapter 1, in Industry's Reaction. Individual managers' fears are shown on p. 182.)

Extremist attitudes at each end of the spectrum (Altruistic and Hostile) are equally dangerous and destructive. The middle two attitudes (Apathetic and Positive Unplanned) tend to be unproductive.

The Positive Planned positioning is the best place to be: it indicates that management is positive but disciplined in its approach.

Green corporate attitudes are also important for recruitment. In a survey of UK students, almost three-quarters (74 per cent) said they would prefer to work for a socially responsible employer. At a time when fewer younger people are entering the market-place, this has important implications for recruitment.

A total of 60 per cent of the students in the survey by KPH Marketing said they had a strong interest in environmental matters, with 56 per cent saying they would take an employer's environmental track record into account when considering whether to accept a job offer.

In another survey, KPH found a high level of environmental interest among managerial staff. A substantial minority (23 per cent) would take a drop in salary to work for an environmentally responsible firm. According to KPH, the next generation of senior managers will be much more green than their predecessors.

The personnel department has an important role to play, in ensuring that key appointments are made, and in developing environmental employment policies. Moreover, Personnel will need to guide line management in ensuring that environmental policies are implemented with full staff co-operation. But the first stage is getting top management's commitment.

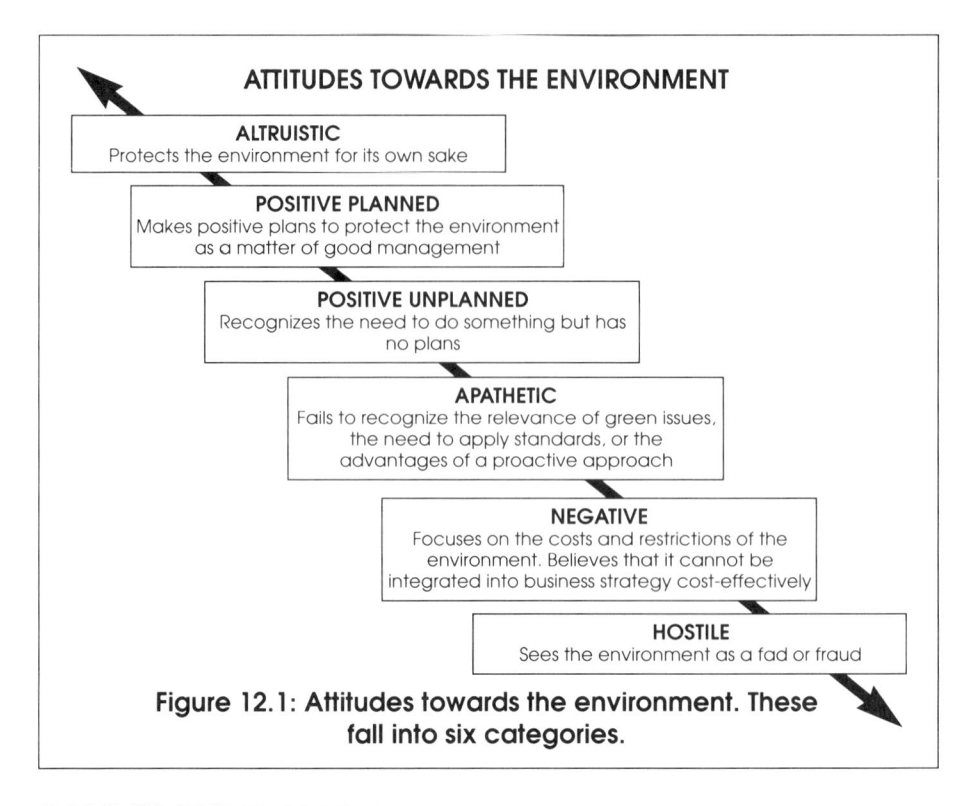

ATTITUDES TOWARDS THE ENVIRONMENT

ALTRUISTIC
Protects the environment for its own sake

POSITIVE PLANNED
Makes positive plans to protect the environment as a matter of good management

POSITIVE UNPLANNED
Recognizes the need to do something but has no plans

APATHETIC
Fails to recognize the relevance of green issues, the need to apply standards, or the advantages of a proactive approach

NEGATIVE
Focuses on the costs and restrictions of the environment. Believes that it cannot be integrated into business strategy cost-effectively

HOSTILE
Sees the environment as a fad or fraud

Figure 12.1: Attitudes towards the environment. These fall into six categories.

COMMITMENT FROM THE TOP

If more than lip service is to be paid to the environment, there must be strong direction from the top. This is said about most corporate activity, such as quality programmes, and it is just as much a requirement for success in environmental issues. Top management must be seen to be concerned about the environment, if employees are not to get conflicting messages.

Changes introduced for environmental or ethical reasons should apply equally to all staff. One firm has decided to ban alcohol completely. It had never been allowed in the factory for safety reasons, but it had been accepted in the senior managers' dining rooms and for entertaining. The decision to ban alcohol came after full consultation throughout the company. 'We didn't want the hypocrisy of allowing alcohol for some people and not for others,' says the firm.

By contrast, senior managers at one of Britain's biggest builders fail to wear safety helmets during their site visits, although ordinary construction staff are expected to wear them.

A company should start by appointing a board member to take environmental responsibility. For most companies environmental activities will be a small part of such an executive's overall work. They will include presenting environmental information at board meetings, and overseeing the changes.

This person could be any one of the directors, and key candidates are as follows. The Managing Director is the figurehead; the Marketing Director is in touch with customers; Finance understands the monetary implications; Personnel covers the human resource issues; Production produces most of the pollution, while Quality acts as a watchdog. Any one of them could take Board responsibility. This being the case, it should go to the person with greatest commitment to making it work.

IN-HOUSE VERSUS EXTERNAL AUDITORS

The appointment of auditors is a crucial task. Until an audit report is produced, and hard facts and figures are available, no plans can be made.

The audit can be carried out in-house, if the expertise exists. It is unwise to let managers audit their own departments: the results will be fairly meaningless. Their knowledge and perspective will be limited, and they will not want to criticize themselves. Some companies appoint an Environmental Affairs Manager, who is asked to audit the business; he will come under internal political pressure to pronounce himself satisfied.

Other companies set up a head office team to audit subsidiaries. This system generally works well; however, it is a heavy overhead for all but the biggest companies.

If the audit is carried out by in-house personnel, the audit team must contain at least one member who does not work at the site. This will ensure a minimum of objectivity.

A third solution is to appoint outside consultants. External consultants are objective, and will have broader experience than in-house staff. They may identify dangers present in activities that in-house staff may overlook; and they are more immune to political pressure. Independent verification is also essential if the company wants to reassure customers or the local community. An in-house audit is rarely credible to outsiders.

On the other hand, consultants can be expensive and they can lack the detailed knowledge of corporate staff. Some firms use external consultants when it comes to assessing a potential purchase, but use their own staff for continuous or routine environmental auditing.

The cost of using outside consultants will depend on the size and type of the organization, and the length of time needed to complete a survey. A list of UK consultants is contained in the ENDS Directory.

HIRING OUTSIDE CONSULTANTS

Before selecting consultants, you should ascertain whether they have:

○   **Qualifications**. What qualifications do they have? Are they members of an association?

- **Experience**. What other work have they carried out? Can they provide references? Avoid being used as a 'guinea pig'.
- **Proper equipment**. Can they measure air pollution or noise levels? But avoid being sidetracked by technical issues. Most businesses need to determine the management issues and formulate a plan. Many scoping audits concentrate on these points. Bear also in mind that, because jobs are so varied and increasingly specialized, even the largest consultancies rely on outside laboratories. For a consultancy to maintain a large staff of scientists and equipment may add an unnecessary overhead.
- **Enough people** if you have many sites or a large organization. Many consultants are one-man bands. Some have specialities (such as marine pollution).

Ensure that you brief consultants properly. Do not keep information back to see whether they discover it for themselves. This will simply waste their time and increase your costs.

Establish the objectives of the audit clearly. What exactly are you hoping to get out of the activity?

Set an agreed fee for each part of the assignment. Make sure that it is presented as a set number of days' work. Check that it includes visits to all relevant sites, and meetings with all relevant personnel. Ask for a plan of campaign.

Agree a timetable, including a date for presentation material. Ask for the information to be presented personally — this will give you a clearer understanding than pages of documentation.

It is often better to audit a small, relatively clean part of the organization first. This will let you evaluate the consultants, and let you absorb extra knowledge on a minor part of the organization.

PERSONNEL STRATEGY CHECKLIST

- Ensure that top management have a real commitment to the environment before any major programme is undertaken.
- Appoint a Board member to take responsibility for environmental affairs.
- Decide whether to use internal or external auditors.
- Evaluate external auditors' knowledge.

THE ENVIRONMENTAL AFFAIRS MANAGER

To ensure that policies are carried through, all companies need an Environmental Affairs Manager. Large companies need a full-time appointment; smaller companies should allocate this responsibility to an existing

ENVIRONMENTAL RESPONSIBILITIES AND COMMUNICATIONS

```
┌──────────────┐      ┌──────────────┐
│    WORK      │◄────►│    LINE      │◄────┐
│   FORCE      │      │  MANAGERS    │     │
└──────┬───────┘      └──────┬───────┘   ┌─┴──────┐
       │                     │           │  THE   │
       │                     │           │ BOARD  │
┌──────┴───────┐      ┌──────┴───────┐   │        │
│ ENVIRONMENTAL│◄────►│ ENVIRONMENTAL│◄──┘        │
│  COMMITTEE   │      │   MANAGER    │            │
└──────────────┘      └──────────────┘   └────────┘
```

Figure 12.2: Environmental responsibilities and communications. The environment involves everyone.

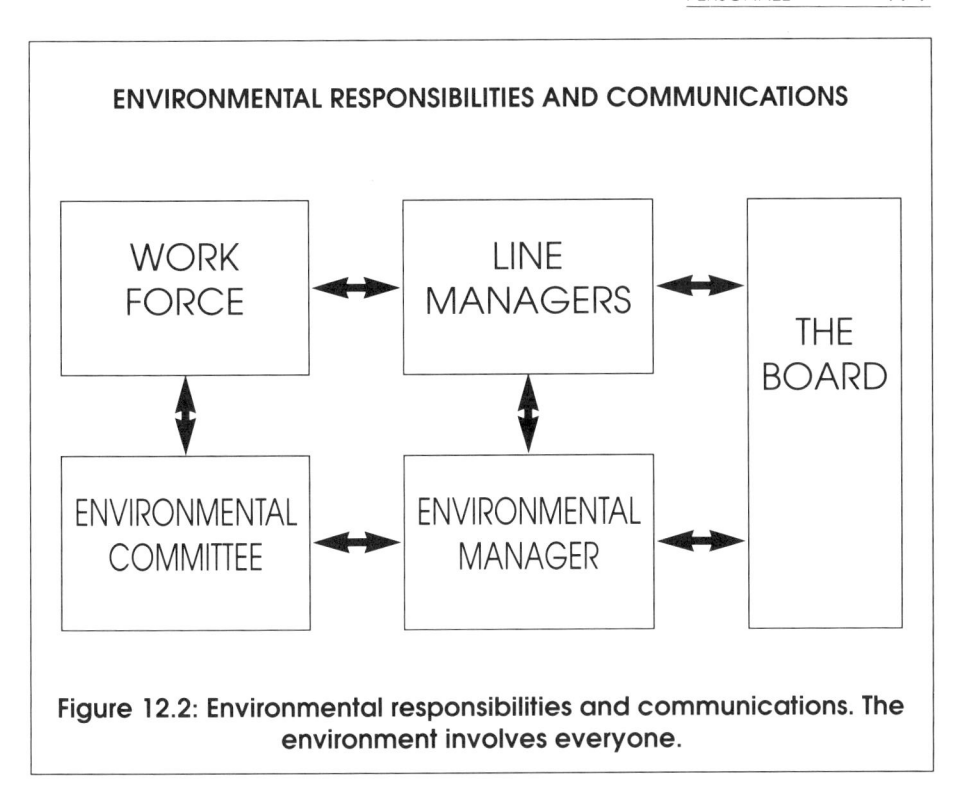

member of staff. Whereas the director will be responsible for policy decisions, the manager will actually implement them. In the absence of an Environmental Affairs Manager, green developments will be carried out much more slowly.

For smaller companies, the employee's motivation is more important than environmental skills. In other words, background discipline is relatively unimportant. Few individuals will be knowledgeable about all aspects of the company's operations. An engineer, for example, will know a lot about pollution control, but relatively little about how to communicate the company's achievements to the outside world.

Some companies add environmental responsibility to an existing job. Some executives are styled Public Affairs and Environmental Manager. Others are called Health, Safety and Environmental Manager. Du Pont uses the title 'Director, Product Safety, Quality and Environmental Affairs'.

As shown in Figure 12.2, the Environmental Manager will often be supported by a committee (discussed in Staff Involvement, below), will work with line managers, and will report to a member of the Board.

THE PART-TIME ENVIRONMENTAL MANAGER

A person whose environmental activities are subsidiary to their main work will need certain characteristics. He or she should:

- Be sufficiently senior in the company to effect change. This means they should be of middle to senior manager status.
- Possess managerial skills (the ability to listen, to evaluate, to prioritize, to motivate, to delegate, to communicate and to persuade).
- Be interested in environmental issues. There is no point in appointing someone who is not interested. The job will not be done properly.

FULL-TIME ENVIRONMENTAL MANAGER

A full-time post will require more experience and qualifications. The individual is likely to be a graduate with:

- a science-based degree
- proven experience in environmental matters
- substantial industrial experience.

RESPONSIBILITIES

Whether full-time or part-time, the Environmental Manager will have a wide remit.

JOB DESCRIPTION – ENVIRONMENTAL AFFAIRS MANAGER

To carry out environmental audits on all aspects of the organization.

To ensure that environmental standards are maintained and improved.

To ensure that the company's products are environmentally friendly.

To reduce the environmental impact of the company's processes.

To provide specialist advice to line management.

To educate staff on the need for better environmental standards.

To communicate the company's high standards to the outside world, by liaising with green groups, local residents, opinion formers, local authorities and national government over environmental issues.

To advise the company on the implementation of better environmental policies.

To protect the company against unfavourable legislation.

To monitor the changes in the local environment through surveys and pictorial records of the site.

To maintain records relating to the company's environmental strategy, and monitor progress.

In making the appointment, you will need to be aware of the dangers of duplicating effort and causing overlapping responsibilities. These problems should be fully thought through and the organization chart revised before the job is advertised. Some conflicts cannot be avoided. The role of the Environmental Manager is that of a catalyst, to persuade others to pay more attention to the environment. Toughness will need to be combined with tact.

The Environmental Manager should report directly to the Board member who has responsibility for the environment. Otherwise, the message will be diluted or stopped from getting through.

At Ciba-Geigy, responsibility for environmental protection rests with line management at each plant. A supporting and 'overview' role is played by a central Health, Safety and Environmental Protection group at the company's Macclesfield headquarters.

The group's functions are to plan and co-ordinate the implementation of corporate policies, act as a source of technical advice, participate in environmental auditing activities, and scrutinize new projects for their environmental impact.

Each Ciba-Geigy site has an Environmental Protection (EP) manager. The post is full time at the five manufacturing locations, and shared with safety or health responsibilities at the three formulation centres. The officers report to local management, but maintain close links with the technical centre at Macclesfield. They meet at least four times a year to exchange information and experience.

ENVIRONMENTAL MANAGER CHECKLIST

◆ Draw up a job description for an Environmental Manager.

◆ Provide the function with the necessary authority to perform the job.

◆ Revise the organization chart to take the new position into account.

◆ Appoint an Environmental Manager, either full or part time.

◆ Communicate with staff about the new appointee's role, to prevent suspicion and conflict.

GETTING STAFF COMMITMENT

Staff commitment is essential to any environmental programme. Taking unilateral action can leave staff confused or even hostile, while obtaining staff involvement will improve motivation and productivity.

The first stage of an environmental programme could start with a 'climate survey' – research undertaken to ascertain staff attitudes. The survey can discover what staff feel about their environment. It can also find out whether they think the company should take greater steps to protect the environment. The survey can assess where staff feel the greatest improvements can be made.

There are many other ways to check staff attitudes and opinions: through a survey of all staff, through a questionnaire in the internal newspaper, or through a staff liaison committee.

As we have seen at the start of this chapter, managers often feel threatened by green initiatives. This especially happens when a green audit is mooted and when outside auditors are involved. Managers' fears can be categorized in the table below. These fears must be allayed in order to reduce conflict and to prevent the project from being ambushed or sidetracked.

MANAGERS' FEARS ABOUT GREEN INITIATIVES

Objection: I'll lose control of my operation.
Response: The audit won't tell you how to run your department. It will merely point out where changes could be made. Any action will be your decision alone.

Objection: The audit will push me into high-cost solutions.
Response: The audit won't dictate solutions. We know that the business must be run at a profit. A surprising number of green solutions save money.

Objection: The audit will produce extremist views.
Response: We've examined the credentials and attitudes of the auditors. We're satisfied that they are businesslike and supportive of our aims. They aren't fanatics.

Objection: The audit will blow the whistle on things I don't want publicized.
Response: The audit is an internal document. It will only be shown to departmental heads like yourself. We all know the main problems that the business faces, so there are unlikely to be big surprises. We have to be proactive, to ensure that we're clean before legislators force us or pressure groups embarrass us.

Objection: It will be used to reprimand managers.
Response: The aim is to investigate and assist, not to punish. We will not be allocating blame, and we will be pleased to discuss problems. But we *will* be concerned about problems that are hidden, or problems that, once identified, are not attended to.

It is best to resolve these issues before the auditors start work. Managers should be invited to voice their queries and concerns, perhaps in a management meeting. But this should not be allowed to block the audit: the auditors must be able to inspect the whole site, including its worst areas.

Auditors should give advance notice of their arrival. Clearing up problems before the auditors arrive is an ideal solution.

The audit report should not be wholly negative: it should praise examples of good practice. The report should concentrate on findings rather than solutions. Suggestions for future action may be broadly defined, but if managers think solutions are being forced on them, they will react in an obstructive way. Corporate strategists should trade a degree of control of the audit against its acceptance and ownership by line managers.

Line managers should also take responsibility for routine auditing, monitoring and control, with formal external audits being undertaken by outsiders every couple of years.

STAFF INVOLVEMENT

Environmental improvements can only be achieved through staff involvement. People must assume ownership of environmental issues, such as recycling and energy reduction. Shared goals will improve morale and make for a happier atmosphere. To gain this, the company needs good upwards and downwards communication.

To succeed, the Environmental Manager will need to draw upon the skills and motivation of other departments. The company should therefore set up an Environmental Committee to assist him. Its members will be drawn from all relevant departments, and it will meet monthly to discuss environmental issues and make recommendations to management.

An alternative is to have an Environmental Protection Team at each factory. These teams will be responsible to line management for monitoring environmental performance, and for liaising across sites where several of the company's plants have a common problem.

Another solution is quality circles (or, in this case, environment circles). These will be small groups of people who come together to discuss problems and find ways of solving them.

THE DEPARTMENTAL REPORT

Managers as well as non-managerial staff must be sensitized to environmental issues. The Environmental Manager may achieve this by asking each department to report on its environmental impact.

Each department's report will be compiled by the departmental representative to the committee. Its contents will be generated through a meeting attended by all members of the department and chaired by the departmental manager. At the meeting, members of the department will discuss the environment and analyse how they can help to protect it.

These reports will be considered by the Environmental Manager and the Environmental Committee, and will be incorporated into the company's Environmental Plan.

Later, there will follow departmental briefing meetings. Departmental managers will explain what the company is trying to achieve, and will discuss the department's role.

OTHER FORMS OF INTERNAL COMMUNICATION

You can communicate a variety of information, including case histories, statistics, reports, press clippings or graphs showing key corporate environmental indicators.

You can also circulate minutes of meetings, but these are usually too dry to be read. Try adapting them into a news-sheet. Other environmental information can be communicated by a staff newsletter, on notice boards, via a video, or in the employees' annual report.

Suggestion Scheme

A suggestion scheme will help the company find good ideas for improving the company's environmental performance and saving money. A committee should investigate each suggestion, and make awards for each one used. Provide a basic financial award, augmented by a proportion of savings made.

Recognition

3M has an awards day on which plaques and official recognition are awarded to individuals, especially technical people, for their contribution to environmental protection. Managers and supervisors are recognized only if they have made a hands-on contribution.

Nominations for awards are made on a standard form, which is evaluated by a co-ordinating committee made up of representatives from all the technical groups. The committee meets quarterly to discuss the entries for all 3M locations.

Du Pont has its Respect awards. These go to any person or team that has created and implemented projects with significant environmental impact. There are eight categories – waste management, wildlife habitat enhancement, product stewardship (for safety improvements), community outreach, public policy (working with the public or environmental groups), innovative technology, personal commitment and other.

Each Respect award lets the employee donate $5 000 to an organization or project benefiting the environment. All individuals also get 'personal recognition items'. The first Respect awards honoured 17 outstanding achievements, and the 'honorees' donated a total of $100 000 to outside organizations.

Branding the programme

The environmental programme will be easier to communicate if it has a name. 3M has 3P (Pollution Prevention Plus); Du Pont, as we have seen, has Respect and Chevron has SMART (Save Money and Reduce Toxics).

REVISING RESPONSIBILITIES

All staff should be set environmental responsibilities or objectives. This could include pollution reduction, careful motoring, avoidance of waste on a particular machine, or ethical marketing claims. At their performance reviews, employees should receive an assessment of their environmental achievements.

Environmental performance should form an element of manufacturing management's pay. In other words a plant that pollutes excessively would reduce the production manager's bonus. Environmental performance should also be taken into account when making decisions about promotion.

Where possible, job descriptions should be amended to prevent damage to the environment. Company cars should not be given unless essential for the job or in response to market pressures. Research suggests that employees choose lower-rated cars if they are given cash in lieu.

REDUCING WASTE IN STAFF COMMUNICATIONS

While many companies communicate poorly with staff, there are some who deluge employees with information. For example, minute papers are often widely circulated, using huge amounts of paper in the process. This can lead to a waste of paper. You could reduce the volume of paper by posting the information on notice-boards.

You could also examine what newsletters are produced internally, and whether these are wanted by staff.

The company's environmental record should be mentioned in recruitment brochures and advertisements. Some companies have separate brochures about their environmental record.

ENVIRONMENTAL TRAINING

Staff need to be trained in environmental awareness. Introductory training courses should move from the general to the specific (starting with global problems and ending with practical solutions the employee can undertake). They should also be interactive (with the employee providing the solutions). Figure 12.3 shows the outline of a training programme, which covers:

○ Global environmental issues (global warming, the greenhouse effect, pollution, habitat destruction, extinction of species, consumption of non-renewable resources).
○ The legislative framework in the UK, Europe or the US.
○ The impact of our industry on the environment – how we affect the environment – cars, pollution etc.
○ Our company – our policy, our strategy, how we compare with others. The steps we are taking. What else needs to be done.
○ My department – the extent of its impact, its interface with suppliers or customers. Ways of reducing environmental impact.

AN ENVIRONMENTAL TRAINING COURSE

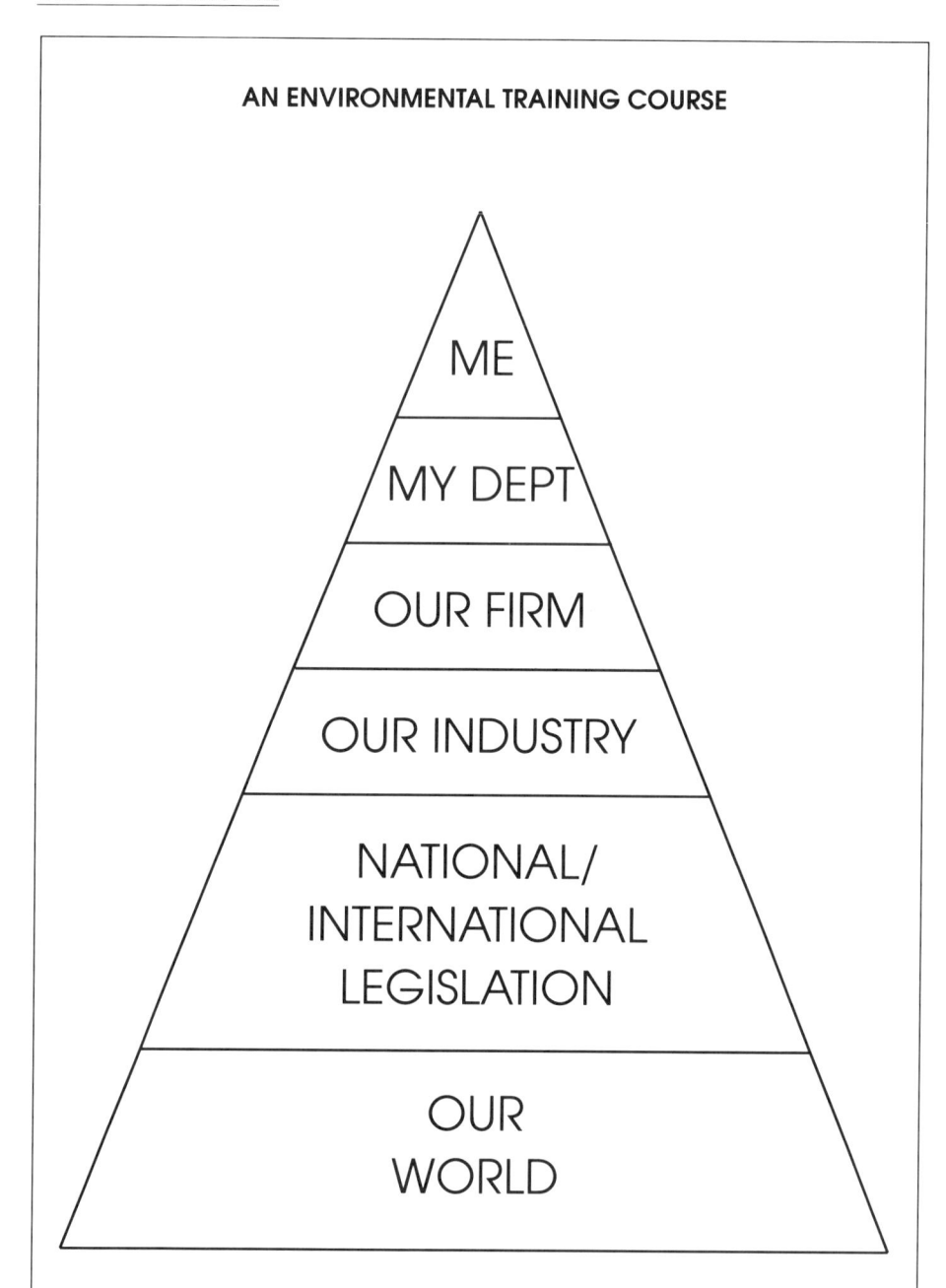

- ME
- MY DEPT
- OUR FIRM
- OUR INDUSTRY
- NATIONAL/ INTERNATIONAL LEGISLATION
- OUR WORLD

Figure 12.3: An environmental training course. The modules of this course become successively more focused. By the end of the course, attenders are thinking about the practical steps they should be taking.

○ Me – what I can do to help.

For example, an off-licence multiple organized a one-day seminar for senior management, and a one-hour briefing for area managers. The briefing topics included:

○ Our world: global topics
○ EC and UK: legislation and standards relating to containers, waste, labelling, shops and advertising
○ Our industry: packaging and containers; production methods, including pesticides and organic production
○ Our business: policy and products; measures taken
○ My group of stores: energy use; recycling; communicating with the thinking, drinking customer
○ Me: feedback on problems and initiatives.

Environmental training should be supported by fact sheets and a workbook. These will help individuals determine what steps they should be taking to improve the environment. New staff should also be educated as to the company's environmental policy.

> At the Allied Dunbar cafeteria, there are racks containing information from local conservation groups and educational material about the environment.

Staff also need to be trained in safety. Regular safety training has many benefits: it reduces the risk of injury to staff, customers and the public, as well as damage to the environment. Some industries, especially construction, need higher safety standards. In 1989 there were 36 deaths and 413 serious injuries on construction sites in London alone.

HUMAN RESOURCES CHECKLIST

◆ Evaluate staff attitudes through research.
◆ Communicate environmental policy and procedures to all employees.
◆ Set up an environmental committee.
◆ Request environmental reports from all departments.
◆ Organize departmental briefings.
◆ Assess whether line managers have obtained their subordinates' consent over new environmental policies.
◆ Nominate relevant people, with adequate resources, to carry out specific development projects.
◆ Agree a newsletter or other forms of written communications.
◆ Set up or revise a suggestion scheme.
◆ Brand the environmental programme.

- Revise employees' responsibilities, targets and job descriptions to incorporate environmental protection. Document these revisions.
- Include environmental performance in performance reviews.
- Set up an awards scheme for environmental effort.
- Provide a continuing training programme for all employees (including new recruits) in environmental awareness.
- Avoid waste in employee communications.
- Include environmental information in recruitment literature.

HEALTH AND SAFETY MANAGER

The company may have a Safety Manager, or this post may be combined with environmental or quality responsibilities. The Safety Manager will mirror the functions of the safety representatives (see below) – making sure that the health and safety of employees and customers are not endangered. Again, it is important that unnecessary overlaps are not created. The manager's responsibilities will be:

- To evaluate the safety management system
- To arrange the training of first aid staff at each site
- To maintain and upgrade COSHH material
- To conduct safety audits
- To recommend improvements to line managers
- To provide safety training
- To liaise with safety representatives.

SAFETY REPRESENTATIVES

Safety is closely connected with the environment. Hazardous materials can damage the environment, poison employees and kill wildlife. That is why a company of any size should have safety representatives and a safety committee. Safe workplaces are less likely to suffer accidents or cause accidental pollution.

Safety representatives should be the company's ears and eyes, watching for hazardous practices and procedures. They should constantly be asking themselves the question, 'What if...?' What if a fork-lift driver pierced those containers? What if the resin caught fire? What if someone fell on the mezzanine level?

Safety representatives should be treated as a valuable resource to be tapped, not as a threat or to be ignored or sidelined. They should promote a dialogue between the company and its workforce, with the aim of providing a safe work environment.

The safety representatives should have the right to go wherever they choose, to investigate potential hazards, and to draw them to management's attention.

Unsafe or unhealthy working practices and unsatisfactory welfare arrangements come within their scope. They should be able to examine machinery, equipment and documents. They should also seek outside advice on technical matters which are beyond their expertise.

They should also examine the circumstances surrounding an accident, and make recommendations to prevent it happening again. The company must give them the information and facilities they need to do the job properly.

Safety representatives are usually appointed by a trade union, and they are given paid time-off for training. Typically, a safety inspection will be concluded with a report that covers:

- Location
- Date
- Activity inspected
- Observations
- Recommended action
- Name of safety representative
- Date for next review
- Action subsequently taken
- Received by employer (signature)

SAFETY COMMITTEE

A safety committee should receive submissions from safety representatives. Its scope could include all matters relating to employees' health, safety and welfare. On the committee should be a mixture of management, supervisory and manual staff. The Safety Committee can:

- Study accident reports and disease statistics, and report finding and conclusions to management.
- Consider reports by Health and Safety Executive and other bodies.
- Consider reports submitted by safety representatives.
- Help develop safety rules and safe procedures.
- Monitor safety performance.
- Check the effectiveness of safety training and safety communications.
- Consider the safety representatives' reports, draw conclusions and make recommendations.

SAFETY CHECKLIST

- Appoint a Health and Safety Manager.
- Facilitate the appointment of safety representatives.
- Ensure the safety representatives are properly resourced.
- Set up a safety committee.

13

THE CAFETERIA

◆

Company food varies enormously. At the bottom end of the range, companies provide just a vending machine with crisps and chocolate bars. A mobile sandwich business may arrive at lunchtime. At the other end of the spectrum, the Board dining room is loaded with fine china and crystal. But whatever the location, most companies give little thought to 'green' food.

Any machine, if properly maintained, will give years of faultless service. But if we use cheap lubricants or feed it the wrong voltage, it will perform badly and eventually seize up. Our bodies are the same. Mostly we mistreat them by our poor diet. Healthy food is the cornerstone of a green lifestyle. The cafeteria is where this can be put into practice.

The first stage is to review current eating facilities and menus. A cafeteria that is only for the manual workers will never have high standards. Having one cafeteria for all staff will encourage the creation of better food.

Menus need to cater for the traditional 'meat and two veg' consumer, but they should also educate the diner into healthier eating. A green food strategy is the starting point.

A GREEN FOOD STRATEGY

A green food strategy will involve the following factors:

○ **Serve wholefoods**. They are more nutritious and less adulterated. Serve wholemeal bread instead of white, and wholegrain rice in place of white rice. Serve fruit for puddings.
○ **Specify organic food** where possible – it will be less polluted with chemicals.
○ **Use fresh food** rather than processed ready meals. It is almost certain to be more nourishing and more free of chemicals. Avoid the excessive use of highly processed foods like sausages whose precise contents are unknown.

- **Vegetarian food should always be available**, because it does not harm the world or any of its creatures. According to the Vegetarian Society's 1991 Food Survey, there are 3.1 million adult vegetarians in Britain, 7 per cent of adults, compared with 1.6 million in 1990. A further 4.6 million people totally avoid red meat. The main reasons are health issues and animal welfare.
- **Reduce the amount of meat served**. It contains no dietary fibre; and the majority of meat comes from intensively farmed animals whose lives are a disgrace to a caring society. All the protein, vitamins and minerals the body needs can be obtained through cereals, vegetables, fruit, nuts and beans.
- **Eat low on the food chain**. Serve simple foods containing rice, wheat or beans.
- **Avoid battery-farmed food**. These include battery eggs – the hens that produce them live a sorry life in cramped cages, denied the opportunity to fly or lead a normal life. If free-range eggs cost more, they are still incredibly cheap for the nourishment they provide.
- **Serve raw foods** (such as salads). Cooking reduces the nutritional value of food.

FOOD SOURCES

Use local suppliers. You can exercise greater control over them, and you will be able to check the conditions under which the food is produced.

Although it is easiest to buy catering packs of convenience food, they rarely provide such nourishing or tasty meals. Cultivate links with local suppliers of organic foods, and arrange delivery of organic fruit and vegetables. Ignore labels like 'farm fresh': they are meaningless.

In the chapter on Land and Buildings we discussed setting up your own vegetable plot – the viability of this project will depend on how many people you have to feed.

THE CAFETERIA

The cafeteria needs to be a clean and pleasant place to eat. Yet all too often the tables are spartan and the chairs are ingrained with dirt, especially where a manufacturing workforce eats. This type of cafeteria will not attract management staff, nor will it foster an interest in good food.

Avoid using disposable cups, plates and cutlery. They are a waste of resources, and generally end up in a landfill site.

SERVING LESS MEAT

There are many reasons why you should reduce the amount of meat served in the cafeteria. Here are a few of them:

The illness argument

Vegetarians have a 20 per cent lower cholesterol level than meat eaters and a 30 per cent reduced chance of coronary illness. They also have 40 per cent less cancer of the colon. In 1988, the German Cancer Research Centre in Heidelburg published the results of a five-year study showing that vegetarians have 80 per cent fewer deaths from heart attacks.

Most meats contain antibiotics, growth hormones and other unhealthy substances injected or fed to the animal by the farmer.

The vegetarian diet is closely in line with the two major UK governmental reports on nutrition (NACNE and COMA).

The humanitarian argument

Intensive rearing of animals (especially hens and pigs) causes them pain and suffering. According to the Vegetarian Society, five hens are kept in a cage measuring only 18×20 inches. They cannot spread their wings or even turn around freely. Up to 90 per cent of eggs sold are battery-produced by hens that will never see daylight and whose feet are deformed by the sloping wire-mesh floor.

As for pork, the sow is an intelligent sociable animal, yet she is deprived of companionship, exercise and fresh air. After giving birth she is restrained in a crate that prevents her from turning round.

The Third World argument

According to Christian Aid, a child dies from starvation every two seconds. That is 15 million children every year. Yet half the world's cereal harvest goes to feed livestock.

Ten pounds of grain produces only 1 pound of beef. The conversion is wasteful.

An area of 10 acres of land will support 24 people on a diet of wheat, but only 2 people on a diet of cattle meat. Britain could support 250 million people on a plant-based diet. Yet over 90 per cent of our agricultural land is used to feed animals.

Since World War II there have been 38 major famines, and during 33 of these, food has been exported from the starving to feed cattle in the West. We even import cereal from Ethiopia during its famines.

The rainforest argument

A total of 60 per cent of Brazil's rainforest has been destroyed by cattle ranching. Trees absorb carbon dioxide. But the burning rainforests actually contributed 20 per cent of all greenhouse gases in 1988.

Tropical rainforests help to produce the oxygen we breathe, yet in 40 years the world's rainforests will be gone forever. Another greenhouse gas is produced by cattle – 200 litres of methane per cow per day.

The pollution argument

Meat production is a significant contributor to river pollution. Slurry (which is 100 times more polluting in terms of oxygen depletion than human sewage) contains heavy metals, nitrates and drug residues.

So what can the caterer do? A leaflet called 'Catering for Vegetarians' is available from the Vegetarian Society. It contains useful suggestions for menus. However, strict adherence to the Society's regimen (avoiding milk, eggs, fish and ordinary cheese) would make life very difficult.

EDUCATING THE DINER

Place small education leaflets on the tables – they will be well-read by the captive audience. Use the leaflets to explain the dangers of an unhealthy diet. Entice people to try a new dish by describing its contents on a blackboard at the cafeteria entrance.

CAFETERIA CHECKLIST

- Ensure the cafeteria is clean and attractive.
- Develop a green food strategy.
- Serve more vegetarian food.
- Serve wholefoods.
- Serve fresh food and uncooked food.
- Buy local organic food.
- Educate the diner.
- Avoid over-processed food.
- Avoid battery-farmed food.

ENTERTAINING AT WORK

What do you serve visitors when they stay for lunch? Most business buffets look the same, and most managements pay little attention to their contents. This is your chance to achieve higher standards. Below are some items that should be banished from the table, and others that should be introduced.

OUT

Chicken drumsticks (battery-farmed)
Ham (highly processed)
Sausage rolls (full of additives and colourants)
Sugared cola
Corned beef (do you know its contents?)
Processed cheese
White bread sandwiches (little fibre)
Meat paté (from battery animals and loaded with additives)
Jelly (a chemical cocktail)
Ice cream
Chocolate cake (full of fats and sugar)
Biscuits (high in sugar)
Mousse

IN

Wholegrain rice dishes
Bean dishes (full of fibre and protein)
Egg dishes (rich in protein)
Filled baked jacket potatoes
A variety of interesting cheeses
Quiche (meat-free)
Crusty wholemeal bread
Mackerel (an oily fish that staves off heart attacks)
Fish paté
Organic wine (try it)
Filtered water
Orange juice
Milk (one of the most perfect foods)
Salads
Smoked salmon or mackerel
Crudités with celery, carrot and other raw vegetables
Crispbreads
Fresh fruit

BEHIND THE SCENES

What goes on behind the counter is just as important as the food that passes over it.

PACKAGING

Avoid excessive or environmentally unfriendly packaging. Do not buy eggs in expanded polystyrene boxes – they might have been made with CFCs. Buy eggs in cardboard boxes, and offer them back to your supplier after use.

Avoid the use of pre-packaged UHT milk and cream in one-shot plastic containers. These 'ecological time bombs' are a gross example of over-packaging, unnecessary adulteration of good food and sheer waste. Bring back the milk jug.

WASHING UP

Large amounts of dishwasher powder are not good for the environment. They contain chlorine bleach and phosphates. When washed into the rivers, phosphates feed algae which grow furiously, turning the water green and taking all the available oxygen. This suffocates the fish and other animals. The plants clog up the river and rot, and the river becomes lifeless.

Use only a small amount of cleaner – check how much the dishwasher manufacturer recommends, and do not exceed it. Try to use cleaners which do not contain phosphates or chlorine.

SURFACE CLEANERS

While every cafeteria has to be scrupulously clean, you should avoid the over-zealous application of bleaches.

Clean floors and work-surfaces by regular sweeping and washing, rather than using powerful chemicals. Check the contents of any cleaning liquid for the presence of ammonia and chlorine, which are highly toxic.

INSECTICIDES

Do not use slow release strips or cakes. They fill the air with dangerous insecticide. Use a machine that attracts flies with ultraviolet light and then electrocutes them.

HAND-CLEANING

Use soap that is guaranteed not to have been tested on animals. Testing cosmetics on animals is not a pretty sight. In the Draize test, for example, the substance is smeared on a rabbit's eyeballs to see what happens.

RECYCLING

Recycle all main waste materials. You will need a separate bin for:

- Glass and jars (milk bottles should be given back to the milkman)
- Paper and card

○ Aluminium (this will include milk bottle tops, aluminium food trays and baking foil)
○ Organic waste (that is, waste food)

Ascertain the location of your nearest recycling point, and make regular trips there. Alternatively, offer your waste aluminium or other valuable waste to Oxfam or a local charity group. Consider also whether organic waste could be used to make compost or feed animals.

UNUSED FOOD

A large independent supermarket in West London gives all its unsold bread to a local convent for distribution to the homeless.

This example could be followed by other organizations. Giving away unused food would reduce the waste of valuable food, and provide a meal for needy people. Check what food is thrown away at the end of the day, and decide how much could be salvaged. Check whether there are any Salvation Army hostels, or centres for the homeless in your area. But be aware of the dangers of food poisoning. Waste food can also be used as compost or for animal feed.

BEHIND THE COUNTER CHECKLIST

◆ Avoid excessive packaging.
◆ Minimize the use of toxic chemicals.
◆ Do not use dishwashing powder that contains phosphates or chlorine.
◆ Use the minimum recommended quantity of cleaning fluids.
◆ Do not use insecticide vapour strips or cakes.
◆ Recycle the rubbish.
◆ Offer unused food to a worthy cause.

14
MEDICAL

◆

Appalled by the Victorian squalor that they saw around them, business philanthropists like William Lever created model homes for workers and instituted health care.

With the advent of the National Health Service, philanthropy fell out of favour. But the politicians' failure to provide adequate health care for all, allied to workers' growing environmental awareness, has put the onus back on to companies to protect their workers' health.

Today, the far-sighted Victorian philanthropists' ideals seem strikingly modern. The company occupies a large chunk of its workers' time and energy. It provides the network of friends. It probably provides the main meal of the day. And unless it takes care, it can also provide occupational illness or even death.

Being in such a powerful position, the company has a responsibility to maintain its workers' health, just as it has a responsibility to safeguard its customers' health and the cleanliness of the planet.

Unfit and unhealthy workers are a drain on resources. Absenteeism, lost production, quality failures, recruitment costs, industrial disputes, all can stem from poor working conditions and an unhealthy lifestyle. By contrast, the fit and healthy worker will cost the company less, and is likely to be motivated and flexible.

To maintain the workforce's health, there are several complementary strategies. They focus on diet, lifestyle, management and treatment.

In introducing these strategies, management must set an example. If the Managing Director smokes cigars, the Marketing Director has large lunches, and the Production Director has a beer belly, the workers will not get healthier.

THE FACTS OF LIFE

THE PROBLEMS

Heart disease is the biggest cause of premature death in the industrialized world. It took 140 000 lives in England in 1989, 26 per cent of all deaths. Its main causes are cigarette smoking, high blood cholesterol levels, raised blood pressure, overweight and lack of exercise. All these can be reduced by changes in diet and lifestyle.

Strokes cause one in eight deaths. As a result 5 000 people aged under 65 die each year. High blood pressure is the main cause, accounting for 60 per cent of all strokes. People can reduce this by not being overweight, not drinking too much alcohol, and not eating too much salt.

Cancer: up to 85 per cent is avoidable. The biggest factor is tobacco, accounting for one in three of all cancer deaths. England has one of the highest rates of breast cancer in the world, which kills 13 000 women each year. Screening can significantly reduce breast and cervical cancer.

Mental illness now afflicts one in ten of the UK population. That means 50 people in a firm of 500 employees could be ill. Mental illness claims a quarter of the NHS's £30 billion budget.

THE SOLUTIONS

Cutting out smoking: In the UK, 33 per cent of men and 30 per cent of women smoke. Cigarettes are the biggest preventable cause of death, according to the government in its 1991 Green Paper.

Improving the diet: We are becoming a nation of fatties. A total of 8 per cent of males and 12 per cent of females are not just overweight but obese. There has been a 2 per cent rise in six years.

Reducing alcohol intake: One in four men and one in 12 women are drinking over the recommended limits. These are 21 units a week for men and 14 units for women, a unit being half a pint, a glass of wine or a single measure of spirits.

Exercise: Only one person in ten takes enough vigorous exercise to protect against heart disease, according to the Royal College of Physicians. Most people are so unfit that even a short stroll tires them out. The College urges employers to encourage people to adopt the fitness habit.

Providing good management: Good management will reduce stress and conflict by providing clear objectives, adequate training and clear communication. Job enrichment, career progression and a supportive culture will reduce staff turnover and mental problems. Health care will warn of impending problems and reduce their scale.

THE HEALTHY DIET STRATEGY

Reports have shown a clear link between diet and health. If staff exist on burgers and chips, if they do not eat green-leaved foods, and if they drink too much beer, their health will suffer.

Heart disease is a significant killer in the western world. The arteries get increasingly blocked, and the heart has to work overtime. Eventually a clot forms, obstructs the blood supply, and the patient suffers a heart attack.

So what are people supposed to eat? Attitudes to diet change with alarming speed. Not so long ago, people were encouraged to avoid potatoes and bread, and to eat margarine rather than butter. Now dieticians are encouraging people to change again.

The real answer is very simple. Avoid fatty and sugary foods. Avoid highly processed foods. Avoid foods that have been adulterated with additives and colourants. Eat simple peasant foods like rice, bread and fish.

Avoid meats from animals kept in inhuman conditions. This includes battery eggs, battery chickens, and intensively reared pork and veal. If you want to eat meat, choose wild animals like pheasant and grouse, or go for free-range meat.

Avoid products whose appearance has been changed beyond all recognition. Sausages, 'turkey steaks' and meat pies should be avoided. But if the packet of fish fingers says '100 per cent cod', and you can see the flakes, there is unlikely to be much wrong with it.

Keep cooking to a minimum. In cooking food we lose much of its goodness. And in overcooking vegetables, we turn greens into the soggy mess that every schoolchild hates.

Avoid excessive amounts of fatty foods. Eat butter, but spread it thinly. Drink milk, but exercise on a regular basis.

In the Cafeteria chapter we looked in more detail at healthy menus and strategies.

THE HEALTHY LIFESTYLE STRATEGY

Too many people have an unhealthy lifestyle. They smoke. They fail to take exercise. They drink excessive amounts of alcohol.

Company exercises, Japanese-style, at 9.30am in front of the office, will not be acceptable in all cultures. But there are many ways in which the company can help employees to better health.

Create a path within company grounds, broad enough for walkers and joggers to pass. Introduce along its length some interesting and calming features – a pond, a clump of trees or some benches.

Introduce bicycle racks and workplace showers as Allied Dunbar has done. Encourage people to cycle to work. Get top management to set an example.

Set up a rolling annual health-check for employees. Start in a small way. Buy a treadmill and give everyone a two-minute test. Concentrate resources on the least fit – this is the group with the greatest opportunity for making improvements.

Identify smokers, and offer them free chest X-rays. Provide them with counselling. Give them information about the dangers of smoking, and the advantages and methods of giving up. Institute an incentives programme.

Provide health insurance. Not just for executives, but for all staff. Anything less is divisive and will cause friction in the business.

Build leisure facilities – a gym or a swimming pool. If your company or site is too small to justify your own pool, provide a free annual pass to the municipal pool.

THE PREVENTION STRATEGY

Introduce training to avoid occupational injury. Show workers how to lift weights without incurring back strain.

Introduce plant and equipment that minimizes injury or pain. Buy lifting gear, conveyors and safety guards.

> Azimo makes thermal-imaging and laser-guided sights for tanks and rifles. Concerned about its employees' welfare, it introduced free twice-yearly eye tests. Employees liked the idea so much they were queuing up for eye tests. Now the company has had to restrict the service to people who are directly involved in manufacturing.

Check secretarial and clerical staff for RSI, which we discussed in Chapter 4, The Office. Offer women cervical smear tests and mammography.

THE HEALTHY MANAGEMENT STRATEGY

Encourage line managers to enrich the jobs of their subordinates. Ascertain how many boring, repetitive and menial jobs exist. See whether they could be enriched by letting the worker complete the whole job. A worker who screws wheels to passing car bodies will not be as happy or as healthy as someone who can point to a car that he and his team assembled in full.

Encourage better management techniques. Do managers know how to deal with hostile workers, poor performers and people with bad time-keeping? Do they know how to motivate workers, how to involve them and how to be a good listener? Discourage managers from shouting at staff or ridiculing them in front of others. Teach them to become more participative. Also consider introducing more caring social policies. These can include better welfare, more egalitarian practices, and a greater commitment to all employees.

In the old days, British companies often organized an annual outing to the seaside. This has been replaced by the annual dinner dance, a much inferior substitute. With the guests dressed in uncomfortable formal clothes and imprisoned at a numbered table, the dinner dance is a stressful event, whose only escape lies in alcohol.

High-tech companies in California's 'silicon valley' have Friday evening beer events, at which all members of staff can get together on an informal social basis on company premises. It is a healthier, more relaxing and more social event. Large companies may have to operate on a departmental basis, but management should be required to attend.

THE HEALTHY TREATMENT STRATEGY

Despite management's best efforts, people will fall ill or hurt themselves. The company needs a treatment strategy for when this happens.

The days are long since gone when medical staff thought that pills were the solution to all problems. Although we still rely heavily on western medicine, complementary medicine is gaining ground.

The solution to some ailments is obvious. If a worker breaks a leg, it will need setting in plaster. But other ailments are more difficult to diagnose. Aches and pains that come and go are not usually taken seriously by western medicine – medical staff often hand out a paracetamol tablet.

Complementary medicine is a growing force. Although some branches are decidedly cranky, others produce results that are superior to western medicine. Their starting point should be holistic – they should concern themselves with the whole of the individual, not just the specific ache. Looking at the wider lifestyle will often reveal stresses, mental or physical, that must be relieved before the pain will disappear.

Aromatherapy is the practice of massaging essential oils into the body. It is used to treat depression, anxiety, arthritis, rheumatism, poor circulation and multiple sclerosis. Nurses who care for confused or disturbed elderly people report that aromatherapy can substantially reduce the need for sedatives. Others have found that pains from old injuries disappear when given this treatment.

Another growing interest is homoeopathy. This involves the patient ingesting minute quantities of natural substances. The amounts are too small to have any effect, according to conventional wisdom, which ascribes the success of the treatment to wish-fulfilment. Yet controlled tests have shown that homoeopathy appears to work. In introducing a homoeopathic practitioner, a company will benefit by avoiding invasive or drug-based therapies, and employees can be relieved of illnesses where conventional medicine has failed.

Other treatments include yoga, acupuncture and osteopathy, all of which have achieved success without drugs.

MEDICAL CHECKLIST

- Provide an effective diet in the company cafeteria. Encourage better eating habits among staff.
- Encourage a healthier lifestyle.
- Provide safer working conditions.
- Ensure effective management of staff.

- Provide health screening and counselling.
- Introduce weekly informal get-togethers.
- Introduce social benefits and welfare.
- Provide job enrichment.
- Introduce complementary medicine.

15
FINANCE

◆

Finance Directors are often appalled by the green investment proposals that pass across their desks. Trained to look for improvements in profitability, they find it difficult to justify new calls on money for environmental projects, many of which do not have an easily quantifiable payback.

But there are good financial reasons for going green. As the grid in Figure 15.1 shows, there are four possible positions for a company to adopt.

○ **The Laggard** does nothing. It spends no money on environmental protection, and it has a grey or dirty image. But as new laws come out, the Laggard can easily find itself in the Punished category.

○ **The Punished** company has failed to adapt to changing circumstances. It is punished by customers who start buying competitors' products, or by legislators who require pollution controls to be retrofitted. Substantial cost often follows, but the company retains its grey image. The expenditure has come too late.

○ **The Conformer** aims to stay within the law by spending as little as possible. It concentrates on no-cost or low-cost solutions. Many companies like to adopt this strategy; and it is quite feasible to have a green image for mimimum outlay.

○ **The Leader** takes a high-cost route, and gains a high profile. It may achieve superiority in technology and innovation, and may become the standard by which other companies are judged.

The matrix shown in Figure 15.1 has an anti-clockwise movement. Leaders who rest on their laurels become Conformers; Conformers who stop running become Laggards; and Laggards become Punished.

Conformers sometimes take an initiative in one aspect of environmental protection. They make a foray into the Leader's quadrant. This brings them favourable publicity or a reduction in costs. Such companies do not have to expend as much energy as a Leader, but they obtain positive benefits due to the focused nature of their green activity.

> Two companies had to install degreasing equipment to prevent water pollution. Company A decided to solve the issue once and for all. It spent

STRATEGIC OPTIONS

	GREEN	GREY
HIGH COST	LEADER High profile, high-investment policy	PUNISHED Retro-fitting required; loss of market share
LOW COST	CONFORMER No-cost, low-cost measures	LAGGARD Do nothing

Figure 15.1: Strategic options: a company can choose which segment it wants to occupy.

£500 000 on an innovative system which cured the problem completely, and produced savings of £75 000 a year.

Company B spent £100 000, only to find that its solution did not work. It spent another £200 000, trying to resolve the problem. Later, an inspector from the regulatory authority visited the plant and told the company that it would have to adopt Company B's £500 000 solution.

So Company B ended up Punished. It had spent reluctantly, and that money had been entirely wasted. This does not mean that costly solutions are always right; it merely indicates the problems that finance departments have to grapple with.

For companies that pollute, finance will become increasingly difficult to get hold of. In the UK, bankers are considering the environmental implications of loans, and in the USA they may be held liable for pollution caused by companies to which they have lent money.

The same applies to insurance. As insurers pay out increasingly heavy sums for pollution compensation, they will be unwilling to cover poor risks.

Waste disposal will become more controlled and costs will therefore rise. Landfill will no longer be a simple low-cost method.

Court costs will also rise. Today, a visitor to any regulatory authority office will find zealous staff debating whether to press charges against well-known companies for pollution offences.

There are also real benefits from going green, especially in increased sales and new product opportunities.

COSTING THE FUTURE

Yet the Finance Director is hampered by the difficulty of costing the environment. At one time pollution was free, and would not have been included in the management accounts. Now costs are appearing in the form of consents.

The Finance Department has to forecast the future costs of pollution consents, waste disposal and compliance costs. It also has to include in the equation a figure for court fines in the event of non-compliance or accidental pollution.

AN ENVIRONMENTAL FINANCIAL ANALYSIS

	Year 1	
	With investment	Without investment
Value of goods produced (noting production increases following investment)		
Value of improvement in product quality		
Value of recycled goods sold		
Less:		
Raw materials (including reduction due to recycling)		
Labour (including reduction in turnover, improved labour relations)		
Depreciation (including new equipment)		
Maintenance costs		
Energy and water consumption		
Costs of handling, storing and treating products and waste		
Cost of consents		
Cost of waste disposal including transportation		
Insurance		
Management time spent on 'fire-fighting' and complaints		
Contribution		

An Environmental Financial Analysis chart should show whether investment in environmental protection will provide a return in terms of reduced waste disposal, cheaper raw materials, or reduced energy.

A factor not clearly seen in the chart but which will eventually show up in the figures is the 'Cost of Quality' that is, the cost of scrap, of quality controllers, the cost of reworking, and returns from customers. If modifications reduce scrap or boost quality, the company will achieve a greater output and reduce costs. There is often a close link between environmental protection and improved quality.

Another factor is increased price. Companies with green products are able to charge more for their products, a factor that will be reflected in the profit and loss account.

Some environmental issues are relatively easy to evaluate. Take energy reduction. It is simple to forecast the payback period for a new heating system. If the capital cost is three times the value of the annual saving in energy, the payback period is three years and therefore justified.

Other factors are less easy to quantify. Take the cost of a filtration system to clean waste water. The investment might not produce cost savings. Nor could it be justified under a 'least cost' financial regime. However, the department might forecast rising water pollution charges, which would make the investment cost-effective.

The regulatory authority might decide to reduce the consent levels, which would then require the company to retro-fit at greater cost. A national newspaper might publish an article on the company's pollution, which would reduce sales by 5 per cent. Or a local resident might decide to take the company to court over a skin complaint allegedly caused by the company's pollution.

These situations may be some distance from the area of hard data, but this does not make the possibility of future costs any less real.

The Finance Department can measure the value of an investment project by using a standard capital appraisal technique such as NPV (net present value). It will need to add into the equation all the forecast costs and revenues, including those we have mentioned above. Many costs will have to be estimates. As Figure 15.2 shows, green investments vary in their ability to produce long- and short-term profit.

> Until now, departments have rarely had to worry about their wastes. But now Avon Rubber is considering the introduction of 'The polluter pays' principle within its organization. Departments producing waste will be penalized. This could lead to a reduction in waste, with major benefits to the business.

A NEW FORM OF ACCOUNTING

There is a further, more esoteric stage. Following publication of the Pearce Report in the UK, some accountants are trying to distinguish between man-made capital (such as machinery, infrastructure or human skills), natural capital (such as oil or a bay), and natural critical capital (such as the ozone layer). In making this distinction, companies can track movements between different types of capital, in particular monitoring whether critical capital is

THE IMPACT OF SELECTED ENVIRONMENTAL PROTECTION MEASURES ON SHORT- AND LONG-TERM PROFITS

| SHORT-TIME: | MAJOR | MODERATE | MINOR | MINIMAL |
LONG-TERM:	MAJOR	MAJOR	MAJOR	MINIMAL
	Waste minimization	Environmental audit	Employee training	Wildlife protection
	Energy reduction	Occupational health	Safety checks	Conservation of non-renewable resources
	Product quality audit	Impact assessment for new projects		
	Acquisition/ divestment audit	Pollution audit		

Figure 15.2: The impact of selected environmental protection measures on short- and long-term profits. Some measures have an immediate effect on profit. Most have their biggest impact in the long term.

being reduced. Putting a value on environmental assets is fraught with danger, but the aim is 'intergenerational equity' – passing on a stock of assets no smaller than we inherit.

Not everything can be reduced to figures. For a smoker, the cost of smoking is simply the cost of each packet of cigarettes. But for non-smokers, the danger of getting lung cancer is an added consideration. For them, the cost of the packet is a small part of a much bigger equation, most of which cannot be costed.

> 3M has decided to spend what is necessary to protect the environment, with or without cost savings. According to Chief Executive Officer, A F Jacobsen, all new air pollution control installations will be judged not by return on investment but by their technical acceptability and environmental benefit. That benefit is defined as an improvement in air quality.

3M has made this bold decision in the light of experience that shows pollution control is cost-effective. Without aiming for savings, the company has made operating savings of $420 million between 1973 and 1988. These are conservative estimates, based on first year only results – how production costs were affected in the first year of project operation.

As the Chairman of Du Pont has said, 'Natural systems have worth independent of their economic value. That's what the citizens of this country are telling us, and it's a value I share.'

ENVIRONMENTAL COST ANALYSIS

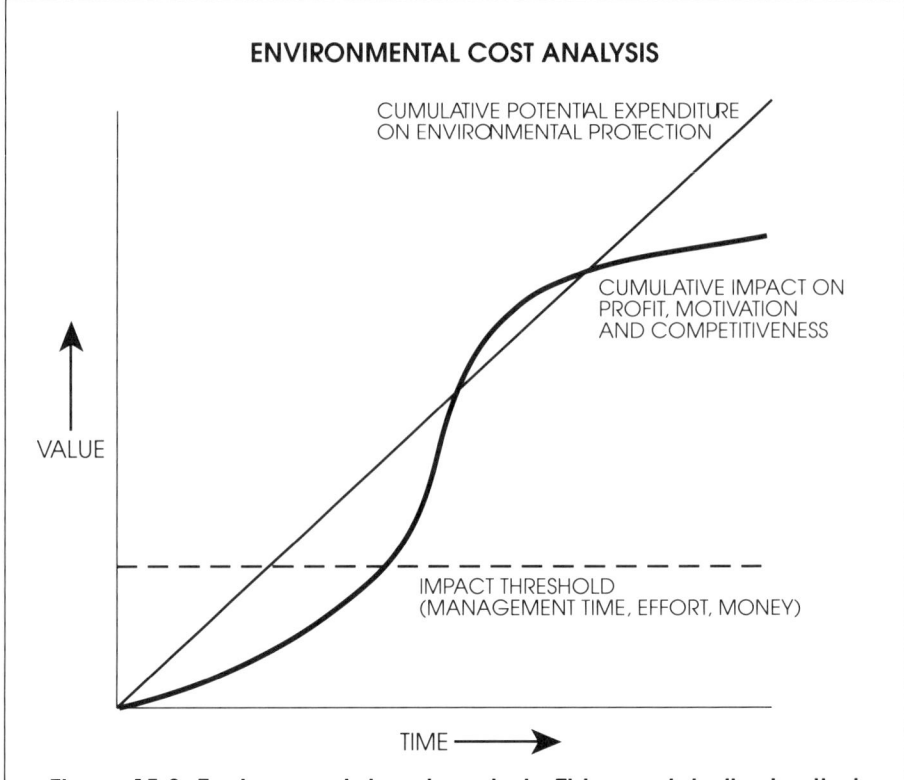

Figure 15.3: Environmental cost analysis. This graph indicates that environmental activity has to be above a certain threshold to have any impact. It also suggests that the benefit takes the form of an S shaped curve, offering low initial benefits, high medium term benefits with a falling off in later periods.

EXPENDITURE STRATEGY

Many elements of environmental control are no-cost or low-cost items. Prime among these are energy reduction and waste reduction.

The greatest savings are the earliest ones. As a company reduces its pollution and issues less waste material, the opportunity for savings will reduce. Figure 15.3 shows how the apparent financial return levels out in the long term. When this stage is reached, the company will need to increase its research and development, and concentrate on staff motivation and input. At this point the company will be focusing on the causes of pollution (such as product formulation) rather than the pollution itself.

Expenditure is most cost-effective in the long term when it prevents pollution from occurring, rather than minimizing its effects once created. That

FACTORS IN THE INVESTMENT ANALYSIS

HIGH INVESTMENT ← Concern over higher disposal costs | The bank → **LOW INVESTMENT**
← Government regulations | Cash flow →
← Improved insurance rating | Shareholders' profits →
← Demands made by line managers and budget holders | Value for money →
 | Return on investment →
← Fear of pollution | Competing investment opportunities →
← Threat of litigation

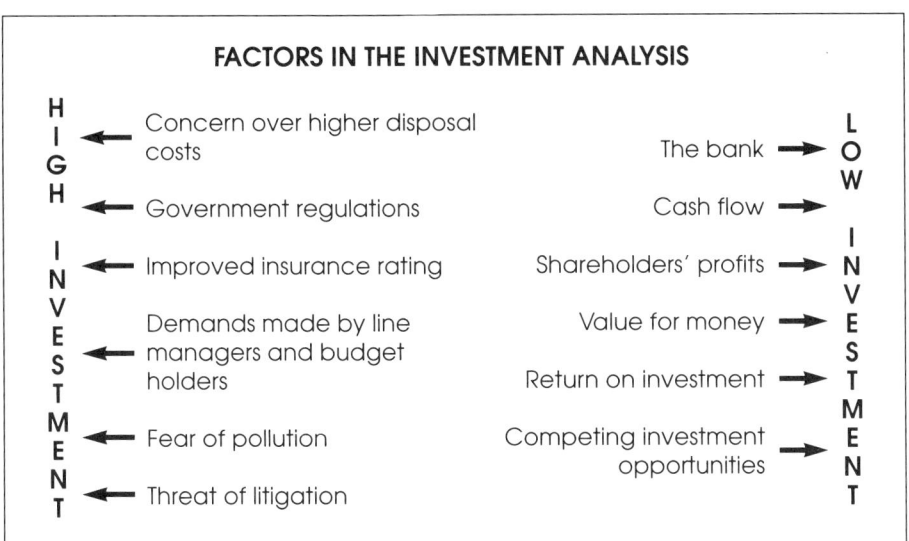

Figure 15.4: Factors in the investment analysis. Different factors pull the finance director in opposite directions. The final decisions will be based on executive judgement.

is why environmental control is best tackled through product reformulation, process modification and equipment.

HOW MUCH TO INVEST

The amount a company should spend will depend on need. Every company will have to make its own objective review of the company's exposure to environmental risk. Figure 15.4 illustrates the conflicting demands made on the Finance Director.

According to ENDS, the UK chemical industry is spending 12 to 15 per cent of its total capital expenditure on ecology and safety. Other estimates suggest that up to 25 per cent is being spent. Ciba-Geigy is spending 19 per cent of its total capital expenditure in the UK (£50 million over five years). To this it is adding another £50 million in revenue spending.

ENVIRONMENTAL COSTING CHECKLIST

- Assess the costs of all possible environmental improvements.
- Analyse the benefits that result from each measure. Include forecast future externalities – the cost of consents and other factors.
- Rank environmental protection measures in terms of cost benefit.
- Assess the capital cost of environmental protection as a percentage of total investment.

INFORMATION SYSTEMS

Financial and management information will need to accommodate environmental legislation and new corporate policies.

Each company will need to monitor its compliance with legislation, in terms of hazards handling and employee health-checks, for example. COSHH legislation requires companies to record the use of substances that can harm health. The information flow starts with suppliers' reports, which may come in a variety of formats.

Considerable paperwork can amass, which is why it is worth transferring COSHH information to a computer database. Inventories, storage, descriptions, assessments, exposure monitoring and disposal can be included.

Existing technical information will need to be captured and processed in new ways to provide green statistics.

Systems will also be needed to evaluate the cost of BATNEEC (best available techniques not entailing excessive cost), and to quantify the effect of environmental protection.

It is particularly important to allocate costs to the department which creates them. Some activities may presently be considered a general overhead, such as energy. If these are re-allocated back to the individual cost centre, staff will become more conscious of the opportunities to reduce costs or minimize environmental impact. Information needs include:

- **Personnel**: Health and safety measures (for example, accidents)
- **Production**: Scrap levels; waste levels
- **Engineering**: Noise levels; air and water emissions; quantities of waste disposed
- **Finance**: Units of energy used
- **Maintenance**: Number of species of plants, animals, birds or insects present; area of grass (m^2)
- **Purchasing**: Percentage of purchases that are environmentally friendly
- **Company Secretary**: Percentage of vehicles either diesel or fitted with catalytic converter. Mpg achieved by cars.

Information about environmental impacts needs to be circulated to the relevant staff. Rhone-Poulenc set up a waste accounting system to keep track of the waste generated and the costs of disposing of it. When the monthly data first reached each plant, staff were surprised by the true product costs that it revealed.

ANNUAL REPORT

With environmental data flowing into the computer system, the Finance Department can more easily organize a feature on the company's environmental practice in the annual report. This will help to communicate the company's green activities, and will show shareholders that it is a socially responsible organization. The feature could contain:

○ Environmental policy statement
○ Environmental action, including case studies showing environmental action
○ Environmental protection expenditures in the accounting period
○ Future expenditures, including contingent liabilities
○ Performance indicators such as emissions, discharges and compliance with legal standards.

ACQUISITIONS

Always evaluate the environmental implications of any company you propose to acquire. Points to consider are:

○ Does the potential acquisition have hazardous products?
○ Does it operate from an environmentally sensitive location?
○ Does it dump hazardous wastes?
○ Could consumers start a lawsuit for injuries caused, and if so what would this cost?
○ Are its products likely to be banned in future?
○ Are its products likely to be superseded by greener products?
○ Does it have interesting green products in development, or under-developed green brands?
○ To what extent is the industry under threat from pressure groups?

This same checklist should be used for new projects or capital investment and strategic corporate development.

INFORMATION SYSTEMS AND ACQUISITIONS CHECKLIST

◆ Determine what data needs to be collected, and with what frequency.
◆ Assess how often the information needs to be output, and in what manner.
◆ Agree who will collect the data, and who will use it.
◆ Analyse how this can be integrated into existing data-processing activities.
◆ Introduce environmental information in the annual report.
◆ Screen new acquisitions or developments for their green implications.

INSURANCE

Well-publicized disasters such as the *Exxon Valdez* oil spill are encouraging companies to take out pollution insurance, and demand is outstripping supply.

In the past, insurance for accidental pollution has been relatively easy to obtain: you could get cover for 'sudden, unintended and unexpected pollution'. But gradual pollution insurance (such as might occur from landfill leaching) has become more difficult to arrange. Such pollution can take place over a number of years, and the insurer may face a claim for the maximum amount in each period. As a result, insurers have been unwilling to provide this type of insurance.

One insurer that offers gradual insurance is Swiss Re, which provides quotations to individual companies following an environmental audit. The Chemical Industries Association also has a new insurance policy. It involves a questionnaire and a survey by an environmental consultant, and if all is satisfactory, a chemical company can be covered for gradual pollution, excluding pollution caused by negligence.

All types of pollution insurance are likely to become more expensive and difficult to find in the coming years. At Lloyds of London, Wellington Underwriting assessed that the ultimate cost of pollution claims could be £60 billion for the world insurance industry over the next 20 years. Syndicates reporting 1988 results (the market works on a three-year time lag to allow for claims) suggested that the ten biggest syndicates would lose £215 million in that year.

The magazine *Insurance Age* believes that pressure from insurers could force more companies to look at their environmental record. It quotes a survey by Touche Ross Europe Services which shows that only 9 per cent of companies had changed products because of pressure from insurance companies, as opposed to 48 per cent who had responded to public pressure. But as environmental legislation takes root, insurance companies may become more involved with companies in helping them control risks.

Insurers are also concerned that their clients should comply with COSHH regulations, on the grounds that a complying company will cause fewer injuries and therefore suffer fewer claims. Many insurers now have COSHH assessment departments which can help companies get their plant in order.

But environmental insurance is expensive and has limited cover. The best solution is to pre-empt the need for insurance by having environmentally friendly products and processes, coupled with effective controls and systems.

INSURANCE CHECKLIST

- Determine the extent of the company's exposure to litigation or other costs arising from environmental issues.
- Check the company's insurance policies to see whether they cover such contingencies.

- Check for limitations in terms of type of pollution, and the limits of any claim in terms of time-scale or value.
- Assess whether to seek added cover in the light of increased environmental pressures.

ETHICAL INVESTMENT

Rather than simply putting profits and pension fund into ordinary investments, consider investing in a green fund.

Since 1984 a number of socially-responsible funds have grown up, and the evidence suggests that green investments perform at least as well as ordinary funds. Enlightened management is likely to be more successful than a management which occupies itself solely with the pursuit of profit without consideration for its community, customers or workforce.

The first and best-known is Friends Provident, whose Stewardship Fund does not invest in companies that are involved in the arms trade, that experiment on animals, harm health, dump waste at sea or pollute the atmosphere.

Its track record is impressive. The sum of £1 000 invested in 1985 would have grown to £2 219 by the end of 1990, compared with £2 050 for the average UK equity growth unit trust, a performance which *Money Management* magazine described as 'excellent'. Funds in this trust now total over £100 million.

The Stewardship Fund is an account based on ethics, a wider definition than some of the newer trusts which only invest in 'green' organizations. One of these is the TSB Environmental Investor Fund. It invests in companies that demonstrate a positive commitment to the protection and preservation of the environment.

A specifically green unit trust is the Merlin Ecology Fund. It buys into companies that are trying to reduce their impact on the environment, rather than restricting itself to environmentally pure products. It looks at active improvement rather than simply refusing to invest in companies that pollute or build nuclear weapons.

A different type of company is Mercury Provident plc, an authorized institution under the Banking Act 1987. This company finances socially beneficial enterprises in education, organic agriculture, natural medicine, care for the handicapped, and co-operative housing and commerce. Depositors can direct their savings to projects of their choice from the company's list of loans.

With Mercury, investors can make a proportion of their investment as a gift, or accept a lower return than they could get elsewhere. Mercury has a variable rate account, in which depositors choose the rate of interest they require – from zero to a maximum of around seven per cent. The interest rate charged to the projects bears a direct relationship to the interest chosen by the depositor.

There is also a green building society. The Ecology Building Society (EBS) lends money to companies as well as individuals. It lends for the purchase of ecologically sound property, such as small-scale workshops, derelict but sound houses which would otherwise have been abandoned, organic small holdings and farms, and homes for people running small businesses with an ecological bias (such as paper recycling or craft workshops).

The society lends on property which will lead to the saving of non-renewable resources, the promotion of self-sufficiency or the most ecologically efficient use of land.

Founded in 1981, the Ecology Building Society is tiny compared with the financial giants; but even though it strictly limits the type of property on which it lends money, it has been growing at 30 per cent a year.

According to the society, saving with the EBS means that investments become a statement of concern about the earth, about people and animals and their interdependence. The society is part of the investors protection scheme, and is regulated by the ombudsman. Investments therefore are as safe as with any other authorized building society. The EBS has assets of £4 million.

If, on the other hand, you want to build up your own ethical investment portfolio, you can contact EIRIS (Ethical Research Information Service). This independent organization conducts research into companies' activities, and makes recommendations about green investments.

PAYROLL GIVING

Employees can now give money to charity in a painless way – through their payroll. Just three years old, Oxfam's Payroll Giving scheme earns over £300 000 a year for its overseas projects. So far Oxfam's scheme has generated over half a million pounds.

The scheme generates funds on a regular and reliable basis which guarantees Oxfam the money it needs to find long-term solutions to poverty.

Donations are simply deducted from gross pay at the end of the month; and the money goes further by not being taxed. According to Oxfam, if four people in an office gave the price of a newspaper each day, they would raise £450 in a year.

The scheme projects a positive and caring image to the workforce, and many employers have welcomed this cost-effective way of helping the world. Some companies match the amount raised by their staff – thereby doubling the contributions.

INVESTMENT CHECKLIST

- Consider investing in a green or ethical fund or lending institution.
- Set up a payroll giving system. Publicize the opportunity to staff and provide request forms.

16

PUTTING IT ALL TOGETHER: THE ENVIRONMENTAL MANAGEMENT SYSTEM

◆

The Conservation Concept (shown in Figure 16.1) is not easy to achieve. The company has to be lean and efficient, with an excellent product range and a dedicated work-force. Quality must permeate the entire organization. It is an ideal that many companies aspire to, and one that will be highly profitable.

Yet there is often a gap between what companies aspire to and what they achieve. Environmental affairs is a case in point: inaction is a great problem. There is a danger that, once the environmental audit is executed and the policy written, little will follow.

Many companies and local authorities produce policies which are full of fine phrases and good intent, but often these are not converted into action.

To reach the Conservation Concept stage calls for effective planning and controls as well as a commitment to excellence and the environment.

It also requires a management system. Companies which lack a system will 'cherry pick' their environmental activities: a bit of recycling here, some landscaping there. It does not add up to serious or comprehensive environmental management. Many company can point to specific actions they have taken to improve the environment, but fewer can point to a complete system. As a British Airways report said (in consultant-speak):

> There appears throughout the organization to be support for one-off 'green' initiatives, but this perception of environment falls short of the more fundamental requirement to consider environmental perspectives of all activities. It is important that environmental 'culture' becomes part of the total quality management concept which is already under development within British Airways.

The link between quality control and the environment, mentioned in the quote above, will be a crucial management issues during the 1990s. Figure 16.2, adapted from *Costing the Earth* by Frances Cairncross (The Economist Books Ltd., 1991), suggests that the cheapest solutions come from management systems, while the most expensive and least satisfactory solutions lie in correcting faults once they have occurred.

THE CONSERVATION CONCEPT

RAW MATERIALS	FACILITIES AND PROCESS	PRODUCT	AFTER-USE
Minimum resources	Low energy	Maximum life	Recyclable
Maximum use of recycled and renewable materials	Minimum emissions and discharges	Minimum packaging	Reusable
	Minimum waste	Minimum adverse environmental impact	
	Maximum safety	Maximum benefit to the environment	

Figure 16.1: The conservation concept. The ideal situation that business can aim for. Perfection may not be feasible, but all companies can aspire to achieve it.

Several organizations have developed systems that involve environmental management. These include the British Standards Institution (BSI), the European Community and the International Standards Organization (ISO).

Several of these systems are based on quality management systems. This makes life simple for companies familiar with quality concepts. But they also have disadvantages. The systems can be bureaucratic and defensive.

Nevertheless, implementing an environmental management standard will help many companies. In the short term they will find that having the standard will give them a competitive advantage: it will be something they can boast about. In the longer term, it will be a requirement for selling into many market. Companies that lack the standard will not be allowed to tender: this has already happened with BS 5750 and ISO 9000.

It also means that responsibility for the environment may pass into the hands of quality control managers, who will have to learn new tricks.

This chapter is designed to help companies understand the arcane requirements BS 7750, but it will also help organizations which simply want an effective system for protecting the environment.

At the heart of the British Standard is an environmental management system (EMS), which is illustrated in Figure 16.3. In the various chapters of this book we have already met most of its elements, but the EMS brings them all together in one disciplined and cohesive system.

There are three key elements in the system: these are the audit, the policy and the plan. We discussed the audit and the policy in Chapter 2, while the plan is discussed later in this chapter. As we shall see, the plan is the engine which drives the company forward and leads towards the Conservation Concept

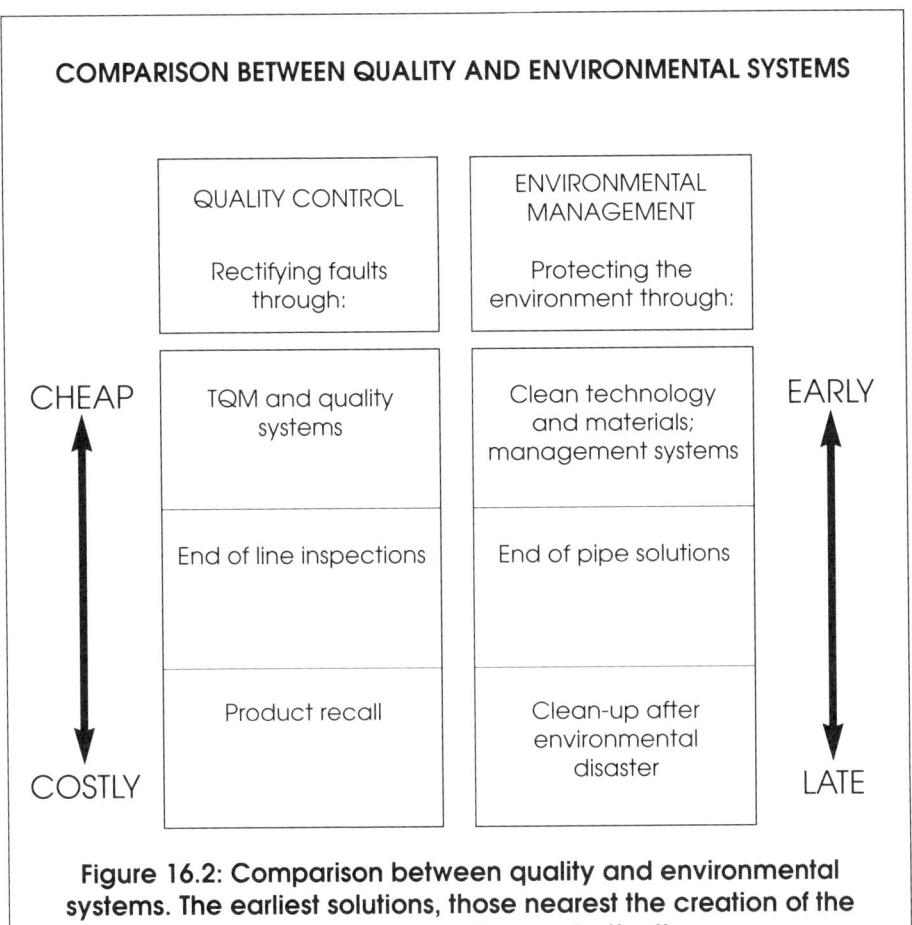

COMPARISON BETWEEN QUALITY AND ENVIRONMENTAL SYSTEMS

	QUALITY CONTROL Rectifying faults through:	ENVIRONMENTAL MANAGEMENT Protecting the environment through:	
CHEAP ↑↓	TQM and quality systems	Clean technology and materials; management systems	EARLY ↑↓
	End of line inspections	End of pipe solutions	
COSTLY	Product recall	Clean-up after environmental disaster	LATE

Figure 16.2: Comparison between quality and environmental systems. The earliest solutions, those nearest the creation of the product, are always the most effective.

ideal. This action-led approach is paramount. An EMS should not be just a passive defence but should make an active contribution to the company's corporate strategy.

Bolted on to the three-part process of audit, policy and plan are a set of structures to keep the system turning (these include the written procedures).

We will examine the system by moving through the process, then we will look at the supporting structures. First, we start with internal and external information.

INTERNAL INFORMATION

Information is the key to success for an EMS, and internal records are crucial. Environmental information needs to be routinely captured and analysed. The

Figure 16.3: An environmental management system. The control elements are the audit, policy and action plan.

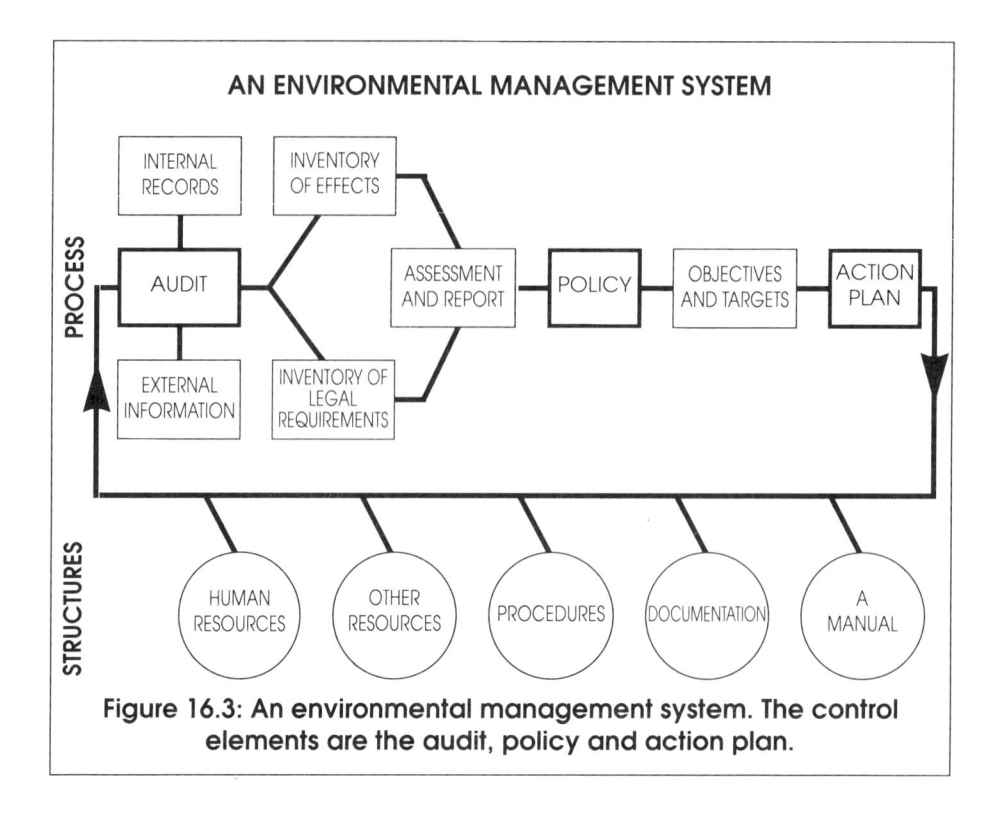

'headline' information should be presented at a monthly environmental meeting, considered at board meetings, and reviewed in the annually updated Environmental Plan.

Typical information that the organization needs to collect is listed under 'Documentation' below.

EXTERNAL INFORMATION

Management should be capable of anticipating change. To do so, it must stay abreast of new products, legislation, technologies and issues. This requires an external information system which could include magazine subscriptions, attendance at conferences, and other means.

It should also include dialogue and liaison with conservation groups, other organizations and the statutory bodies; they are valuable sources of information and a good working relationship is important in this area.

Both internal and external information should be widely disseminated throughout the company if it is to create interest and produce new ideas.

THE AUDIT

The internal and external information (discussed above) make an essential contribution to the next stage: the audit.

The audit or review should cover the topics mentioned in Chapter 2, and should be regular. By the time one set of environmental improvements has been implemented, the world will have moved on. Customers and legislation will require further changes.

Audits should be carried out by independent and competent people, whether internal or external. The auditors should:

- Visit the site and inspect it, rather than relying on computer print-outs or postal questionnaires
- Check whether the environmental system is operating properly
- Review the suitability of current policy, targets and systems
- Review external information about markets, legislation and technology.

In addition to the normal independent audits, self-assessment procedures may also be developed to help line managers assess whether they are complying with the company's green policy and plan.

The audit should not be an *ad-hoc* affair. It should be properly structured and planned. Procedures for carrying out the audit should be described in an audit plan (outlined next).

AUDIT PLAN

The audit plan will describe how, where and when the audits should take place, and who should carry them out. It will detail what documentation should be used, what records should be made, and how the findings should be presented (see p. 21).

INVENTORIES

The audit should produce a list of materials, activities and releases that have environmental effects. The list will describe:

- What is the impact of suppliers' activities?
- What materials, fuels and energy are consumed in the business?
- What releases have taken place, in what volumes and concentrations, and using what paths? This will include emissions to air and water, solid waste and energy use
- What are the effects of these activities on the environment (including staff, local residents and habitats)?
- What happens to the product after leaving the factory? How is it used and disposed of?

The audit will also produce a list of legislative and regulatory requirements.

This may include planning law, discharge consents, and UK and EC legislation. However, it is essential that not all management time is focused on legally controlled impacts. There are many opportunities for cost reduction which stem from the regular review of non-legislative impacts.

ASSESSMENT AND REPORT

The audit will be followed by an analysis of the findings, and a report to management. The report should define the extent of the problems, and should prioritize them. The report should cover:

- Levels of performance against objectives and policies
- Areas of non-compliance, and reasons for this
- Implementation and effectiveness of corrective actions recommended in previous audits
- Conclusions and recommendations.

A POLICY

Environmental policy cannot be created in isolation: it must stem from the facts that are produced from the audit. The policy should cover all key areas (especially waste, pollution, product design and resource use). The environmental policy is fully discussed in Chapter 2 (p. 29).

OBJECTIVES AND TARGETS

The company needs to translate its environmental policy into targets for meeting legislation, reducing pollution and minimizing any impact on the environment.

The organization also needs to identify the skills, knowledge, equipment, processes and monitoring systems that are needed to achieve the required environmental performance.

It may also need to redesign products, services and operations in order to reduce impacts. The implementation of these activities is described next in the Action Plan.

THE ACTION PLAN

The plan will describe how the environmental objectives are to be met. It should assess the significance of the company's impacts, prioritize action and set targets.

It should plan, control and monitor activities to ensure compliance with policy. The plan should cover existing and new products. It should assign responsibilities and introduce co-ordination.

The plan should include all the areas mentioned in the audit in Chapter 2, and should incorporate the following:

- **Management summary**: This should highlight and prioritize the areas for improvement. The most cost-effective changes should be implemented first, along with changes to products or procedures that could cause catastrophe. Companies should prioritize areas which are exceeding consent levels (polluting a river, for example), or which contribute to a polluted environment (for example, a smog-bound inner-city area).
- **Policy Review**. If the plan is an annual update, it should review the company's environmental policy and consider updating it.
- **Processes, equipment and materials**: Wasteful or hazardous processes may need to be altered. Inefficient, noisy or polluting equipment may be replaced or guarded. Dangerous, polluting or non-renewable resources may be changed.
- **Research** into substitutes may be part of the plan. This could be market research, research among suppliers, or scientific research.
- **Marketing**: A new product development plan may need to be created. Research will need to ascertain customer attitudes to environmental issues.
- **Human Resources**: Responsibilities need to be allocated, and performance monitored. This should take place within the company's normal personnel procedures.
- **Finance**: Assessment of costs and benefits. Each section of the plan must be costed. How much will it cost to replace or muffle noisy machinery? What is the opportunity cost of withdrawing a product from the market? The plan must indicate whether investment plans are environmentally friendly.
- **Time plan**: The plan must show when activities will be implemented.
- **Monitoring**: The plan should state how the progress of the plan will be reviewed, and how and when the environment will be reviewed.

EMERGENCY PLAN

An incident plan should be created as part of the Action Plan. This will define the likely incidents or emergencies, their impact on the environment, and the actions to be taken. An incident might include an oil spillage or the accidental release of toxic fumes.

If they happen, accidents and incidents should be analysed and steps taken to prevent their reoccurrence. Events and actions should be documented.

The emergency plan should aim to achieve a fast response: a delay in notifying the regulatory authorities may increase the chances of being taken to court.

The emergency plan may grade different levels of problem. It should map out the potential for catastrophe, and detail the action to be taken in the event of each main type.

THE DESIGN OF THE ACTION PLAN

COMPANY CAR LEASING

The issues

Discussion on the pollution caused by cars generally. The company's need for company cars. The need to find mitigating solutions.

Statutory/legal requirements and considerations

Vehicle emission controls. Higher taxes on cars with larger engines.

Current position

The number of company-owned cars, including pool cars. Breakdown of diesel and petrol, and percentage with catalytic converter. Leasing and servicing arrangements.

Assessment and options for future action

The options considered, and the costs and benefits of each. For example:

- Introduction of an environmental car policy
- Introduction of season ticket loans
- Recommendation that executives travelling to plant B use the train
- Etc.

Action

The best solutions. The action to be taken to achieve them. A time plan. People responsible.

Cost implications

How much will this cost to implement? What elements are self-financing? What capital cost is involved?

The environmental plan should be structured by department: this will match problems to responsibilities. This is an abbreviated entry for a company car manager's department.

We have now been through the EMS process. As Figure 16.3 showed, there are five structures attached to it: human resources, other resources, procedures, documentation and a manual. (The latter two points could be combined into

HUMAN RESOURCES

Humans make the business operate, and they can ruin even the best of plans. Hence the organization structure should include lines of environmental authority and communications. A new organization chart (showing reporting structures) may need to be drawn up.

To ensure that the system works properly, a board member should have overall responsibility; to him/her should report a functional manager who will be given responsibility for implementing the system.

Additionally, all line managers in the organization should recognize their own responsibilities, as should every employee. The humblest operative can have the biggest environmental impact.

Managers should communicate to their subordinates the company's policies, objectives and targets, and they should organize systems and controls.

The company should communicate clearly about environmental issues with all relevant people. It should ensure that its personnel possess awareness, skills and motivation. Training should be provided, and performance reviews may incorporate an environmental appraisal. Co-ordination between departments will be vital: a committee may be one solution.

OTHER RESOURCES

Enough resources should be provided to ensure that the EMS operates effectively. This may include a financial budget; machinery and equipment for monitoring discharges; new production equipment for reducing pollution; and equipment for testing goods, designing new products or handling waste. Computer systems will also be required.

PROCEDURES

Procedures will define how activities should be carried out to minimize their impact on the environment. Existing procedures and systems may need to be changed:

> At Marks and Spencer, unwanted plastic hangers are returned to the manufacturer to be recycled. This has meant changing a procedure among store staff. Labelled recycling boxes have been placed by the tills, and the number of hangers collected has since quadrupled.

Controls need to be introduced on all aspects of the organization (for example, purchasing, processes and transport). These need to be documented, and regular measurements obtained.

Accuracy needs to be specified, and calibration verified; standards (for emission levels, for example) also need to be agreed.

Procedures for corrective action need to be defined. These will ascertain the cause of problems, initiate preventative action and make records.

Accounting procedures should identify the costs and incomes related to environmental management, investment and improvements.

DOCUMENTATION

The organization should keep proper records. These will demonstrate compliance with the EMS, and will record the extent to which objectives have been met.

The records should be comprehensive and easily retrieved. They should also be systematic and orderly. They will include:

- Supplier documentation
- Product composition data
- Inspection and maintenance reports, monitoring data, results of audits, list of releases
- Incident reports
- Failures to comply with policy and action taken
- Financial information
- Waste records
- Policy documents, emergency plans
- Regulations and permits
- Operating procedures
- Environmental committee minutes

A greater sensitivity to the environment inevitably involves capturing more data and analysing it. The company will need to assess what environmental information should be captured in future. How will it be disseminated and used? What are the implications for data processing?

It is essential that information be presented clearly (notably in graph or bar chart form).

THE MANUAL

The organization needs one or more manuals to collate the information and documentation. For larger companies, there may be one manual covering the whole organization, with separate manuals for each division or specialized manuals for individual functions. The manual will describe how the EMS is to be implemented. There should be rules for its control, review and amendment.

The manual will include policies, objectives and the action plan. It will cover procedures, interfaces, roles and responsibilities. Information in the manual and in all other documentation should be clear and simple.

There is a trend away from huge manuals: no one ever reads them, and as a result they are poor at communicating information. You should not presume that information in the manual will be read. The manual should therefore be as slim as possible, and its contents should be shown and explained to all recipients.

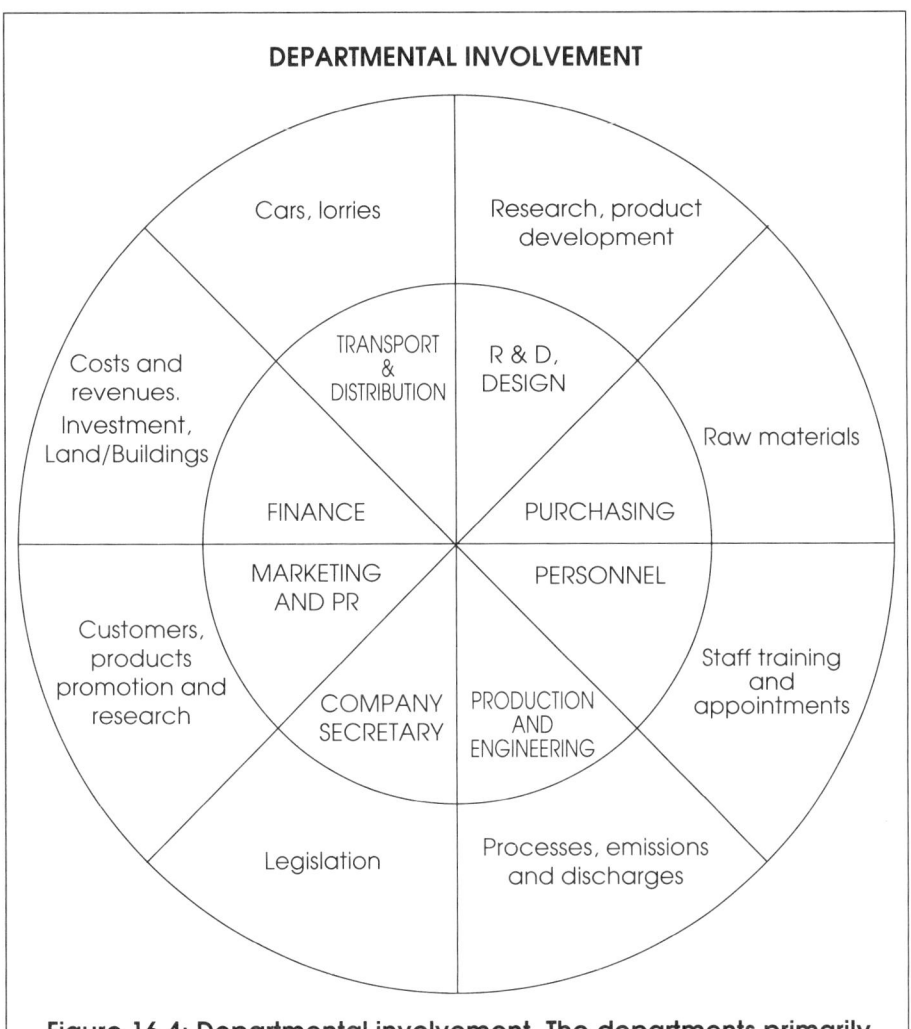

PUTTING IT ALL TOGETHER: THE ENVIRONMENTAL MANAGEMENT SYSTEM 225

Figure 16.4: Departmental involvement. The departments primarily involved in the EMS, together with key topics.

POINTS COMMON TO ALL PARTS OF AN EMS

Certain common principles apply to all aspects of the EMS. They will be familiar to organizations which have introduced quality systems, with which this system shares a common purpose.

All aspects of the EMS need to be regularly reviewed and updated. Any changes should be documented and communicated.

The system should fit with the specific needs of the company, and reflect its organization. Make the EMS fit existing systems, not vice versa.

The system should encompass the whole organization and every department, as suggested in Figure 16.4. Proper co-ordination between functions is essential.

The system should cover all stages of the product's life. This means there should be an analysis of how the product is made, and what happens to it after leaving the factory gate.

The system should include direct and indirect effects (for example, the impact of production processes and of office activities).

The system should encompass every aspect of the environment. Apart from air, water and land, it should include people (especially staff, local residents and customers), and any living things that might be affected.

Every analysis should describe normal, abnormal and emergency situations. The company should be prepared for any problems that might arise.

ENVIRONMENTAL MANAGEMENT SYSTEM CHECKLIST

- Are internal environmental records maintained?
- Is there an external information gathering system?
- Are audits regularly carried out?
- Is an inventory of effects maintained?
- Is an inventory of legislation maintained?
- Are audits assessed and reported on?
- Does senior management review the information?
- Does an audit plan exist?
- Does the company have an environmental policy?
- Does it have environmental objectives and targets?
- Is an action plan in place?
- Does an emergency plan exist?
- Are staff properly assigned, trained and supported?
- Are sufficient other resources allocated to the environmental management system?
- Are procedures in place to make the EMS work?
- Is documentation in place to make the EMS work?
- Is an EMS manual maintained?
- Does the EMS cover all departments and products, and all stages of the products' life?
- Are all aspects of the EMS regularly reviewed and updated?
- Is there a system for ensuring that legislative and regulatory requirements are complied with?
- Does the EMS cover normal, abnormal and emergency situations?
- Does the company communicate with interested parties over its environmental impacts?

APPENDIX I
ENVIRONMENTAL LAW

◆

This appendix is designed to guide managers quickly to the legislation that affects them. It condenses the law to a manageable size; but, as the reader will appreciate, the law is both wide and ever changing, so the appendix cannot cover every point. It is not intended as a substitute for professional advice on the circumstances of particular cases. If you are in any doubt, seek professional legal advice.

The checklist uses terms like 'hazardous substances' or 'special wastes': these terms are usually defined in the appropriate law. If any of your operations and products is contentious, there will almost certainly be a law affecting it, and you should investigate further.

EC legislation has not been included here. EC Regulations are directly binding on the UK and do not require British legislation, while EC Directives have to be implemented by Britain in the form of a UK law. EC laws that have been passed in the last few years, or are in the process of becoming law in Europe, will eventually affect businesses in the UK.

PRODUCTION

ITEM	STATUTE REFERENCE (see below for key)
Do you employ people?	AH1
Do you operate a factory?	AF1
Do you use hazardous substances?	RC3
Do you use toxic, explosive or flammable substances?	RC4
Are your operations noisy, smelly or smoky?	AE1, AC3, RN1
Are you involved with farming?	RS1, AW1
Is your plant potentially a hazard?	RC4
Do you keep hazardous substances?	AP1, RC3

Do you produce or dispose of radioactive substances?	AR1, AN1
Do you operate a nuclear installation?	AN1

POLLUTION

Does the business emit air pollution?	AE1, AC1
Do you discharge waste water to rivers, lakes, estuaries or coastal water?	AW1
Do you own sea-going oil tankers or explore for oil?	AP3, AM1, AM2, RM3, AO2, AD1
Do you use premises that could discharge oil into the sea (for example, an oil terminal)?	AO2
Do you pollute water from land-based sources (for example, sea dumping)?	AF3
Do you discharge pollution or waste water to the drains?	AP5
Do you dump waste in the sea?	AM1

TRANSPORT

Do you transport radioactive substances?	RR1
Do you transport 'special' (that is, dangerous) wastes?	RC2
Do you carry dangerous goods by road tankers?	RD1
Do you transport hazardous substances by sea or air?	RM1, RD3
Do you operate ships?	AE1, AO2, AF3
Do you transport hazardous waste across national boundaries?	RT2
Do you transport radioactive substances?	RR1, RI1

LAND AND BUILDINGS

Do you operate an office or shop?	AO1

Do you suffer from litter?	AE1
Do your premises occupy buildings of historic or architectural interest?	AP2
Do your premises operate from conservation area, SSSI, or national park or similar?	AP2
Do you intend to change your buildings?	AT1
Do you construct buildings, roads or large scale projects?	AC3, AT1, AP2, RN1, RT1
Are staff involved in electrical installation, maintenance or repair?	RE1
Do staff remove asbestos?	RA2
Is your property on 'contaminated land'?	AE1

WASTE

Do you own or use a landfill site, whether old or new?	AE1
Do you produce waste?	AE1
Do you operate a waste disposal business?	AE1
Do you discharge waste to sea?	AF3, AP3

PRODUCTS

Do you sell pesticides?	AF3
Do you import, use or supply injurious substances?	AC3, AE1, RC3
Are you involved with radioactive substances?	AR1, AN1
Do you process or sell food?	AF4

PRIMARY LEGISLATION

AC1	Clean Air Acts 1956, 1968
AC2	Consumer Protection Act 1987
AC3	Control of Pollution Act 1974
AD1	Deep Sea Mining (Temporary Provisions) Act 1981

AE1	Environmental Protection Act 1990
AF1	Factories Act 1961
AF2	Fire Precautions Act 1971
AF3	Food and Environment Protection Act 1985
AF4	Food Safety Act 1990
AH1	Health and Safety at Work etc Act 1974
AM1	Merchant Shipping Acts 1974, 1979, 1984, 1988
AM2	Merchant Shipping (Oil pollution) Act 1971
AN1	Nuclear Installations Act 1965
AO1	Offices, Shops and Railway Premises Act 1963
AO2	Oil Pollution Act 1971
AP1	Planning (Hazardous Substances) Act 1990
AP2	Planning (Listed Buildings and Conservation Areas) Act 1990
AP3	Prevention of Oil Pollution Act 1971
AP4	Public Health Act 1961
AP5	Public Health (Drainage of Trade Premises) Act 1937
AR1	Radioactive Substances Act 1960
AT1	Town and Country Planning Act 1990
AW1	Water Act 1989

REGULATIONS

RA1	Air Navigation (Dangerous Goods) Regulations 1985
RA2	Asbestos Regulations 1983
RC1	Classification, Packaging and Labelling of Dangerous Substances Regulations 1984
RC2	Control of Pollution (Special Wastes) Regulations 1980
RC3	Control of Substances Hazardous to Health Regulations 1988 (COSHH)
RC4	Control of Industrial Major Accident Hazard Regulations 1984 (CIMAH)

RD1	Dangerous Substances (Conveyance by road in road tankers and tank containers) Regulations 1981
RD2	Dangerous substances (Notification and Marking of Sites) Regulations 1990
RD3	Dangerous Substances in Harbour Areas Regulations 1987
RE1	Electricity at Work Regulations 1989
RH1	Health and Safety (Emissions into the Atmosphere) Regulations 1983
RI1	Ionising Regulations 1985
RM1	Merchant Shipping (Dangerous Goods) Regulations 1981
RM2	Merchant Shipping (Chemical Tankers) Regulations 1986
RM3	Merchant Shipping (Prevention of Oil Pollution) Regulations 1983
RN1	Noise at Work Regulations 1989
RN2	Notification of Installations Handling Hazardous Substances Regulations 1982
RR1	Radioactive Substances (Carriage by Road) (Great Britain) Regulations 1974
RR2	Reporting of Injuries, Diseases and Dangerous Occurrences Regulations 1985
RR3	Road Traffic (Carriage of Dangerous Substances in Packages) Regulations 1985
RS1	Sludge (Use in Agriculture) Regulations 1989
RT1	Town and Country Planning (Assessment of Environmental Effects) Regulations 1988
RT2	Transfrontier Shipment of Hazardous Waste Regulations 1988

Please note: The classification used here (AC1 – RT2) is designed for this appendix, and has no official status.

APPENDIX II
PRESCRIBED PROCESSES AND SUBSTANCES

◆

Many processes and substances are now regulated by the Environmental Protection Act. If your business carries out any of these activities, you should consult the Environmental Protection Regulations 1991 or your regulatory authority to find out how you are affected. You may need a consent to carry out the process.

The regulations exclude processes that are below certain threshold volumes. They also distinguish between heavy and moderate polluters, and they define different controls for each.

This appendix is intended to alert companies to their possible need for information and action. It is not intended to be as detailed, comprehensive or as current as can be obtained from a solicitor.

The processes are followed by lists of substances whose release to air, land or water is prescribed.

Acid: Manufacture, processing or recovery of sulphuric acid, sulphur oxides, nitric acid, nitrogen oxides, phosphoric acid.
Animal and plant treatment: Processes involving prescribed emissions to water or air, or which produce offensive smells. Maggot breeding. Fat rendering, vegetable oil processing. Offal processing. Tripe production.
Asbestos: Processing, manufacture, finishing.
Carbonization: Production and processing of carbonaceous materials.
Cement and Lime: Making or grinding cement clinker, related storage and handling. Heating of calcium; related lime slaking. Cement storage, blending and handling.
Ceramic: Firing clay or refractory goods.
Chemical fertilizer: Manufacture or conversion.
Chemical bulk storage: Storage of anhydrous ammonia, acrylates, acrylonitrile, toluene di-isocynate, vinyl chloride monomer, anhydrous hydrogen fluoride.
Coating and printing: Boatyards using TBT; textile treatment involving releases to water; processes involving special waste. Other industries releasing particulates and VOCs, coating materials and solvents. Vehicle respraying.

Combustion: The regulations control combustion plants producing >0·4MW.

Di-isocynates: Manufacture, including foam and elastomer. Hot wire cutting and bonding.

Dyestuffs, inks and coatings: Processes involving hexachlorobenzene, organic solvents, powder coatings.

Gasification: Production of natural gas and other carbonaceous materials.

Glass manufacture: Manufacture of glass, and use in related processes.

Halogens: Manufacture or processes involving releases to air.

Inorganic chemicals: Manufacture or processes using or releasing HCN or H_2S. Production etc of Sb, As, Be, Ga, In, Pb, Pd, Pt, Se, Te, or Tl. Production etc of Cd, Hg, Cr, Mg, Mn, Ni, Zn. Any metal carbonyl. Processes involving the release to air of ammonia or phosphorus.

Iron and steel: Ore handling and storage, smelting, electric arc production, other small furnaces.

Non-ferrous metals: Extraction or recovery of aluminium or other non-ferrous metal by chemical or thermal means. Zn or Sn mining, releasing Cd to water or air. Stand-alone refining, batch processing. Processing alloys containing Be, Cr, Mg, Mn, Pb, Cu, Sb, As, P, Pt, Se. Cd and Hg processes, Be or Se processes. Heat-based scrap recovery. Batch processing. Cu, Al and Zn recovery, Zn galvanizing, die-casting.

Organic chemicals: Manufacture etc. of styrene, vinyl chloride. Release to air of acetylene, aldehydes, amine, isocynate, nitrile, organic acid, organic sulphur, phenol. Manufacture etc. of carbon disulphide. Manufacture etc. of pyridene etc. Any organo-metallic compound. Acrylate.

Other mineral fibres: Manufacture of glass fibre, fibres from non-asbestos minerals.

Other mineral processes: Processing of clay, sand, or other minerals, slag, coal, ash, gypsum, bricks, tiles, concrete, glass. Coal handling.

Paper and pulp: Chemical-based, involving prescribed release to water.

Pesticides: Manufacture involving prescribed release to water or production of special waste.

Petrochemicals: Olefin manufacture, processes and polymerization.

Petroleum: Handling, storage and treatment of primary products and chemical feedstocks.

Pharmaceutical production: Involving release to water of prescribed substances, or special waste.

Rubber: Primary processes involving carbon black; related finishing processes.

Smelting: Smelting or calcining sulphides.

Tar and bitumen: Manufacturing and processing.

Timber: Processes involving release of prescribed substances to water. Preservation processes involving special waste. Sawmilling.

Uranium: Treatment, manufacture using compounds or alloys.

Waste-derived fuel: Heat-based production.

Waste incineration: Chemical or plastic manufacturing wastes. Destruction of Br, Cd, Cl, Fl, Hg, I, Pb, N, P, S, Zn or compounds. Other incineration, metal container burning out; crematoria.

Waste recovery: Oil or solvents by distillation. Filter cleaning involving release of prescribed substances to air, land or water.

THE MOST POLLUTING SUBSTANCES

The following substances have been prescribed under the Environmental Protection Act. Special attention must be paid to prevent or minimize their emission, which may require a consent.

PRESCRIBED SUBSTANCES FOR RELEASE TO AIR

Oxides of sulphur and other sulphur compounds

Oxides of nitrogen and other nitrogen compounds

Oxides of carbon

Organic compounds and partial oxidation productions

Metals, metalloids and their compounds

Asbestos (suspended particular matter and their fibres), glass fibres and mineral fibres

Halogens and their compounds

Phosphorus and its compounds

Particulate matter

PRESCRIBED SUBSTANCES FOR RELEASE TO WATER

Mercury and its compounds

Cadmium and its compounds

All isomers of Hexachlorocyclohexane

All isomers of DDT

Pentachlorophenol and its compounds

Hexachlorobenzene

Hexachlorobutadiene

Aldrin

Dieldrin

Endrin

Polychlorinated biphenyls

Dichlorvos

1,2-Dichloroethane

All isomers of Trichlorobenzene

Atrazine

Simazine

Tributyltin compounds

Triphenyltin compounds

Trifluralin

Fenitrothion

Azinphos-methyl

Malathion

Endosulfan

NB These form the government's 'Red List'

PRESCRIBED SUBSTANCES FOR RELEASE TO LAND

Organic solvents

Azides

Halogens and their covalent compounds

Metal carbonyls

Organo-metallic compounds

Oxidizing agents

Polychlorinated dibenzofuran and any congener thereof

Polychlorinated dibenzo-p-dioxin and any other congener thereof

Polyhalogenated biphenyls, terphenyls and naphthalenes

Phosphorus

Pesticides: any chemical substance for destroying any organism harmful to plants, wood, water, buildings or animals.

Alkali and alkaline earth metals and their oxides.

APPENDIX III
HAZARDOUS SUBSTANCES

◆

The COSHH regulations apply to all workplaces where dangerous substances are present. Schedule 5 of COSHH lists substances and processes which require medical surveillance. These are summarized below, but the list is not definitive. More information can be obtained from the Health and Safety Commission, from whom this information was obtained.

SUBSTANCES OF RECOGNIZED SYSTEMIC TOXICITY

These require health records to be kept, biological monitoring and professional advice from an occupational health nurse or a doctor.

Substance	*Typical processes*
Mercury and organomercury compounds	Chemical manufacturing Measuring instrument manufacture and servicing Explosives manufacture
Cadmium	Brazing and soldering Pigment manufacture Refining scrap metals Metal manufacture Battery manufacture
Arsenic	Chemical manufacture Glass production Wood preservation
Beryllium	Alloy manufacture Manufacture of fluorescent lights
Phosphorus and organophosphorus compounds	Chemical manufacture Contract sheep dipping Crop spraying by specialist contractors

Diethylene dioxide (dioxan)	Manufacture of cosmetics Paint stripping
Acrylamide	Manufacture of paper, dyes, artificial leather, photographic emulsion, adhesives.
N-Hexane	Printing
Methyl bromide	Pest control and fumigation

SUBSTANCES THAT CAUSE ASTHMA

These require routine checks for respiratory symptoms among employees. The checks should be carried out by a trained person, following the instructions of a nurse or doctor. All symptoms must be reported to the doctor or nurse for further investigation.

Substance	*Typical processes*
Platinum salts	Metal refining and use of compounds
Isocyanates	Plastic foam manufacture Applying certain paints, inks, adhesives, varnishes and lacquers.
Epoxy resin curing agents	Fumes and dust arising from manufacture, transport or use.
Azodicarbonamide	Plastics manufacture Food processing
Acid anhydrides	Chemical manufacture Resin curing
Reactive dyes	Use in tanning and textile industries
Colophony fumes	Electronics industries Soldering
Antibiotics and sulphonamides	Pharmaceuticals manufacture
Proteolytic enzymes	Detergent manufacture
Red cedar dusts	Woodworking
Grain dust	Grain handling and processing, harvesting, milling and mixing, feeding to livestock.
Flour	Baking

Substance	Typical processes
Animal dander and urine	Intensive livestock production (pig and poultry) Work in animal houses
Proteinaceous materials finely divided (for example, dust from bird droppings, mushroom compost and hay/straw compost dust).	Agriculture Mushroom farming

SUBSTANCES THAT CAN CAUSE SEVERE DERMATITIS OR OTHER SKIN AILMENTS

Train a responsible person to inspect hands and forearms once a month (or twice a week in the case of chrome solutions) or as advised by a doctor. Employees should be encouraged to report sore, red or itching skin. Cases must be referred to a health care professional for investigation.

Substance	*Typical processes*
Epoxy resins	Use as adhesives Electronic component manufacture
Cutting oils	Engineering Production processes
Hard metal powders containing for example, cobalt, chromium	Refining Powder manufacture and use
Acrylates and methacrylates	Manufacture and use of plastics, paints, inks, varnishes and lacquers Dental work
Plating solutions	Electroplating
Reactive chemical intermediates	Chemical and pharmaceutical manufacture
Biocides	Paint and detergent manufacture Humidifier maintenance
Organic solvents	Degreasing Chemical synthesis
Cement	Construction
Strong solutions (for example, brine)	Food processing
Bleach	Widespread uses

Hair dyes and shampoos	Hairdressing
Soaps and detergents	Domestic contract cleaning Catering
Sap of plants of the Compositae family, daffodils etc.	Plant handling Floristry and horticulture
Chrome solutions	Electrolytic plating Dyeing processes Liming and tanning of hides

CARCINOGENS

These are marked on suppliers' labels with the risk phrase R45 'may cause cancer'. Other substances appear in Appendix I of the COSHH Carcinogens Code of Practice (from HMSO).

Skin carcinogens include coal soots, pitch, coal tar, certain mineral oils and used mineral and engine oils, and arsenic. These warrant regular skin inspections by a trained person. Other carcinogens include MbOCA, whose use should be subject to biological monitoring.

OTHER HAZARDOUS SUBSTANCES

These may require health surveillance procedures similar to those already discussed.

Typical substance	*Effect*
Alkyl phenols, alkyl catechols and hydroquinones.	Skin depigmentation
Cutting oils	Oil acne
Dibenzo-dioxins	Chloracne
Penicillin, inhalants, certain plants	Uticaria (hives)
Strong acids and alkalis, Cement	Skin ulceration
Silica (quarrying)	Silicosis
Benzene (for example, in chemical manufacture and coal tar distillation)	Toxic, carcinogen

Plant dusts and spores	Extrinsic allergic alveolitis (Farmers lung)
Oxides of nitrogen (explosives manufacture)	Throat and eye irritation.
Hazardous micro-organisms	Respiratory illness

HEALTH RECORDS

Some situations require only health records to be kept, without the need for health checks. These are:

- Man made mineral fibres
- Rubber process dust and fume
- Leather dust in boot and shoe manufacture
- Pottery production (excluding lead)
- Pesticides application (other than organo-phosphorus pesticides)

APPENDIX IV
GLOSSARY

◆

Acid rain: acidic deposits from power stations and other sources that can damage trees, lakes and stonework.
BATNEEC: 'Best available techniques not entailing excessive cost': a government formula for reducing pollution. Certain processes are required to adopt it.
Biodegrade: to decompose.
Catalytic converter: a device for removing harmful emissions from car exhausts.
CFCs: chlorofluorocarbons. Used as refrigerants and propellants. When released into the air, they damage the ozone layer. Their use is being phased out.
CHP: combined heat and power. A power station that makes use of the heat produced in generating electricity.
Compliance: conforming to legislation, regulations or corporate policy.
Conservation: saving energy, wildlife, or raw materials.
COSHH: Control of Substances Hazardous to Health Regulations. These regulations apply to organizations handling dangerous substances.
Cradle to grave: term for considering a product's total impact on the environment. This includes raw materials, production, use and disposal.
Deforestation: clearance of jungle for logging, agriculture or housing.
Desertification: growth of desert areas (caused by overcropping, soil erosion and other factors).
Duty of care: legal requirement for companies to monitor what happens to their waste.
Eco-label: product label containing environmental information.
Environmental Audit: analysis of an organization's effect on the environment.
Environmental Impact Assessment: review of the potential impact of a new development.
Environmental Management System: system for ensuring that a company safeguards the environment.

Environmental Policy: written statement about an organization's attitude towards the environment.

Ethical investment: investing in socially responsible funds (avoiding, for example, companies that produce tobacco or military equipment).

Eutrophication: process whereby rivers become clogged with weeds and green algae. Caused by fertilizer and sewage leaking into the water.

Fossil fuels: oil, coal and gas. Produce greenhouse gases and acid rain when burnt, and are non-renewable.

Global warming: gradual increase in average world temperatures.

Greenhouse effect: process whereby gases such as carbon dioxide trap the sun's rays inside the earth's atmosphere. This leads to global warming.

Hydrocarbons: hydrogen/carbon compounds emitted from petrol evaporation and car exhausts. They react with nitrogen oxides to form ozone.

Incineration: burning of waste. Incineration can release toxic substances unless carried out at very high temperatures.

IPC: Integrated Pollution Control. A system for controlling all wastes (whether to air, land or water) by one regulatory authority.

Landfill: what used to be called rubbish dumps. The disposal of solid waste in the ground.

LCA: Lifecycle Analysis. Assesses a product's environmental impact at all stages of its life.

Leaching: percolating through soil, usually into a river (often applied to nitrates).

Methane: greenhouse gas, produced by cows, landfill sites and rice fields.

NIMBY: 'Not in My Back Yard'. Applied to people who approve of controversial developments (such as nuclear power stations) as long as they are not located close to their home.

Nitrate: substance that promotes plant growth, and is used in agricultural fertilizers. Excessive use causes eutrophication.

Ozone: layer in the stratosphere that shields the body from harmful rays of the sun; but ground-level ozone acts as an irritant.

PCBs: Polychlorinated biphenyls. Fire retardant chemicals once used extensively in electrical equipment and other applications. Now known to be toxic.

PET: plastic used to make drinks bottles.

Phosphate: plant nutrient and water softener. Can lead to eutrophication.

Photodegradable: material that decomposes in sunlight.

Polluter Pays Principle: making a company pay for its pollution, whether by taxation, consents or court action. Designed to reduce pollution by making it expensive.

Recycling: the reuse of materials rather than disposing of them.

Renewable energy: power from permanent energy sources (such as wind or wave power).

Retrofit: to modify equipment after it has been installed. Usually refers to the fitting of pollution-control devices. Generally more expensive than incorporating them into the original design.

RSI: Repetitive Strain Injury. Upper limb pain in a keyboard user.
Sick building syndrome: the tendency of some modern buildings to cause illness among staff who work in them.
Solvents: substances used to dissolve other substances; used in paints and glues. Can cause pollution.
Sustainable development: growth that does not prevent future generations from meeting their needs.
Toxic: poisonous.

APPENDIX V
USEFUL ADDRESSES

◆

Association for the Conservation of Energy, 9 Sherlock Mews, London W1M 3RH. Trade association, information on energy conservation.
Association for Environmentally Conscious Building, Windlake House, The Pump Field, Coaley GL11 5DX. Information about environmentally sound building.
Board of Trade, Environment Unit, 123 Victoria St, London SW1E 6RB. Helps industry respond to environmental challenges and opportunities.
Board of Trade, Environmental Enquiry Point, Warren Spring Laboratory, Gunnels Wood Road, Stevenage SG1 2BX. Advice for industry.
British Glass, Northumberland Rd, Sheffield S10 2UA. Information about the use of glass.
British Library, Environmental Information Service, 25 Southampton Buildings, London WC2A 1AW. Reference point for information on the environment.
British Plastics Federation, 5 Belgrave Square, London SW1X 8PD. Trade association, information about the use of plastics.
British Steel Tinplate, PO Box 101, Velindre, Swansea SA5 5WN. Information about recycling steel.
British Wind Energy Association, 4 Hamilton Place, London W1V 0BQ. Information on wind energy.
Building Research Establishment, Bucknalls Lane, Garston, Watford WD2 7JR. Certification scheme for commercial buildings; information about energy use in buildings.
British Standards Institution, 2 Park St, London W1A 2BS. Environmental standard.
Can Makers, 36 Grosvenor Gardens, London SW1W 0ED. Aluminium and steel can recycling.
Centre for Alternative Technology, Machynlleth, Powys, Wales SY20 9AZ. Environmentally sound technologies.
Charities Aid Foundation, 48 Pembury Road, Tonbridge, Kent TN9 2JD. Information about charities that need used materials for recycling.

Chartered Institution of Building Service Engineers (CIBSE), 222 Balham High Road, London SW12 9BS. Information about energy in buildings.
Chemical Industries Association, Kings Buildings, Smith Square, London SW1P 3JJ. Trade association for chemicals.
Confederation of British Industry, Environment Management Unit, Centre Point, New Oxford St, London WC1A 1DU. Environmental information for members.
Department of the Environment, 43 Marsham St, London SW1P 3PY. Works to improve the environment.
Department of Transport, 43 Marsham St, London SW1P 3PY. Transport issues, emission standards.
Ecology Building Society, 18 Station Rd, Cross Hills, Keighley BD20 5BR. Finance for ecologically sound properties.
Electricity Council, 30 Millbank, London SW1P 4RD. Information on better use of electricity.
ENDS, 24 Finsbury Business Centre, 40 Bowling Green Lane, London EC1R 0NE. Monthly environmental publication and annual report.
Energy Efficiency Office, Eland House, Stag Place, London SW1E 5DH. Information on energy saving.
Environment Council, 80 York Way, London N1 9AG. A programme to boost awareness of environmental issues.
Environmental Transport Association, 15a George St, Croydon CR0 1LA. Roadside assistance and lobbying.
Farming and Wildlife Advisory Group, nac, Stoneleigh, Kenilworth CV8 2RX. Practical conservation advice.
Friends of the Earth, 26 Underwood St, London N1 7JQ. Pressure group.
Food Commission, 88 Old St, London EC1V 9AR. Research and campaigning organization.
Friends Provident, Castle St, Salisbury SP1 3SH. Ethical investment.
Health and Safety Commission, Broad Lane, Sheffield S3 7HQ. Protects the health and safety of workers.
HMSO, PO Box 276, London SW8 5DT. Government publications.
Industry Council for Packaging and the Environment (Incpen), 10 Greycoat Place, London SW1P 1SB. Trade body. Information on packaging.
Intermediate Technology, Myson House, Railway Terrace, Rugby CV21 3HT. Enables people in the Third World to develop and use methods which give them control over their lives.
International Maritime Organisation, 4 Albert Embankment, London SE1 7SR. Promotes pollution prevention and safety at sea.
Mercury Provident, Orlingbury House, Lewes Rd, Forest Row RH18 5AA. Ethical lending institution.
Ministry of Agriculture, 17 Smith Sq, London SW1P 3HX. UK government department responsible for farming, fisheries and food.
National Association of Waste Disposal Contractors, 4 Carmelite St, London EC4Y 0BH. Trade association.

National Society for Clean Air, 136 North St, Brighton BN1 1RG. Campaigning organization, information on clean air.

Oxfam, 274 Banbury Rd, Oxford OX2 7DZ. Charity.

Renewable Energy Enquiries Bureau, ETSU, Harwell OX11 0RA. Information on renewable energy.

Soil Association, 86 Colston St, Bristol BS1 5BB. Promotes organic agriculture.

Steel Can Recycling Information Bureau, 536 Kings Rd, London SW10 0TE. Information on recycling.

Vegetarian Society, Parkdale, Dunham Rd, Altrincham WA14 4QC. Campaigns for vegetarianism.

Waste Watch, 26 Bedford Square, London WC1 3HU. Promotes recycling.

INDEX

◆

Acetic acid, 36
Acid rain, 82–83
Accounting, 206–207
  Acquisitions, company, 211
Action plan formulation, 220–224
  documentation, 224
  emergency, 221–223
  human resources, 223
Active solar energy, *see* Solar energy
Activity audit, 20
Addresses, of environmental agencies, 244–246
Advertising, and environment, 160–161
Aerosols, 37, 62
  see also CFCs
After-sales support, 152–153
Air-conditioning, 53
Air fresheners, 66–67
Air pollution, 84–87
Air quality, offices, 54
Alcohol, 57
Aluminium, 106
Animal testing, 142–143
Annual reports, 210–211
Aquifer power, 117
Aromatherapy, 201
Asbestos, 53
Asthma-inducing agents, 237–238
Audiences, of companies, *see* Marketing
Auditors, 177–178, 219–220
  see also Environmental audits

Bacteria, 53, 66, 101
BATNEEC, 84, 210
Bats, 36
Batteries, 62
Benzene, 54
Bicycles, 128–129
Biodiversity, 40

'Bio-diesel', 122
Biofuels, 116–117
'Body Shop' practice, 154
Borax, 36
Bottled water, 57
Bottles, glass, 62–63
Brands, green, 151–152
BREAM, 51
Building exteriors, 37–39
Building societies, green, 213–214
Buildings, 34–51
Business, and green issues, 162
  attitudes, 4–6
  problems facing, 10
  see also Industry
Buying, 69–80
  cars, 119–120
  criteria for, 69–71
  information, 71–74
  materials to avoid, 78–80
  packaging, 76–77
  paper, 77–78
  policy, 69
  timber, 77

Cafeterias, 190–196
  diner education, 193
  entertainment and, 193–194
  food sources, 191
  kitchens of, 194–196
  meat and, 192–193
Cans, 57–58
Carbon dioxide, 53, 84–85
Carbon monoxide, 85
Carcinogens, 239
Car pooling, 124–125
Cars, 121–127, 129
  diesel, 121
  drag coefficient, 121

248 INDEX

engine size, 121
fuel, 121
green issues and, 120–123
life of, 121
mileage, 125–126
petrol, 121
rail and, 127
safety of, 121
types of, 121–123
Catalytic converters, 122
CFCs, 37, 49, 50, 53, 62, 66, 69, 76, 129, 153, 195
Chairs, 55
Charity
food, 196
money, 214
Chemicals, R&D, 144–145
CHP system, 114
Christmas cards, 61
Cigarettes, see Smoking
Claims, by companies, 144–145, 157–160
Clean Air Act 1956, 1
Cleaning, of waste, 101–102
Commitment, by staff, 181–184
departmental reports, 183
involvement and, 183
Communication, and PR, 167–171
Company PR, see PR
Complaints, 172–174
Complementary medicine, 201
Compliance audit, 20
Compost, 88
Computers, 65
Conservation concept, 215–217
Construction strategy, 48
Consultants, 177–178
Contaminated land, 43
Control of Substances Hazardous to Health 1988, 6, 16, 93–94, 210, 212
implementing, 94
Corporate audit, 20
Corporate research, 149
Costing, 205–206
Cyanide, 91
Cycling, see Bicycles
Cypermethrin, 36

Data analysis, 27–29
Daylight, 49, 112
DDT, and water pollution, 91
Degradable plastics, 107
Department integration, 224–226
Departmental reports, 183
Dermatitis-inducing agents, 238–239
Design, engineering, 100

re–, 102
Design, of equipment, 100, 102
Desks, 55, 64
Detergents, 195
Diesel engines, 122
Diet, 198–199
Diner education, 193
Direct mail, 161–162
Disasters, environmental, see Environmental disasters
Dishwashers, 195
Drag coefficient, 121
Draughts, 111–112
Drinking water, 57
Drinks, in offices, 57
Driving, see Cars and also Lorries

Eco-label mark, 157
Ecology Building Society, 213–214
Education
of diners, 193
and PR, 171–172
see also Training, staff
Electric cars, 122–123
Electrical plugs, 151
Electricity pylons, 47
Electronic mail, 68
Emergency action plans, 221–223
Emissions, see Air pollution
Energy, 48–49, 108–111
information, 108–109
labelling, 157
management, 108
offices, 65–66
renewable, 114–118
solar, see Solar energy
strategies, 109–111
water, 116
wind, 115–116
Engineering, 98–118
Entertainment, at work, 193–194
Envelopes, 59
Environment
attitude by business, 4–6
concern for, 1
interest in, 2
promotion, 160–161
see also Green issues
Environmental affairs manager, 178–181
full-time, 180
job description of, 180
part-time, 179–180
and staff commitment, 181–184
Environmental agencies, list of, 244–246
Environmental audit, 18–33

INDEX

benefits, 18
choosing, 20–21
data analysis, 27–29
definition, 19
measurement, 25–27
planning, 21–25
policy definition, 29–33
strategy, 18–19
targets, 32–33
see also Audits
Environmental disasters, 3
blame for, 10–13
Environmental impact, 24
Environmental impact assessment (EIA), 20, 44–47
Environmental Impact Statement (EIS), 44
accidents, 45
effects assessment, 45
mitigating measures, 45
organizations consulted, 45
project description, 44
site description, 44–45
Environmental indices, 26–27
Environmental law, *see* Legislation
Environmental management systems, 215–226
Environmental policy, 29–31
Environmental process chart, 81–82
Environmental Protection Act 1990, 6–7, 83, 87
Environmental terms (glossary of), 241–243
Environmental training, 185–188
Ergonomics, of offices, 55
Ethical investment, 213–214
Ethical marketing, 157–160
Exercise, 199
Expenditure strategy, 208–209
External records, 23
Exxon Valdez, 1, 212
Eye tests, 55

Filtration, 101
Finance, 203–214
Finishes, 49–50
Fire extinguishers, 64
Fires, 97
Food
cafeterias, 190–196
unused, 196
Formaldehyde, 49, 52, 54, 77
Friends Provident, 213
Fuel, 105
diesel, 122
petrol, 122
Fungi, 36
Furniture, office, 64

Gardening, 40–42
Glass bottles, 62–63
Glass recycling, 107
Global warming, 8–9, 86–87
Green brand development, 151–152
Green buying policy, 70
see also Buying *and also* Finance
Green investment companies, 213–214
Green issues
and business, 10–16
inaction on, 13
intensity, 31–32
local authorities and, 16
problems, 8–10
transience of, 7–8
see also Environment
Green new buildings, 48–51
Green office assessment, 51
Green Party, 7
Gulf War, 7

Hazardous substances, 79–80, 93, 236–240
Hazards, of land/buildings, 47–48
HAZCHEM label, 93
Health & Safety managers, 188–189
committees and, 189
representatives and, 188–189
Healthy lifestyles, 199–200
Heating, 49, 113–114
Homoeopathy, 201
Human resources, 223
staff training and, 185–188
Hygiene, in cafeterias, 195

Incineration, 88–90
Industry, and green issues
pollution and, 82–83
reaction of, 13–15
reasons for becoming green, 10–12
ways of helping by, 15–16
Information gathering, 22–23
external records, 23
inspection, 22
internal records, 22–23
interviews, 22
Information needs
for buying, 71–74
for EMS, 217–218
for R&D, 136–137
for finance, 210
for waste reduction, 98–99
Inland waterways, 133
Insecticides, 36, 195
Insects, 36
Insulation, 111–112

Insurance, 212–213
IQ, 53
Irradiated foods, 141
ISDN, 68
Inspection, 22
Internal records, 22–23
Interviews, 22
Investment, 209
   ethical, 213–214
Issue audit, 20

Karin B, 12
Keyboards, 55

Labelling, 155–157
   energy, 157
   ingredients, 156
Land, 34–51
Landfill, 87–88
   energy from, 117
Land holdings, 42–43
Landscaping, 40–44
Lavatories, 66–67
Laws, on the environment, 6–7, 83–84, 227–236
Lead, 53, 85
Legionnaires' Disease, 49, 53, 113
Legislation, 6–7, 83–84, 227–236
Lighting, 112
Litter, 39–40
   use, 40–42
Litter Abatement Order, 39
Local authorities, 16, 39
Local research, marketing and, 148
Lorries, 129–130

Machinery, 114
Mail, 60, 161–162
Maintenance materials, 35–37
Marketing, 146–162
   direct mail, 161–162
   and environment, in promotion, 160–161
   ethics, 157–160
   sales literature, 161–162
Measurement, and environmental audit, 25–27
Meat, 192–193
Media, and PR, 171
Mercury Provident, 213
Merlin Ecology Fund, 213
Metal recycling, 106
Methane, 47, 105
Mileage reduction, 125–126
Milk bottles, 63
Municipal solid waste, 88

NAP analysis, 27, 29

New building green policy, 50–51
New buildings, vs. refurbishment, 34–35
Newspapers, 60
Nitrogen oxides, 85–86
Noise, 92–93

Occupational health, 96–97
   see also Offices *and also* Sick Building (Office) Syndrome
Offal, 141–142
Offices, 51–68
   drinks, 57–58
   equipment, 64–66
   photocopying, 63–65
   smoking, 56
   stationery, 58–62
   telecommuting, 67–68
   washrooms, 66–67
Oil waste, 101–102, 129
Ozone, 85

Packaging, 76–77, 153–155
   cafeterias and, 195
Paints, 36–37, 53
Paper, 77–78, 195
   packaging, 76–77, 153–155
   used, 59–63
Paperless offices, 61
Paradichlorobenzenes, 67
Particulates, 86
Passive solar heating, 117–118
Payroll giving, 214
PCBs, 36, 88
Personnel, 175–189
   auditors, 177–178
   commitment by, 181–185
   environmental affairs manager, 178–181
   health & safety manager, 188–189
   training and, 185–188
PEI bottles, 63, 76, 152
Petrol consumption, 125
Petrol engines, 122
Photocopiers, 63, 65
Planning, of audit, 21–25
   information gathering, 22–23
Plants, 54
Plastic cups, 57
Plastic recycling, 106–107
Plastics, 63
Policy, *see* Environmental policy
Pollution, *see specific forms of*
Pollution attitudes, 82–83
Posture, 55
Power, and heat, combined, 114
PR (public relations), 163–174

communication improvement, 167–171
communities and, 166–167
critics and, 172–174
education, 171–172
environmental impact, 164–165
media and, 171
Product improvement (R&D), 140–141
Product research, marketing and, 149
Production, 81–97
Public Health Act 1937, *see* Legislation
Public relations, *see* PR
Purchasing, *see* Buying *and also* Finance
Pyrethroid insecticides, 36

Radiation, 86
Radon, 47
Rail, 126–127, 130–131
and road, 127
R&D, 136–145
see also Marketing
Records
external, 23
internal, 22–23
Recycled materials
glass, 107
metal, 106
paper, 59–61, 77–78, 103–108
plastic, 106–107
Recycling, of paper, 59–61, 77–78
external use, 59–60
internal use, 59
waste, 103–108
Refurbishment, 34–35
Repetitive Strain Injury, 55
Reporting, 28–29
Reports, 183–184
annual, 210–211
Responsibility, revision of, 184–185
Reverse osmosis, 101
Risk, to employees, 96–97
see also Offices *and also* Sick Building (Office) Syndrome
Roads, *see* Cars *and also* Lorries

Safety, of company staff, 188–189
committees for, 189
representatives for, 188–189
Sales literature, 161–162
Scoping audit, 20
Scrap, 102–103, 105
Sea pollution, 134–135
Sea transport, 133–134
Shelving, 64
Ships, 133–134
Sick Building (Office) Syndrome, 52–55

Site audit, 20
Site appearance, 37–39
Skin irritants, 238–239
Smoking, 199
litter and, *see* Litter
in offices, 56
Soda, 36
Solar energy, 48–49, 115, 117–118
Staff, *see* Personnel
Stamps, 60
Standards, for business associates, 162
Stationery, 59
Steel, 106
Stewardship, 213
Street Litter Control Notice, 39
Sulphur dioxide, 86
Supplier audit, 20
SWOT analysis, 27–28

Take-over audit, 20
Targets, and audit, 32
corporate strategy checklist, 33
international perspective on, 32–33
Telecommuting, *see* Teleworking
Teleworking, 67–68
Thermostats, 49
Tidal barrages, 117
Timber, 77
Tinplate, 106
Titanium dioxide, 36, 104
Tiolet paper, 66, 147
Toxic agents, *see* Hazardous substances
Training staff, 185–188
Transport, 119–135
cars, 121–126, 129
cycling, 128–129
inland waters, 133
lorries, 129–131
rail, 126–127
sea, 133–135
waste, 131, 133
Trichloroethylene, 54
Turbines, wind, 116
Typing, 55

'Unpopular' products, 141–142
Urinal flushing, 67

VDU's, 55
Ventilation, 49
Volatile organic compounds, 86

Washing powders, 195
Washrooms, 66–67
Waste cleaning, 101–102

Waste disposal
  emission, 84–87
  incineration, 89–90
  landfill, 87–88
  water pollution, 90–91
Waste reduction, 98–103
  controls for, 100
  design, 100, 102
  information, 98–99
  process modification, 100–101
  redesign, 102
  scrap and, 102–103, 105
  standards, 100
Waste transport, 131, 133
Water, 57
  heating, 113
  pollution, 90–91
  power, 116
  temperature, 53
  use reduction, 118
  in washrooms, 67
Water Act 1989, 6
Waterways, 133
Wildlife, 50
  rare, 43
Wind energy, 115–116
Wood preservatives, 36
Wood products, 77
  see also Paper

Zero emission vehicles, 123

RELATED RESOURCES FROM GOWER

◆

MANAGING TO BE GREEN   VIDEO

'the Managing to Be Green Package is one of the most comprehensive on the market . . . an ideal forum for provoking group discussion.' Management News

Managing to Be Green is a three part video training programme that examines attitudes to the environment and puts forward practical ideas for managers and staff at every level of an organization to follow.

Part One – The Challenge

A 12 minute introduction to the subject, designed to motivate all levels of staff.

Part Two – Green Leadership

A 25 minute video aimed at managers. It gives ideas and strategies for action based on what some of the leading green organizations around the world are doing.

Part Three – Green Power

This 14 minute video for staff and workers aims to empower them to act with or without an organizational policy on the environment.

Duration: 51 minutes
Origin: Australia
Released: 1991

The three-part package is available for rental or purchase.

THE GREENING OF BUSINESS   BOOK

Edited by Rhys David

Contains all the papers given at a conference organized by Business Magazine, where distinguished figures from the worlds of industry, marketing, public relations and government got together to discuss their views on, and experiences with, becoming green.

August 1991   115 pages   hardback   0 566 07281 5

ENVIRONMENTAL ASSESSMENT: A PRACTICAL GUIDE   BOOK

C.A. Fortlage

A guide to the process of environmental assessment that reviews the history and background to assessment; summarizes the current legislation and provides useful advice on the skills and management techniques needed to run a successful environmental assessment project.

January 1990   168 pages   hardback   0 566 09045 7

HAZARDS AND THE COMMUNICATION OF RISK   BOOK

Edited by John Handmer and Edmund Penning-Rowsell

Practical techniques – with a range of case studies – for assessing the risk of any sudden or long-term disasters and making sure that those at risk are alert to the danger.

August 1990   352 pages   A4 hardback   0 566 02784 4

WASTE MANAGEMENT   BOOK

O.P. Kharbanda and E.A. Stallworthy

A simple, straightforward approach to a growing problem, managing our waste. Waste Management looks at the extent of the problem; examines present methods for disposal and explores the real solution – a 'non-waste' technology.

January 1990   288 pages   hardback   0 566 09052 X

For more information on any of these products, call our customer service department on 0252 317711 or write to: The Customer Service Department, Gower Publishing Company Limited, Gower House, Croft Road, Aldershot, Hampshire GU11 3HR. Tel: 0252 317711, Fax: 0252 344405.